YOU ARE
NOT
AMERICAN

YOU ARE NOT AMERICAN

Citizenship Stripping
from
Dred Scott
to the
Dreamers

AMANDA FROST

BEACON PRESS
Boston, Massachusetts
www.beacon.org

Beacon Press books
are published under the auspices of
the Unitarian Universalist Association of Congregations.

24 23 22 21   8 7 6 5 4 3 2 1

This book is printed on acid-free paper that meets the uncoated paper
ANSI/NISO specifications for permanence as revised in 1992.

Text design and composition by Kim Arney

Library of Congress Cataloging-in-Publication Data

Names: Frost, Amanda, author.
Title: You are not American : citizenship stripping from Dred Scott
    to the dreamers / Amanda Frost.
Description: Boston : Beacon Press, 2021. | Includes bibliographical
    references and index.
Identifiers: LCCN 2020024819 (print) | LCCN 2020024820 (ebook) |
    ISBN 9780807051429 (hardcover) | ISBN 9780807051436 (ebook)
Subjects: LCSH: Citizenship—United States—History. | Civil rights—
    United States—History. | Political culture—United States—History. |
    Scott, Dred, 1809–1858.
Classification: LCC KF4700 .F76 2021 (print) | LCC KF4700 (ebook) |
    DDC 342.7308/3—dc23
LC record available at https://lccn.loc.gov/2020024819
LC ebook record available at https://lccn.loc.gov/2020024820

*To Richard,
and to all Americans
denied their rightful citizenship,
along with those who fought on
their behalf to get it back.*

CONTENTS

THE SIGNIFICANCE
OF CITIZENSHIP

On a foggy day in January 1913, Ethel Coope Mackenzie left her home in the fashionable Nob Hill neighborhood of San Francisco to exercise her newly won right to vote. Although the ratification of the Nineteenth Amendment to the US Constitution was still seven years away, California had recently joined the handful of states allowing women to vote—thanks in part to Mackenzie, who had given her "heart and soul" to the suffrage movement. Heiress to the celebrated Ben Lomond vineyard in Santa Cruz, Mackenzie was well known in San Francisco's elite social circles. The press adored her, describing her as "possessed of beauty and charm of manner that have won her much admiration" and running flattering photos of her and her dashing husband. Although the papers failed to mention it, she also had a will of steel and a media savvy gained from years on the front line of the women's suffrage movement. Mackenzie had reason to suspect that her fight for the right to vote was not over, so she made sure that members of the press corps came with her to the San Francisco Registrar's Office that January day to record what happened next.[1]

As Mackenzie had feared, the registrar informed her that she had lost her right to vote before she ever had a chance to use it. Four years earlier, she had married the celebrated Scottish tenor Gordon Mackenzie, an event reported at length in the San Francisco papers hungry for every detail (right down to her choice to do "without the conventional veil," as the San Francisco Call noted with a whiff of disapproval). As the registrar explained, under a federal law enacted in 1907, her marriage to a noncitizen meant she had not only forfeited the right to vote that she had fought so hard to obtain; she had lost her status as a US citizen.[2]

Mackenzie was outraged. "I have done nothing criminal unless it be a crime to marry a foreigner," she declared, and she challenged the law all the way up to the US Supreme Court. As she explained at the time, she fought not only for herself but also for the thousands of other American women who lost their citizenship—and some their right to vote—solely because they had married a foreigner. But a unanimous Supreme Court ruled against her. Although claiming to "sympathize" with her "earnest . . . desire to retain" her citizenship, the nine justices were firm, explaining that it is an "ancient principle of our jurisprudence" to "merge" the identity of husband and wife and to "give dominance to the husband." The "marriage of an American woman with a foreigner has consequences," they declared. "Therefore, as long as the relation lasts, it is made tantamount to expatriation."[3]

Just a few years earlier, twenty-eight-year-old Haw Moy had returned to the United States after a visit to her extended family in the Guangdong province in China. Upon arriving by boat at the port of San Francisco in October 1908, she produced documents proving she had been born in the United States and was allowed to enter as a returning citizen. But ten months later, for reasons that remain unclear, the commissioner of immigration issued a warrant for her deportation. She was "forcibly dragged from her house" and detained in a cramped, two-story wooden shed at the Pacific Mail Steamship Company dock in San Francisco where all immigrants were processed on their way into the country.[4]

At the turn of the twentieth century, the Bureau of Immigration regularly revoked the citizenship of Americans of Asian descent. The Fourteenth Amendment to the US Constitution, ratified in 1868, declared that "all persons born or naturalized in the United States, and subject to the jurisdiction thereof, are citizens of the United States." But the Bureau of Immigration would have none of it. Referring to these Americans as merely "technical" citizens, it adopted practices and policies designed to prevent them from entering or remaining in the United States. Openly flouting the US Constitution's birthright citizenship guarantee, the commissioner general of immigration declared in his 1907 annual report that any native-born American of Chinese descent who "remained in China until after reaching his majority had in effect expatriated himself . . . and was not, therefore, entitled to be regarded as an American citizen." Even after being forced to abandon this policy, the Bureau of Immigration continued to apply higher standards of proof of citizenship to this group. The "testimony of persons of that race is almost universally unreliable," the commissioner general complained, demanding additional documentation or the testimony of white witnesses before a claim of birthright citizenship would be credited.[5]

Moy could not meet those standards. After spending more than two years in detention as she appealed her case to unsympathetic courts, she was deported to China.

Wilfredo Garza was born in Matamoros, Mexico, a bustling border town a stone's throw across the Rio Grande from Brownsville, Texas. In 1979, when he was eight years old, he left his Mexican mother to be with his father, a US citizen who lived in Brownsville. By the age of sixteen, Garza was working full-time doing odd jobs—picking tomatoes, gathering eggs, roofing houses, whatever work he could find that would earn him a few dollars. But he was repeatedly caught by immigration officials, who would send him back to Mexico upon learning he had no immigration papers. Garza would wait a few days and then wade back across the Rio Grande at night. Once, when he was eighteen, US immigration officials pulled him down from a border fence as he tried to scale it, and the fall broke his arm. Undeterred, he managed to cross back later that same day.[6]

In 2005, Garza was caught again, only this time he was charged with illegal reentry into the United States—a felony punishable by up to two years in prison. And yet that proved to be his lucky day. Because he had been charged with a serious crime, Garza was constitutionally entitled to a lawyer, who had good news. As the son of an American father who had lived a sufficient number of years in the United States, Garza had been born a US citizen.[7]

But it took some doing to prove it. Garza, a slight man with a tattoo of a devil on one hand and an angel on the other, lived in fear. "I don't go out in the street very much," he said as he awaited the government's determination of his status. Those fears were justified. Garza was picked up by immigration officials yet again. Even though he insisted he was a US citizen, he was jailed for two months and deported once again to Mexico. "There is nothing to protect someone claiming to be a U.S. citizen if they are unable to substantiate it," explained a spokesman for US Citizenship and Immigration Services. Finally, thanks in part to his lawyer's efforts, Garza received written confirmation from the US government that he was, and always had been, a citizen of the United States—papers that his lawyer warned him to carry with him at all times. He celebrated by cooking chicken fajitas for family and friends. "I can go anywhere now," he said.[8]

On April 9, 1865, General Robert E. Lee and General Ulysses S. Grant met in the parlor of Wilmer McLean's house in Appomattox, Virginia, to formalize the surrender of Lee's Army of Northern Virginia, effectively putting an end to the Civil War. Less clear was what would happen to the white residents of the seceding states, who were arguably no longer Americans. For the past four years, the military and civilian leaders of those states claimed to have established a new nation they called the "Confederate States of America," complete with its own president, court, legislature, flag, currency, stamps, and, of course, army. In effect, they had expatriated themselves. As one contemporary observer described it, the rebels "no longer have . . . any right of citizenship . . . and [have] become *de facto* foreigners." In 1862, Massachusetts senator Charles Sumner declared them "alien enemies" on the floor of the US Senate. The following year, the Supreme Court made it official, concluding that the residents of the seceding states were "enemies" who had "cast off their allegiance" to the United States and so no longer had any claim to constitutional rights.[9]

Shortly after the war ended, President Andrew Johnson proclaimed a general amnesty for residents of the seceding states, allowing them to regain the rights of citizenship and be pardoned for their crimes. But Johnson carved out an exception for thousands of high-ranking Confederate officials such as General Lee, who were required to petition the president directly for a pardon. Lee quickly did so, not only to attain "full restoration of all rights & privileges" of US citizenship but also to save his own life. Lee had been indicted for treason, a crime carrying the death penalty. In the spring of 1865, an article published in numerous newspapers asked, "Does [Lee] feel about his throat, in his dreams, the encircling hemp which he must know his crimes entitle him to?" He did. Painfully aware of his pariah status, Lee wrote to one family member, "I am considered now such a monster, that I hesitate to darken with my shadow the doors of those I love lest I should bring upon them misfortune."[10]

Lee was never tried for treason, and he died in 1870 of natural causes. But President Johnson never granted Lee's petition for amnesty. Lee's citizenship rights were not restored during his lifetime; he was barred from holding public office and, until a few months before his death, from voting.

In 1975, long after Lee had morphed from a despised traitor into a venerated hero, Congress proposed a joint resolution to "right a grievous wrong" by posthumously restoring Lee's citizenship. In the debate leading up to the vote, members of Congress lavished praise on Lee, describing him as a "patriotic citizen" and a man of "great humanity" whom "all Americans would be proud to refer to as their fellow citizen." No one uttered the words "traitor" or "treason," and the only reference to slavery came when Congressman Kenneth

Hechler of West Virginia erroneously declared that Lee had freed his slaves "long before the War began." (In fact, Lee did not free his slaves until the end of 1862, after being forced to do so by a court order implementing the terms of his father-in-law's will.)

In August 1975, President Gerald Ford signed the resolution into law at the Custis-Lee Mansion on the grounds of Arlington National Cemetery, the Lee family's former home. "General Lee's character has been an example to succeeding generations," President Ford told the nation, "making the restoration of his citizenship an event in which every American can take pride."[11]

This book is the story of how a nation attempted to unmake itself by stripping undesirable groups and individuals of their citizenship over the course of two centuries. Ethel Mackenzie, Haw Moy, Wilfredo Garza, and Robert E. Lee appear to have little in common, but they represent the broad array of Americans who lost their citizenship. Although General Lee lost his citizenship first, his story is recounted last because his more recent posthumous redemption illustrates the complicated relationship between citizenship stripping and the ever-shifting perception of who is worthy of being called an American.

The United States has regularly revoked the citizenship of native-born and naturalized citizens alike. Sometimes the goal has been to deprive these individuals and groups of their civil and political rights; other times, to expel them from the United States altogether. At its core, citizenship stripping embodies the view that society can cast out its unwanted and use that process to redefine itself and all those allowed to remain. Historically, citizenship stripping has been primarily reserved for those who appeared "un-American" in some way to government officials—be it their dress, manners, race, accent, marriage partner, religion, traditions, or even their choice of reading material. Mackenzie, Moy, Garza, and Lee were all victims of a policy that reversed the democratic norm: in a country in which the people are supposed to choose their government, the government instead chose the people.

Marital expatriation was the penalty imposed on American women such as suffragist Ethel Mackenzie for seeking a spouse beyond the stock of American men, "polluting" the United States with the children of foreigners. Congresswoman Ruth Bryan Owen, the dancer Isadora Duncan, and President Ulysses S. Grant's daughter were a few prominent examples of the many thousands of native-born American women who lost their citizenship as a result of their choice of spouse.

Women who married noncitizens were just one subset of Americans deprived of their citizenship—a group that included the anarchist Emma Goldman; an unknown number of Americans of Chinese descent; 5,589 Japanese

Americans forced into camps during World War II; soldiers who fought for foreign armies or deserted during wartime; hundreds of thousands of Mexican Americans during the mass "repatriations" of the mid-twentieth century; and thousands of naturalized citizens whose actions suggested to the US government that they lacked the requisite "attachment" to the United States.

Citizenship stripping is a practice more commonly associated with totalitarian regimes than with a democratic government such as that of the United States. The Soviet Union stripped millions of their citizenship under Joseph Stalin's leadership. During the apartheid era, South Africa revoked the citizenship of the black population, amounting to 70 percent of the residents of that country. Over the four years in which the collaborationist Vichy government controlled France, fifteen thousand French men, women, and children—the vast majority Jews—lost their citizenship. But the US experience proves that, left unchecked, a liberal democracy can also give in to the impulse to expel those whom it finds undesirable. For over a century, Congress enacted laws enabling citizenship stripping that the executive branch enthusiastically implemented and the courts upheld. Indeed, the United States often led the way. In the 1930s, prominent Nazi lawyers praised the United States' race-based citizenship laws and practices, some of which served as a model for the 1935 Nuremberg Laws stripping Germany's Jews of their citizenship.[12]

The consequences of expatriation were sometimes fatal. Native-born American Kazumaro "Buddy" Uno had been visiting Japan when World War II began. He was conscripted into the Japanese Army—an event that automatically revoked his US citizenship under federal law, and eventually led to his capture and then detention in an American-run prisoner-of-war camp in the Philippines. While he was incarcerated, his older brother—a US citizen in military intelligence who by coincidence was also stationed in the Philippines—went to visit him, and at first didn't recognize the "enemy alien" with whom he had spent his childhood in Oakland, California. Uno was desperately ill and weighed less than one hundred pounds. His health shattered, he died not long after the war.[13]

For tens of thousands of others, the loss of US citizenship meant the loss of civil and political rights: the right to vote, to own property, to go to court, to hold public office, to work in certain professions, to criticize the government without fear of reprisal, to be reunited with family, and, in at least one state, to own a dog—a privilege that Pennsylvania once reserved to US citizens alone. For naturalized citizens in particular, the government's citizenship-stripping campaigns forced them to live in fear, chilling any inclination to speak out against the government or the norms of mainstream America. Even decades after becoming citizens the government could decide that their words, actions, or beliefs suggested that their oath of allegiance to the United States had been a lie, serving as the basis for denaturalization and expulsion.[14]

For many of the expatriated, the result was permanent exile from the country they had considered their home. After political activist Emma Goldman was stripped of her citizenship, she was deported with 248 others in 1919. The group was marched en masse at dawn onto a boat that set sail for the Soviet Union, accompanied by fifty-eight armed crewmembers to ensure they reached their destination.[15] Goldman spent the rest of her life living in the Soviet Union and Europe, unable to return to the United States. "I am . . . a woman without a country," she wrote in a 1933 essay, because "to have a country implies, first of all, the possession of a certain guarantee of security, the assurance of having some spot you can call your own and that no one can alienate from you."[16]

———————

To be sure, citizenship alone is no guarantee of equal access to political and civil rights. The Fourteenth Amendment to the US Constitution, ratified in 1868, guaranteed birthright citizenship to all born in the United States, and yet African Americans were denied most of the essential political and social rights of citizenship for much of the century that followed. These Americans were barred from voting, holding office, serving as jurors, testifying in court, traveling freely among the states, using public accommodations, and attending integrated schools. Even today, when de jure discrimination on the basis of race is prohibited, citizens of color often find it difficult to exercise their rights to full membership in the community. State laws disenfranchising felons, heightened voter ID requirements, patterns of policing, and discrimination in employment—to name just a few common practices—can all play a role in eroding the rights and privileges that come with US citizenship.

Nor do US citizens have a monopoly on access to US constitutional rights. The Bill of Rights protects "people" and "persons," not "citizens." The government violates the US Constitution when its officials search a home without a warrant, use excessive force, and prohibit freedom of speech, religion, or association, regardless of whether the target is a US citizen, green card holder, or undocumented immigrant.[17]

Nonetheless, citizenship matters, and never more so than today. The fight for equality for the newly freed slaves began with the Fourteenth Amendment's guarantee of birthright citizenship, even if it did not end there. That same provision has protected the rights of many others occupying a precarious position in the United States. Throughout US history, citizenship has been an important marker of the holder's status, a vital component of personal identity, and a prerequisite for participation in democratic governance. In modern times, citizenship's significance has only increased as legal status grounded on race, gender, religion, and property ownership has diminished. To be the holder of US citizenship—to possess that dark blue passport embossed with a golden eagle—has never been more valuable, for it comes with the right to enter and remain in the United States, and thus to access many of the other rights, conditions, and opportunities that enable human flourishing.[18]

Citizenship stripping runs counter to the popular perception of the United States as an open, tolerant, and multicultural nation of immigrants, welcoming not only new*comers* but also new cultures, religions, and beliefs. That perception is rooted in fact. From the beginning of the nineteenth century to the start of the twentieth, the United States became the new home for three-fifths of the world's immigrants, and it continued to take in more immigrants than any other country throughout the twentieth century. Today, the nation still admits a million immigrants each year, and most will be legally eligible to become US citizens within three to five years of gaining that status. Alongside these liberal immigration and citizenship-acquisition policies, the United States has embraced freedom of speech and of religion under the First Amendment, protecting the rights of ethnic, religious, ideological, and racial minorities to live as they prefer.[19]

And yet the United States is often at war with that identity, at times embracing exclusionary and intolerant policies ranging from Jim Crow to racially restrictive immigration rules to McCarthyism. Laws governing the acquisition of US citizenship have long reflected these same contradictions. Even more so, the laws and practices *revoking* US citizenship are overt evidence of a nation struggling with its conflicted identity—snatching back a status that, some conclude, had been given away too lightly. The price paid by those affected is high. The deprivation of political and civil rights, and possibly of family, home, work, and, in Emma Goldman's words, having "some spot you can call your own," is devastating. Acquiring US citizenship carries great practical and symbolic value. Losing it is even more meaningful, and comes at an enormous cost.

I began this project with the conviction that citizenship stripping was of legal, historical, and symbolic importance, but I assumed the number of people affected was relatively small.

I was wrong. When adding up the number of people who have lost their citizenship over the last two centuries—either because it was revoked by law or because government officials refused to recognize their status—it easily reaches the millions. And I began to meet those personally affected. There was the archivist in Texas whose Asian grandmother was the first member of the family to gain citizenship, only to lose it after marrying a noncitizen, barring her from returning to the United States. The mother of an adopted child born outside the United States emailed me about the difficult and expensive process of obtaining the documents that would prove her daughter is a US citizen—a status her daughter is automatically entitled to under federal law. A friend and former colleague described how when she was five years old, she was detained overnight with her sister and grandmother when returning from abroad because government officials questioned her family's citizenship. A woman in Kansas emailed to explain that the State Department had refused to renew her passport, despite having a state-issued birth certificate and having lived in the United States her entire life, because she had been born at home. She only received her new passport after her representative in Congress intervened on her behalf. Friends and colleagues who are naturalized citizens describe the newfound fear that something they say or do will bring them to the attention of government officials, who may then scour their paperwork, searching for an error in the process that could undo their status.

As these stories suggest, citizenship stripping continues to this day. In 2017, the federal government argued before the US Supreme Court that it could denaturalize anyone found to have made even a minor error in a naturalization application—for example, by failing to admit to having driven sixty-five miles per hour in a sixty-mile-per-hour zone. (The government lost.) Even more recently, the Department of Justice announced it was hiring dozens of lawyers to participate in "Operation Janus," a campaign to investigate seven hundred thousand naturalized Americans to determine whether their citizenship had been granted in error. With increasing frequency, the federal government is questioning the citizenship of Americans living near the US-Mexico border, asserting that their birth certificates may be fraudulent and requiring additional proof of the location of their birth. As Wilfredo Garza's story illustrates, a surprisingly large number of Americans are mistakenly detained and deported by immigration authorities because they cannot prove their citizenship status. One expert estimates that 1 percent of the population held by immigration officials at any time are actually US citizens, amounting to about three thousand people a year. And President Donald Trump has repeatedly threatened to unilaterally end birthright citizenship for the children of undocumented immigrants—a legally dubious claim that nonetheless undermines the citizenship status of millions of people with an undocumented parent.[20] As this book went to press, in August 2020, President Trump questioned the citizenship of Senator Kamala Harris, the Democratic vice presidential nominee. Senator Harris was born in California to immigrant parents legally present in the United States. Trump echoed a widely circulating but baseless claim that she was an alien ineligible not only to be vice president but also to continue to serve as a US senator. Indeed, under Trump's view, Senator Harris—as well as the many thousands of others born in the United States under the same circumstances—could be deported at immigration officials' discretion.[21]

At times, citizenship stripping transcends governmental action. Take, for example, the "birther" movement's bizarre claim that Barack Obama was not a "natural born" citizen qualified to serve as president of the United States. Even after Obama produced his long-form birth certificate showing that he was born in Hawai'i, a significant number of Americans were not convinced. The *New York Times* reported that in January 2016, near the end of Obama's eight years as president, 52 percent of those polled questioned whether Barack Obama had been born in the United States. For these doubters, no amount of evidence could overcome their deep-seated belief that the president of the United States was not a real American.[22] As Obama's experience illustrates, citizenship stripping in all its varied forms sends a powerful message. *You are not American*, the nation declares when it denies citizenship, and in doing so it defines not just "you," but also what it means to be an "American."[23]

Dred and Harriet Scott

CHAPTER 1

CITIZEN SLAVE

The Mississippi River was unusually shallow in September 1838, when a very pregnant Harriet Scott boarded the steamboat *Gipsey* in St. Louis for the month-long journey upriver. Steamships were a dangerous and uncomfortable mode of transportation for everyone, but they were especially risky for slaves like Harriet. Boilers exploded with some regularity, scalding to death seven hundred people on the Mississippi River alone in 1838—many of those the slaves consigned to travel below deck. Even when nothing went wrong, the boat's inhabitants suffered from a combination of the sun's "fierce rays down upon the roof" and a deck "heated by the furnaces below," leaving the passengers "panting and exhausted between these two fires." "Hell afloat" is how one nineteenth-century passenger described such travel during the summer months.[1]

Surely, Harriet would have preferred to give birth to her first child anywhere but a steamship crawling upriver in the lingering heat of late summer—a boat so small and crowded that there was no corner of it unoccupied by passengers and cargo. But she had no choice in the matter. She was only about nineteen years old, a "smart, tidy-looking" woman with a heart-shaped face and tired eyes. She had been married a little shy of two years, and her husband's master, military surgeon Dr. John Emerson, now owned her as well. They were traveling with Dr. Emerson from St. Louis to his new assignment at Fort Snelling, near present-day St. Paul, Minnesota. As his slaves, they had no legal right to refuse to accompany him.[2]

As the labor pains began, Harriet knew that a bunk in the communal ladies' cabin was off-limits to any black person, slave or free, and so her only choice would have been to create a makeshift space below decks behind the bales of blankets and boxes of cargo. Wherever she was, no one on that small boat could help but know that a new human being had arrived. Reverend

Alfred Brunson, a Methodist missionary and fellow passenger, would later note in his memoirs that "on the upward trip . . . a girl . . . was born" to Dr. Emerson's "servants."[3]

Eight years later, when Harriet and her husband, Dred Scott, filed their famous lawsuit petitioning for their family's freedom, their owner disputed many aspects of their claim. But all agreed that the Scotts' daughter Eliza "was born on board the steamboat *Gipsey*, north of the north line of the State of Missouri, and upon the river Mississippi."[4]

And that location mattered. The Missouri Compromise of 1820 had declared that territory north of Missouri's southern border was perpetually off-limits to slavery—a line cleaving the United States into a country that was half slave, half free. Both before and after Eliza's birth, Harriet and Dred Scott spent several years living at Fort Snelling in free territory. They had met at Fort Snelling when their respective owners had brought them there and had married with their owners' blessing. In their legal filings, the Scotts asserted that under the then well-recognized rule of "once free, always free," they remained free even after the family returned to the slave state of Missouri with Dr. Emerson. Their daughter Eliza had a double claim to freedom. Not only did the baby girl inherit her free status from her mother, she was born in free territory.[5]

When they filed their lawsuits in 1846, the status question that consumed Dred and Harriet Scott was whether they and their children were slaves or free, not whether they were US citizens. In any case, the Scotts had no reason to doubt they were Americans. After all, they had both been born and raised in the United States, as was their daughter Eliza and her younger sister Lizzie. How could the family be anything *but* US citizens?

And yet their citizenship became a central question in their case—one of the most important of several momentous issues addressed by the US Supreme Court, and one of the few that remains relevant more than one hundred and fifty years later. After the Civil War, when slavery was officially abolished by the Thirteenth Amendment to the US Constitution, the question of citizenship remained—not just for the newly freed slaves, but for all those in the United States whose race, ethnicity, religion, or political preferences struck those in power as undesirable and "un-American." Dred and Harriet Scott's petition for freedom raised questions about birthright citizenship, the nature of American democracy, the permanency of citizenship status, and the rights essential to citizenship—issues that continued to be litigated for decades to come, and which have yet to be resolved even today.[6]

The Scotts' famous lawsuit began on April 6, 1846, when "Harriet, a woman of color," filed a "petition for leave to sue for freedom." Dr. Emerson had passed away, so she named Dr. Emerson's young widow, Irene Emerson, as the defendant—though later Irene's name would be replaced by that of her brother, John Sanford, who served as the administrator of her late husband's estate. Harriet's petition claimed that two days before, on April 4, 1846, Irene Emerson "made an assault upon" her, "then and there beat, bruised, and ill treated her," and "kept and detained her . . . for the space of twelve hours." Harriet argued that she "was and still is a free person," rendering the assault and imprisonment illegal—and yet the "defendant held and still holds her in Slavery." Dred Scott filed an identical petition on the same day, and each sought ten dollars in damages. The Scotts were illiterate, so in place of a signature each scrawled a rough "X" next to their printed names at the bottom of the petitions.[7]

By the time their lawsuits reached the US Supreme Court, Harriet's case had been consolidated with that of her husband, and his name is the one that history remembers. But Harriet Scott was likely the driving force behind the litigation.[8]

Dred Scott was a small man with a "rather light frame" who stood little more than five feet tall, so he was not much use for heavy labor even in his younger years. By 1846, he was approaching fifty years old—the average life span of male slaves at the time. Like most slave states, Missouri required slave owners to provide for elderly and infirm slaves regardless of whether they could work. In other words, by 1846 Dred Scott was a liability, not an asset.[9]

And yet widow Emerson fought tooth and nail against the Scotts' petitions for freedom. Her lawyers raised every technicality and point of error possible to delay and derail the Scotts' case, even though the precedent in Missouri in 1846 strongly supported the Scotts' claim to freedom. Why? As legal historian Lea VanderVelde has explained, perhaps it was because even though Dred was of little financial value to Mrs. Emerson, his case was inextricably intertwined with Harriet's. And Harriet Scott was worth a small fortune.[10]

At twenty-eight, Harriet had decades of useful service left in her when she filed suit in 1846 and, in the parlance of slave advertisements of the day, she would have been described as "likely"—meaning likely to produce more slaves for her owner. She had already proven her fertility by giving birth to four children in eight years: Eliza, Lizzie, and two sons who had died in infancy. Just as important, the slave status of Harriet's children turned on the outcome of her case under the doctrine of *partus sequitur ventrem* (what is born follows the womb). If Harriet won her freedom, Irene Emerson would also lose her claim to the Scotts' two daughters, who, like their mother, had significant value for their reproductive potential as well as for their labor.[11]

The Scotts surely knew that Harriet and her two daughters would command a high price on the slave market, which must have terrified them. Harriet was described as "devotedly attached to her husband and children," and Dred surely felt the same. But their devotion would not be enough to keep them together if Mrs. Emerson chose to sell her property.[12]

On any given day in 1846, Dred and Harriet Scott would have walked by slaves for sale. A slave pen in downtown St. Louis housed slaves awaiting sale down the river, in New Orleans. Slave dealers marched men and women "handcuffed and chained together, in a long two-by-two column" along the city's sidewalks, "driven under the crack of the driver's whip." Every week like clockwork, slave auctions were held at noon on the east steps of the very same St. Louis courthouse where the Scotts had filed their suit. The auctions always attracted a crowd of buyers in black suits and top hats, milling around to watch as slaves were made to walk, jump, and dance to show their physical strength and stamina, sometimes in time with a fiddle. The courthouse took up a full square block at Market and Fifth Streets, in the very heart of the city, and so, like the rest of St. Louis, Harriet and Dred "couldn't help seeing" the rowdy auctions as they passed by.[13] In any case, Dred Scott needed no reminder of the danger—his first wife had been sold away from him decades before, and he had never laid eyes on her again.[14]

The lawsuit not only gave the Scott family a chance at freedom, it also bought them temporary protection. For as long as the litigation was pending, Mrs. Emerson was barred by court order from selling any member of the Scott family. And when she moved to Massachusetts shortly after the lawsuit began, it provided them with a small measure of freedom. The Scotts were left in custody of the sheriff, who hired them out and collected their wages but allowed them to find their own accommodations out from under the eye of a suspicious owner. Having little faith that the justice system would save them, Dred and Harriet "took advantage of the absence of restraint on their movements" to send their two daughters into hiding—so deeply hidden that the location has eluded the historians who have attempted to discover it since.[15]

Whatever the reason, Irene Emerson chose to litigate the Scotts' case up to the US Supreme Court, with momentous consequences. In hindsight, she surely regretted her choice to fight. For the case came at a high personal cost to her and her family, as well as to the family she claimed to own.

At first, no one involved thought of *Dred Scott v. Sandford* as a case about citizenship. But the Scotts' citizenship status became a threshold issue once the case was refiled in federal court—a court that only had jurisdiction to hear the case if the Scotts were "citizens" within the meaning of the US Constitution.

This dry, technical question of federal jurisdiction nonetheless raised contentious issues about the status of free blacks in a country that embraced racialized slavery while at the same time espousing the principles of representative democracy, liberty, and equality for all.

In defense, John Sanford, acting for his sister Irene Emerson, argued that because Scott was "a negro of African descent, whose ancestors were of pure African blood, and who were brought into this country and sold as slaves," he was not a citizen, *regardless* of whether he was a slave or free. The question of whether free blacks qualified as US citizens had divided the lower courts and bedeviled Congress, and the Supreme Court had yet to pronounce on it. Dred and Harriet Scotts' case would put that question squarely before them.[16]

On July 4, 1776, Americans not only invented their own citizenship, they invented the very idea that people could choose their citizenship.[17]

Under English law, almost everyone born on territory controlled by the British Crown "ow[ed] a lasting obedience to his natural superior the king" and had no power to cut the ties that bound. "Once an Englishman, always an Englishman," had been the maxim cited by British courts. But this was *subjectship*, America's Founding Fathers decided, not *citizenship*. The Declaration of Independence and the American Revolution that followed refuted the English conception of perpetual and immutable citizenship, without choice or consent. The Declaration announced that the "people" were entitled to "dissolve the political bands which have connected them with another," because "governments . . . deriv[e] their just powers from the consent of the governed." After the war was won, and after the nation had ratified the US Constitution in the name of "We the People of the United States," it was clear that these "People" were empowered to choose their government. Left unresolved, however, was the question of which of the United States' millions of residents were included within "We the People."[18]

Remarkably, neither the Declaration of Independence nor the US Constitution drafted eleven years later defined the rights and privileges of US citizenship, or even who could claim that status. The Founding Fathers did not explain whether American citizenship was acquired by being born on US soil, or by being the child of a US citizen parent, or whether both were required. Nor was it clear whether the federal government or the states controlled access to citizenship, or whether either could strip citizens of that status.[19]

Nonetheless, the Constitution does hint at what citizenship meant to the founding generation. We know that they conceived of citizenship as a significant marker of allegiance and civic engagement, for the Constitution provides that eligibility to serve as a member of the US House of Representatives requires a minimum of seven years of US citizenship, and to serve in the Senate a minimum of nine. The Framers shared the belief that US citizenship could be automatically acquired at birth, for the Constitution states that the president of the United States must be a "natural born citizen." And even though the Constitution is silent about who acquires citizenship at birth, it explicitly granted Congress the exclusive power to create a "uniform rule of naturalization" governing immigrants' acquisition of citizenship.[20]

The Framers opposed gradations or hierarchies among citizens, as had been the case in ancient Rome and medieval England. The Constitution prohibits both the government of the United States and those of the individual states from granting a "Title of Nobility" that would suggest that one person or group had a status above their fellow citizens. To ensure that each state treated the others' citizens as equals, Article IV of the Constitution provides: "The Citizens of each State shall be entitled to all Privileges and Immunities of Citizens in the several States."[21]

But the Constitution's Privileges and Immunities Clause begged the question of who qualified as a citizen entitled to equal treatment—a tinderbox issue in a nation divided over racialized slavery. As legal historian Martha Jones has explained, if free blacks were considered citizens *anywhere*, the Privileges and Immunities Clause suggested they had to be treated as citizens *everywhere*, entitled to all the political and civil rights that even many Northern states limited to white property holders alone. So if Vermont bestowed citizenship on its free black residents who then traveled to the South, did the Privileges and Immunities Clause require Virginia to treat those transplanted Vermonters as they would their own white citizens? That vexing question repeatedly came before both the courts and Congress in the first half of the nineteenth century, producing clashing oratory but no clear results.[22]

Indeed, the citizenship status of free blacks nearly derailed the Missouri Compromise of 1820—the legislation that kept war between the slave and free states at bay for decades. Congress had been on the verge of voting in favor of the agreement to allow Maine to join the union as a free state and Missouri as a slave state, as well as barring slavery in the Louisiana Purchase territory north of Missouri's southern border. But then Missouri added to its constitution a prohibition against "free negroes and mulattos from coming to and settling in [Missouri] under any pretext whatsoever." Northern congressmen objected, pointing out that free blacks were considered citizens in many Northern states, entitled under the US Constitution to "all Privileges and Immunities of citizens in the several States." Ultimately, Congress dodged the issue, leaving the question whether free blacks were citizens to another day. Now that *Dred Scott v. Sandford* reached the US Supreme Court, that day had arrived.[23]

On a mid-December morning in 1856, the lawyers for Scott and Sanford settled themselves at counsel table in a ground-floor room on the Senate side of the US Capitol building, waiting for the justices to join them under the vaulted semicircular ceiling. After the packed audience had been shushed into silence, the nine men entered "without any flourish of parade, or announcement . . . in their black silk gowns, in procession, ranked according to the dates of their respective commissions." The men took their seats directly in front of an arcade of windows, severe in their priest-like black robes. Perhaps by design, the light flooding from behind them made it difficult for the spectators to read the expressions on their faces.[24]

This was the second time that *Dred Scott v. Sandford* was to be argued before the US Supreme Court. Remarkably, when the case was first presented to the justices ten months earlier, the nation hardly seemed to notice. A few papers reported in small print on their back pages that a case entitled *Scott v. Sandford* had reached the high court, with little fanfare or commentary. The case was so obscure that no one could get the parties' names right. A Supreme Court clerk misspelled John Sanford's last name, adding a *d* where there was none, and at least one newspaper reported Dred Scott's name as "Fred. Scott." Only the abolitionist paper the *National Era* gave the case headline status. "Important Suit Before the Supreme Court," the paper declared in all caps, and then marveled that "little attention seems to have been given" to a case that "involve[s] highly interesting legal and constitutional principles, touching Slavery and the rights of free colored people."[25]

The Supreme Court, at least, recognized that the case raised important issues, allotting it four days of oral argument from February 11 to 14, 1856. And yet even that was not enough. After conferencing, the court asked counsel to reargue the case in December of the same year, requesting that the lawyers focus in particular on the question of "whether or not . . . [Dred Scott] is a citizen" whose case could be heard in federal court. That was an ominous sign for the Scotts, as this was the one issue on which they had won in the court below.[26]

By the time the second oral argument came around, the nation had finally awoken to the enormity of the matter pending before the US Supreme Court. On Monday, December 15, 1856, all nine justices were present to hear what the *New-York Tribune* called the "the most important [case] that has ever been brought before that tribunal." "The Supreme Court was thronged this morning," the *Baltimore Sun* reported on the same day, noting that the audience included "many distinguished jurists and members of Congress," and that the case "daily attracts large crowds of earnest auditors." The Washington *Evening Star*, which had failed to mention the matter when it was argued in February, now described it as "one of the most important cases ever brought up for ad-judication by the Supreme Court."[27]

The Scott family's fate was now in the hands of the nine black-robed men, and in particular those of Chief Justice Roger Brooke Taney. As befit his sta-tus, Taney occupied the center chair, flanked by four justices on either side. By tradition, it was Taney who called for the Scotts' attorney, Montgomery Blair, to step forward to the podium to begin the oral argument.

Taney was six feet tall and did not lack confidence. A contemporary re-marked that Taney issued his pronouncements on questions of law and life alike with an air of papal infallibility. But he walked with a stoop and carried a whiff of "persistent invalidism" that for decades had led each new president to assume he would be looking for Taney's replacement in short order. Yet Taney hung on. By the time the Scotts' case came before the court, he was a few months shy of eighty. He had already served on the court for two decades and would labor on for another eight years until his death in 1864.[28]

Taney was born into a wealthy slave-owning family in Calvert County, Maryland. Although he had freed his own slaves more than thirty years be-fore the Scotts' case reached his court, he remained an ardent supporter of the slave states' right to maintain the institution of slavery, free from interference by the free states or the federal government. And he was not alone. Four other justices were also from slave states, all from slaveholding families. Seven out of the nine justices had been appointed by Southern, slave-owning presidents. As a reporter for the *New-York Tribune* commented, "The members of the Court are not impartial in such a case," so to "expect them to sit, hear, and re-solve, unswayed by the passions of those who placed them where they are, and by the interests of that institution which now controls every other department of the Government, would be to suppose them more than men."[29]

As he sat waiting for oral argument to begin, Montgomery Blair knew that he had his work cut out for him. The lanky forty-three-year-old Blair was a socially and politically prominent Republican from the border state of Ken-tucky who had taken on the Scotts' case pro bono once it reached the Supreme Court.[30]

For over a decade, Dred and Harriet Scott had been dependent on a se-ries of attorneys willing to work for little or no money, so the couple had little say in who represented them.[31] If the Scotts had been able to select their own counsel, Blair would surely not have been their first choice. Although he was against the expansion of slavery into the western territories, Blair was also a former slaveholder who opposed integrating blacks into white society as social or political equals. In 1863, in a passionate speech given while serving as President Lincoln's postmaster general, he declared that the nation was "menaced by the ambition of the ultra-Abolitionists" who wanted to see Negroes "elevated to equality" and who "would make the manumission of the slaves the means of infusing their blood into our whole system by blending with it 'amalgamation, equality, and fraternity.'" Like many supporters of the Union—including, for a time, President Lincoln—Blair advocated that freed slaves be immediately removed from the United States to Africa or Central America. (Abolitionist William Lloyd Garrison attacked Blair for his "vulgar exhibition of senseless colorphobia," concluding, "It is Mr. Montgomery Blair who ought to be banished, if anybody.")

Blair clung to these views throughout the Reconstruction era and beyond. In 1879, a few years before his death, he published an article in the *North American Review* criticizing black suffrage and referring favorably to the idea of deporting the black population, writing that "*Nature* has drawn such indelible lines of distinction between the black and white races that they can not live as equals in the same government."[32]

At 11 a.m. on December 15, 1856, this was the man who rose to his feet before the US Supreme Court to argue that Dred Scott was a free man and a citizen of the United States.

On a clear spring morning almost three months later, Chief Justice Taney slowly made his way through the throng of top-hatted dignitaries gathered on the platform over the steps at the Capitol's east portico. In a few moments he would swear in James Buchanan as the nation's fifteenth president.

Buchanan, a Democrat, won comfortably in the Electoral College, but he lost ten of the fourteen Northern states and received less than half the popular vote in the three-way race for president. His election temporarily put to rest the Southern states' threats to secede had Republican John Frémont won, but the contentious campaign and election had done nothing to soothe sectional tensions around slavery. Buchanan despised abolitionists, viewed slavery as a kindness to the slaves, and had the South to thank for two-thirds of the Electoral College's vote in his favor. He had no hope of bringing the country together.[33]

Buchanan seemed to think that the Taney Court could save him and the country from having to address the schism over slavery. In his three-hour-long inaugural speech, he described the conflict between slave and free states as "a judicial question," promising to "cheerfully submit" to the court's decision in *Dred Scott*, "whatever this may be."[34]

That was easy for Buchanan to say. Violating today's norms of secrecy, several of the justices had communicated with Buchanan to inform him that the court would rule against Dred Scott, and so Buchanan knew that the court would soon deliver a decision he could live with.[35]

Two days later, the rest of the nation learned the result as well. At 11 a.m. on March 6, Chief Justice Taney and his colleagues again took their places in their ground-floor courtroom. Once again, the courtroom was packed, but this time it was the justices and not the lawyers who took center stage. Taney cleared his throat and began. For more than two hours, he read aloud from his opinion defending the outcome, his wavering voice at times so low as to be barely audible.[36]

The opinion was breathtaking in its scope. A seven-member majority of the court had concluded that Dred Scott's residence in free territory was not enough to free him, ending the "once free, always free" rule that had governed in the past. But Taney's opinion then went far beyond that already broad ruling to conclude that Congress lacked any authority to prohibit slavery in the territories. The decision rendered the thirty-seven-year-old Missouri Compromise banning slavery north of Missouri's southern border a dead letter, and it marked the first time in its history that the Supreme Court invalidated a major federal statute. Many in the North, including Abraham Lincoln, thought the decision would inevitably lead to the nationalization of slavery—unless the nation went to war first.

Arguably, however, Taney should not have reached any of those issues. For he also declared that no black person, whether slave or free, could *ever* be a US citizen. That meant the court had no jurisdiction to hear the Scotts' case, and so the court lacked authority to opine on any other matter.[37]

The *Dred Scott* decision is infamous for its perpetuation and expansion of slavery, which pushed a teetering nation one step closer to civil war. But Taney's conclusions about black citizenship were equally sweeping. In one stroke, he stripped national citizenship from half a million free blacks living in the United States and barred four million enslaved blacks from any hope of joining the polity, even if they bought or won their freedom.

Taney couched black citizenship as a question that began and ended with history—a history he skewed to support the conclusion he endorsed. He concluded that only those persons "who were at the time of the adoption of the Constitution recognized as citizens in the several States, became also citizens of [the United States]"—a group that Taney concluded could not have included blacks. "For more than a century," Taney wrote, blacks had "been regarded as beings of an inferior order, and altogether unfit to associate with the white race, either in social or political relations." Then, in a sentence for which he would be pilloried for years to come, Taney said that blacks were considered "so far inferior, that they had no rights which the white man was bound to respect; and that the negro might justly and lawfully be reduced to slavery for his benefit."[38]

As support, Taney pointed to long-standing state and federal laws prohibiting cross-racial marriage, excluding blacks from militias, barring blacks from naturalizing, and preventing blacks from voting. The US Constitution itself endorsed slavery by prohibiting Congress from interfering with the importation of slaves until 1808, and by requiring that any "person held to service or labor" (typically a slave) who flees to another state must be returned to his owner. Taney conceded that *states* could bestow *state* citizenship on black residents if they so chose, but states had no power to endow blacks with citizenship under the US Constitution.[39]

But what of the Declaration of Independence's sweeping rhetoric that "all men are created equal" and are "endowed by their Creator with certain unalienable rights"? Taney admitted that such language would "seem to embrace the whole human family." Yet for him it was "too clear for dispute that the enslaved African race were not intended to be included, and formed no part of the people who framed and adopted this declaration." For if so, the "conduct of the distinguished men who framed the Declaration of Independence," many of whom owned slaves themselves, "would have been utterly and flagrantly inconsistent with the principles they asserted."

Like so many before and since, Taney could not reconcile the Declaration's stirring words with its proponents' actions. He concluded that if the Founding Fathers had intended to include blacks as among the "men" who were "created equal," even as they imported and enslaved so many of that race for their own benefit, then they would have "deserved and received universal rebuke and reprobation" from the rest of the world. The twenty-first-century reader is struck by how Taney perfectly captured the founding generation's hypocrisy, even as he tried to resolve it by enlarging the denial of blacks' humanity at its core.[40]

And so Taney concluded that black inhabitants of the United States "are not included, and were not intended to be included, under the word 'citizens' in the Constitution, and can therefore claim none of the rights and privileges which that instrument provides for and secures to citizens of the United States."[41]

Justice Benjamin Curtis was one of only two justices to dissent, and the only one to attack Taney's views on black citizenship at length. A shade under fifty years old, Curtis was a generation younger than all but one of his colleagues on the bench, and he had served on the court for only six years—a mere whippersnapper from Taney's perspective. Although born and educated in Massachusetts, Curtis was no firebrand for black equality. As the court's first and only Whig, he advocated for compromise on the slavery issue. Curtis was a vocal supporter of the Fugitive Slave Act requiring that Northern states help return fleeing slaves as a key component in such a compromise—a position for which he had been excoriated in his home state. Later, he would go on record as opposing the Emancipation Proclamation. Ralph Waldo Emerson publicly proclaimed that Curtis was a man "without self-respect" and "without character" for such views.[42]

"It is not true," Curtis wrote in a direct rebuke to Taney, "that the Constitution was made exclusively by and for the white race." "Colored persons were not only included in the body of 'the people of the United States' by whom the Constitution was ordained and established," Curtis explained, "in at least five of the States, they had the power to act, and doubtless did act, by their suffrages, upon the question of its adoption." Because some blacks were citizens at the time of the Constitution's ratification—indeed, had voted to ratify it themselves—they were part of "We the People" who, paraphrasing the words of the Constitution's preamble, had "ordained and established" the Constitution for "themselves and their posterity." It "would be strange," the justice observed, "if we were to find in that instrument anything which deprived of their citizenship any part of the people of the United States who were among those by whom it was established."[43]

Curtis's dissent gave a full-throated defense of birthright citizenship, at least for those born free on US soil. Repeating arguments long made by free blacks, Curtis observed that the Constitution's requirement that the president be "a natural-born citizen . . . assumes that citizenship may be acquired by birth." Birthright citizenship was the common-law rule at the time the Constitution was ratified in 1788 and had generally been accepted both before the Declaration of Independence and after, when those born in the former colonies became citizens of the United States. Although Curtis failed to mention it, at the turn of the nineteenth century the federal government had expressly recognized birthright citizenship when it issued certificates of citizenship to black sailors to prevent their impressment by the British navy. The "Constitution has recognised the general principle of public law that allegiance and citizenship depend on place of birth," Curtis declared.[44]

Curtis did not deny that state and federal laws subjected free blacks to a long list of disabilities. But he pointed out that similar laws excluded women, children, and the mentally incompetent from voting, holding office, controlling property, and the like, and yet no one denied that these groups were US citizens within the meaning of the Constitution. "Citizenship, under the Constitution of the United States, is not dependent on the possession of any particular political or even of all civil rights," he explained, "and any attempt to define it must lead to error."[45]

Curtis was technically correct. And yet in making this point, he embraced a view of citizenship that was so thin as to be all but content-less. He would not have the Court resolve questions such as which citizens could exercise the franchise and "what civil rights shall be enjoyed," leaving those matters to "be determined by each State, in accordance with its own views of the necessities or expediencies of its condition." For Curtis, then, free blacks were citizens within the meaning of the US Constitution, but that status seemed to confer on them no rights beyond the ability to file a lawsuit in the US courts.[46]

Curtis's dissent was applauded throughout the North, and his words were reprinted in newspapers across the country. But he took no pleasure in becoming the standard-bearer for Northern abolitionists, and his dissent in this momentous case would ultimately shatter what had once been a successful career. As he explained in a letter to a friend, the political nature of the court's decision, the partisan rancor that followed it, and an acrimonious exchange of letters with Chief Justice Taney about the case had left him without the "confidence in the court . . . [or] that willingness to cooperate with them, which are essential to the satisfactory discharge of my duties as a member of that body." Within six months of the decision, Curtis had tendered his resignation—one of the very few justices in the court's history to leave the position before death or retirement—citing only "reasons growing out of his private affairs."[47]

News of this final complete loss of any hope for freedom must have devastated Dred and Harriet Scott. In the words of St. Louis, Missouri's *Holmes County Republican*, the Supreme Court's decision "dooms [them] to Slavery." The court's ruling crushed not only their own hopes for freedom, but also those of every other slave in a similar position, as well as the claims of free blacks throughout the United States to the rights and privileges of US citizenship.[48]

For the Scotts, the lawsuit had been an eleven-year ordeal that had ended in disaster. Dred Scott told one newspaper reporter that the case had brought him a "heap 'o trouble," and that if he had known "it was gwine to last so long" he would not have filed it. The Scotts had brought the case to keep their family together, but they were now in greater danger than ever before. Irene Emerson would have no interest in retaining the slaves who had battled her for over a decade for their freedom, and there was nothing to stop her from selling Harriet and Dred at the next auction, as well as their two daughters—though only if she could find them first. Eliza, now eighteen years old, and Lizzie, about ten, were still in hiding, likely living under an assumed name with a friend or relative. Their parents must have clung to the hope that whatever happened next, the girls could stay together.[49]

And then, a miracle. In March 1857, the Springfield, Massachusetts, *Argus* ran a story reporting that the Scott family was owned by John Sanford's sister Irene Emerson (now Irene Chaffee) and her second husband, US congressman Calvin Clifford Chaffee. The Chaffees lived in Massachusetts, where slavery was both illegal and unpopular, and Representative Chaffee was well known as an "ultra abolitionist" member of Congress. The *Argus* mocked him for pretending to be an abolitionist while "at the same time enjoy[ing]" the benefits of slavery "under the cover of his wife's crinoline."[50]

Chaffee quickly responded in a letter to the *Springfield Republican* that "neither myself nor any member of my family . . . ever knew of the existence of that suit," and that he had "no power to control" the litigation. His professed ignorance was hard to square with his wife's eleven-year legal battle. The Chaffees became laughingstocks, and Representative Chaffee was derided as a hypocrite. Although he did not resign his seat, life in Washington, DC, must have become "uncomfortable," as the *Argus* gleefully put it. Chaffee lost his next election to Congress, and never served in elected office again.[51]

As one historian asked, did Chaffee "innocently march . . . up the aisle with his Southern bride, unaware that his betrothed was soon to be unmasked as one of the most famous slave masters on the continent?" Or did he know full well that his new wife had spent years defending her right to retain ownership of her slaves? Either way, that an abolitionist member of Congress became the accidental owner of the most famous slaves in America was further evidence that the United States was "a house divided"—at times, literally—on the issue of slavery.[52]

Whatever he may have known before the Supreme Court issued its decision, the humiliated Chaffee moved quickly to defend himself and right the very public wrong. He declared the Supreme Court's decision "monstrous" and expressed his "fullest sympathy with Dred Scott and his family in their efforts to secure their just rights to freedom," writing in the pages of the *Springfield Republican* newspaper, "I believe that, under the Constitution and laws of this Union, these colored persons have become not only freemen, but citizens." In a heartfelt private letter to the Scotts' attorney, Montgomery Blair, Chaffee asked advice on how to help the Scotts. "My whole soul utterly loathes & abhors the whole system of slavery," he wrote, and the court's decision "has made humanity grieve and all true Americans blush."

On May 13, 1857, Chaffee filed papers transferring any ownership interests he and his family "have or are supposed to have" in the Scott family to the son of Dred Scott's childhood owner—a man who had long supported the lawsuit financially, apparently on the strength of his fond memories of Dred while growing up—who promptly freed them.[53]

(Although Representative Chaffee took pains never to concede that his family owned the Scotts, his wife had no such qualms. On May 27, 1857, Irene Chaffee's attorney quietly filed a legal claim for the Scotts' wages earned during the years of litigation, which she received.)[54]

On May 26, 1857, more than eleven years after they filed their case in court, the Scott family was free. In an interview, Dred professed to be "grateful for the boon of liberty which had recently been granted him." His daughters came out from hiding, and the family could live together openly for the first time in many years. Dred and Harriet Scott had filed their lawsuit to keep their family together, and in that they had succeeded. But, as they both well knew, they were free not because a court of law had declared them so. They were free because in their case—and their case only—the court of public opinion had demanded it.[55]

If President Buchanan had truly expected the country to "cheerfully submit" to the court's decision in *Dred Scott*, then he was sorely disappointed. Newspapers throughout the North howled in outrage, competing to find colorful adjectives with which to condemn it. "Barbarous and humiliating," shrieked the New York *Evening Post*. New York's *Independent* spluttered, "There never was, under the whole heaven, a more atrocious, wholesale wickedness perpetrated upon the bench of justice than this." Unable to leave it at that, the paper continued, *Dred Scott* "takes . . . a whole race by the throat, and strangles it, and flings forth the lifeless corpse." Although most of the outrage was reserved for the majority opinion's statements about slavery, editorials also condemned its rejection of black citizenship. The *Evening Post* declared that the Supreme Court "has annihilated at a single blow the citizenship of the entire colored population of the country, and with it all laws and constitutional provisions of the different states for the protection of those rights."[56]

The Southern courts greeted the court's decision in *Dred Scott* with relief. These courts relied in particular on Taney's assertion that regardless of whether some states chose to make their black residents *state* citizens, no black person could ever be a citizen within the meaning of the US Constitution, and no state could be required to grant them the rights of citizenship. In 1859, the Mississippi Supreme Court cited Taney's opinion to reject the claim of a freed slave living in the free state of Ohio that, as a citizen of Ohio, she could inherit property bequeathed to her by her former owner—a white Mississippian who also happened to be her father. "Ohio has . . . the right to degrade and disgrace herself" by "confer[ring] citizenship" on free blacks, or "on the chimpanzee or ourang-outang" for that matter, sneered Mississippi's highest court. But according to *Dred Scott*, Ohio could not force Mississippi to "lower their own citizens and institutions" by granting a free black woman that same citizenship status.[57]

Free! The Scotts must have marveled at their change in fortune. After eleven long years in court, they were finally free. But they still had to live in the world that the divided nation and the Taney Court created for them. They felt secure enough to fetch their two daughters from hiding, living together for the first time in years in a wooden house with a balcony in an alley near Carr and Sixth Streets in downtown St. Louis. Dred Scott found work as a porter at the nearby Barnum Hotel. Aided by her daughters—Eliza now a young adult and Lizzie a teenager—Harriet was employed as a washerwoman, backbreaking physical labor requiring buckets of scalding water, caustic soap, and heavy irons. She was used to hard work, explaining to a reporter that she was proud that she had "always been able to yarn her own livin'." The Scotts must have taken a newfound pleasure in keeping their wages every week rather than be forced to turn them over to their white owner.[58]

But were the Scotts safe? In the months after his case had made the front pages of newspapers across the nation, Dred Scott had become a public figure, "attracting a great deal of attention from strangers" as he walked the streets of St. Louis. One newspaper described him as "the most celebrated character of the present day," and another as "the best known colored person in the world."[59]

All the attention made the Scott family nervous. When newspaper reporters came knocking on the door a few months after the case was decided, Harriet was visibly riled. "Why don't white man 'tend to his own business, and let dat nigger 'lone?" she complained, then worried out loud, "Some of dese days dey'll steal dat nigger—dat are a fact." Harriet had good reason to be worried. It was not unusual for free blacks to be snatched and sold back into slavery, and she feared that the extraordinary media attention followed by their very public emancipation put the whole family at risk of retaliation.[60]

Even if the Scott family could avoid kidnapping, re-enslavement, or other physical harm, their lives as ostensibly "free" persons were deeply circumscribed, as was the case for all free blacks in Missouri. As sectional tensions over slavery increased, white Missourians had grown more paranoid about the risk of free blacks unsettling the enslaved population and had enacted a series of laws intended to curb their influence. Black churches were not permitted to hold services unless a white police officer was present. Free blacks were barred from "bartering in liquors" or assembling in taverns. Although Dred Scott was permitted to work at the Barnum Hotel, no black person was allowed to stay there, or in any other hotel available to whites. Another law set a curfew for free blacks and slaves alike, declaring that "all negroes found in the street after the hour of ten o'clock without a proper pass will be arrested." Free blacks were barred from most professions, and even from obtaining the license required to use a wheelbarrow in the streets, making the job of courier off-limits as well. In 1847, Missouri joined other Southern states by enacting a law forbidding teaching any black person, free or slave, how to read or write. Dred and Harriet Scott were illiterate and had signed their court papers with an "X"; Missouri sentenced their daughters to the same fate.[61]

Even to claim their status as free persons, the Scotts had first to obtain a license from the state, which entailed posting a $1,000 bond to ensure that they maintained "good behavior," along with finding a white man willing to sign as security. A black person without a license could be arrested, jailed, rented out to pay off the large fine, whipped, and then immediately expelled from the state and barred from returning. Not only were the Scotts not citizens; they were just barely free.[62]

The *Dred Scott* decision illustrated how citizenship and freedom were inextricably intertwined. As for so many other Americans, Chief Justice Taney found it impossible to reconcile black citizenship with black enslavement—though he responded to that dilemma by ending citizenship rather than by ending slavery. The existence of one status rendered the other intolerable, perhaps because the social and political rights of citizenship—not only the right to vote and hold office but also to obtain an education, travel freely, own property, access the justice system, use public spaces, and participate in public discourse—suggested not just equality but also a shared humanity incompatible with the institution of slavery.

US senator Hiram Rhodes Revels

Confederate general Robert E. Lee

CHAPTER 2

CONFEDERATE CITIZEN

On the morning of November 10, 1865, two hundred soldiers in their Union blues lined up in the Old Capitol Prison yard, their bayoneted rifles propped before them. The yard housed the Old Brick Capitol, which had served as Congress's temporary home after the British burned down the US Capitol building during the War of 1812. Now a prison, the three-story Federal-style brick building would have been attractive if not for the metal crossbars on every window. Just a few hundred feet to the west loomed the newly renovated Capitol dome, crowned by the bronze Statue of Freedom cast by a slave five years before. Directly in front of the soldiers stood the wooden gallows, the reason they had gathered there that morning.[1]

During the final months of the war, some of these men had themselves been prisoners at Andersonville, the infamous Confederate prison. To be here, they had survived starvation rations, foul water, squalid conditions, and regular beatings that killed more than thirteen thousand of their fellow soldiers. Now they had been invited to watch their former jailor die.

Captain Henry Wirz, commandant of the Andersonville prison, was perhaps the most hated man in America. Just about everyone had seen the newspaper photos of the "walking skeletons" liberated several months before—men so emaciated that the bones of their skulls jutted through wisps of hair. After watching a boatload of released prisoners walk ashore, the poet Walt Whitman wrote, "Can those be *men*—those little, livid brown, ash-streaked, monkey-looking dwarfs? Are they really not mummied, dwindled corpses?" He concluded, "There are deeds, crimes, that may be forgiven; but this is not among them."[2]

At ten minutes past ten on that November morning, Wirz was marched up the scaffolding's weathered steps to catcalls of "Hang the Scoundrel!" Another onlooker cried, "Down with him; let him drop!" as the noose was adjusted around his neck. The executioner pulled out the bolts and pressed the "fatal spring," and the raised platform on which Wirz stood fell away. The spectators cheered as he fell six feet and hung, suspended off the ground. He drew up his legs several times, shrugged his shoulders, and then went still. His body was cut down fifteen minutes later.[3]

Wirz's execution was covered in all the major papers throughout the country, North and South. The news quickly reached bucolic Lexington, Virginia, where the former Confederate general Robert E. Lee now lived. Jefferson Davis, the former president of the Confederate States of America, would have learned about it from his prison cell at Fort Monroe in Virginia. Wirz was the most notorious of the Confederate officers to be executed, and the nation celebrated the event. Lee and Davis must have wondered if they would be next.

These two men had every reason to think that they would soon be mounting the scaffolding of their own gallows. The *New York Times* proclaimed that General Lee had "levied war against the United States more strenuously than any other man in the land, and thereby has been specially guilty of the crime of treason"—a crime carrying the death penalty. In April 1865, in a speech celebrating the fall of the Confederate capital in Richmond, Virginia, then vice president Andrew Johnson was interrupted after mentioning Jefferson Davis's name with catcalls of "Hang him! Hang him!" Johnson broke from his prepared speech to nod in agreement, declaring, "Yes. I say hang him twenty times." Two weeks later, Abraham Lincoln was dead and Johnson was president. When asked at the end of the war how the North should treat Confederate leaders, Johnson replied, "I would arrest them, I would try them, I would convict them, and I would hang them"—a course of action endorsed by his cabinet.[4]

Johnson's words were echoed by thousands of ordinary citizens who sent letters in 1865 urging him to punish the "traitors" who led the rebellion, and in particular Lee and Davis. The Confederate leaders "ought to be hung or driven from the country, their property confiscated, their lands divided up," one insisted. Referring to Davis, a rope maker from Illinois asked if he could "mak[e] the rope, free of charge, with which to hang the scoundrel." The *Cleveland Daily Leader* put it most plainly: "Jefferson Davis must die," the paper declared, and advocated the same for Lee.[5]

Both Davis and Lee were well aware of their precarious position. As one paper described it, Davis had already been "buried alive" in a prison cell in Fort Monroe, Virginia, where he was held on charges of treason. Although Lee remained free, he was formally a "prisoner on parole" after surrendering his Army of Northern Virginia to Union general Ulysses S. Grant at Appomattox

Court House, and he had recently been indicted for treason as well. Lee and Davis, like all those loyal to the Confederacy and not yet pardoned, had also lost their citizenship rights—meaning they could not vote, hold office, or take back possession of their property seized by the federal government. Lee in particular was painfully aware that he had become a pariah, observing in a letter that he had become "an object of censure to a portion of the country."[6]

Not long after Wirz's execution, Hiram Rhodes Revels was packing his bags to travel from his home in Vicksburg, Mississippi, to Jackson, about fifty miles away. Vicksburg, located on a high bluff at the confluence of the Yazoo and Mississippi Rivers, was nestled in a jumble of steep hills and surrounded by swamp, making travel challenging. The route was familiar to Revels, who had taken it many times for his work on behalf of the Freedmen's Bureau, a relief agency established by the federal government at war's end to help the newly emancipated slaves. Revels was a minister by education and profession, but now he spent most of his time establishing schools for the freedmen. Fewer than one in ten former slaves was literate, and schools were what the South's four million freedmen most needed.[7]

Revels was a rarity—an educated black man from the South dedicated to working on behalf of the emancipated slaves. He was born free in 1827 in Fayetteville, North Carolina, but because it was impossible even for free blacks to receive a higher education in that state, he left for a Quaker seminary in Indiana and then earned his degree from Knox College in Galesburg, Illinois. He became a minister in the African Methodist Episcopal Church and traveled throughout the Midwest before the Civil War, attending to the spiritual needs of both free and enslaved blacks. Dred and Harriet Scott surely heard his name when he passed through St. Louis and may even have attended his sermons at their neighborhood church.[8]

Revels was in Baltimore at the start of the war, and he quickly helped to organize the black population to fight for the Union. He served as a chaplain to Maryland's first black regiment, and later assisted in organizing a black regiment in Missouri. Revels came from a politically engaged family whose history stretched back to the founding of the nation. His great uncle, Aaron Revels, had been wounded in the Revolutionary War and then in 1787 had cast his vote in favor of the ratification of the US Constitution. More recently, two of Revels's relatives had fought with John Brown's army at Harpers Ferry.[9]

Revels made a powerful impression. He was physically striking—tall and heavy-set, with a full beard that showed flecks of white as he entered middle age. Employing the obsessive racial classifications of the day, newspapers described him as a "very light mulatto" or "octoroon," and one complimented his "decidedly Caucasian nose." But his intellect and his character were his most notable features. "He is of popular manners and speaks with great ease, fluency, and generally in good taste," one contemporary reported, and another described him as "a man of much energy and character, with excellent and well developed mental qualifications."[10]

Deeply religious, Revels was dogged in his determination to resurrect Mississippi and its population of emancipated slaves from the ashes of war. In 1870, he wrote to a friend, "I am working very hard in politics. . . . We are determined that Mississippi shall be settled on a basis of justice and political and legal equality." To pursue that goal, Revels was often on the road. His wife, Phoeba, had grown used to managing their growing household on her own, though Revels regularly sent home letters enclosing small amounts of money and asking that she "kiss the children for me."[11]

But on this particular evening before his departure, something happened to make the energetic and unflappable Revels change his plans and stay home. He received a "warning"—or perhaps a veiled threat—that a group of "bushwhackers," also known to call themselves "Ku-Kluxers," were planning to ambush him on his journey.[12]

Revels would have heard enough about "Kukluxery" to take the warning seriously. Founded by Confederate veterans in Pulaski, Tennessee, in 1866, the Ku Klux (as it was first known) had quickly replicated itself throughout the South. The group terrorized blacks and their white Republican allies. In the years 1867 and 1868 alone, Kukluxers attacked at least 10 percent of the members of constitutional conventions in the South, killing seven. In 1868, another black leader, newly elected South Carolina state legislator Benjamin Randolph, was murdered in broad daylight while standing on a train platform. Witnesses described his killers strolling slowly away after they shot him, knowing full well that they would never be caught or prosecuted.[13]

Revels—an educated, charismatic black man who was actively encouraging blacks to take over the reins of political power—was just the sort the Ku Klux targeted for attack. Recognizing the very real danger, Revels changed his travel plans, choosing to stay home rather than make the trip to Jackson. But he had a bigger decision to make: Would he step aside permanently, or would he continue his work, taking his rightful place in the governance of his state despite the risk to him and his family?[14]

———————————

In the years following the Civil War, the fate of black men and women like Hiram Revels was intertwined with that of the leaders of the Confederacy such as Robert E. Lee and Jefferson Davis. As the war came to an end, neither group's members were full-fledged citizens of the United States, and both were in jeopardy of being imprisoned, killed, or forcibly banished from the United States—albeit for very different reasons.

As Wirz's execution vividly demonstrated, Confederate leaders were at serious risk of prosecution and, if convicted, execution by the government against which they had spent four years at war. Banishment was the comparatively kinder solution, and the one that President Lincoln preferred. "I should not be sorry to have them out of the country," he told his cabinet in April of 1865, but then added that he would "be for following them up pretty close, to make sure of their going." Many Confederates did flee, setting up communities in Mexico, Cuba, and Brazil, where even today one can find the great-great-grandchildren of these Confederados waving Confederate flags and dressing up in Confederate-gray uniforms for local holidays.[15]

The emancipated slaves were also at risk of coerced removal, though again this was presented as a kindness to both the races. Throughout the 1800s, colonization societies had helped former slaves emigrate to Liberia and Haiti, with encouragement and financial support from the government. President Lincoln was a longtime proponent of colonization. In August 1862, even as he was editing a draft of the Emancipation Proclamation, Lincoln told a delegation of freed slaves that "difference" between the races "affords a reason why we should be separated." He suggested the same in his message to Congress in December 1862 before abandoning the idea by the end of the war.[16]

But even if blacks and former Confederates were permitted to live freely and in relative safety in the United States, it was far from clear in 1865 that either group would exercise the rights of full citizenship in a postbellum United States of America.

When Lee surrendered his Army of Northern Virginia in April 1865, many of the white residents of the Confederate states had lost the legal and political rights of US citizenship. Their leaders had sought to establish a new nation, the "Confederate States of America," and so in effect they had expatriated themselves. During the war, Massachusetts senator Charles Sumner had declared that the occupants of the seceding states should be considered not just criminals but also "alien enemies," and Pennsylvania representative Thaddeus Stevens explained that by "renouncing their allegiance to the Union . . . the Constitution and the laws of the Union are abrogated so far as they are concerned." In 1863, the US Supreme Court labeled even the loyal citizens residing in the seceding states as "enemies" who had lost all constitutional rights because their state governments had "cast off their allegiance" to the United States.[17]

The newly freed slaves were also excluded from citizenship. In 1857, the Supreme Court declared in *Dred Scott v. Sandford* that no black person, slave or free, was a citizen, and that blacks had "no rights which the white man was bound to respect." As the war wound to a close, all agreed that the "peculiar institution" was dead. But the abolition of slavery did not automatically transform the newly freed slaves into American citizens with equal political rights. Most of the white population, North and South, did not support giving freedmen the right to vote, hold public office, serve on a jury, or testify in court. The "Black Codes," enacted by the all-white Southern legislatures immediately after the war, barred the freed slaves from doing all those things, as well as from owning land, entering the professions, and accessing the courts in any capacity other than as defendants in a civil or criminal case brought by whites. "Nothing would make me cut a nigger's throat from ear to ear so quick," one Southerner told a Northern journalist, "as having him set up his impudent face [in court] to tell that a thing wasn't so when I said it was so."[18]

In particular, in 1865, almost no Southerners and few Northerners thought blacks should be allowed to vote—a privilege that in any case had never perfectly aligned with citizenship. In a world in which all white women and many white men were denied the franchise, giving that right to the newly freed slaves struck many as ludicrous. "We don't believe that because the nigger is free he ought to be saucy," one South Carolinian who had remained loyal to the Union declared, "and we don't mean to have any such nonsense as letting him vote."[19]

By war's end, the newly emancipated slaves and the Confederate leaders were in a race to acquire citizenship. The stakes were high. Whichever group first acquired the civil and political rights of full citizens—and in particular, the right to vote and hold state and federal office—would secure their own precarious position in the United States. And if the Confederate leaders won that race, blacks had good reason to fear they would use that regained power to bar blacks from obtaining the same status.

––––––––––––

The 39th Congress was controlled by the Radical Republicans, a faction of the Republican Party who sought equal political rights for the newly emancipated slaves. These political leaders were well aware of the consequences to the nation if the white Southern planter elite—dubbed the "slaveocracy" by antislavery campaigners—regained citizenship rights before the emancipated slaves were awarded theirs.

Before the war, the slaveocracy had dominated the federal government. Although this group was a minority even in the South, they wielded outsized political power thanks to the infamous three-fifths compromise in Article I of the US Constitution. To convince the slave states to ratify the Constitution, the Framers had agreed to count each enslaved African as three-fifths of a person for the purpose of apportioning seats in the House of Representatives and votes in the Electoral College. As a result, the South had somewhere between twenty to thirty "slave seats" in each Congress—seats that corresponded entirely to the enslaved population—giving each white voter in the South two or three times the voting power as those in the North. Most property-less whites were also barred from voting, which further enhanced the planter elites' power. Ending the domination of the slaveocracy, rather than abolishing slavery itself, was the primary reason many Northerners had gone to war.[20]

Paradoxically, however, the South's defeat threatened to enlarge even further the disproportionate political power of its white elite. The Thirteenth Amendment's abolition of slavery rendered the three-fifths compromise a dead letter. The four million former slaves would now be counted as equal to white Southerners when it came to apportioning political power, giving the South at a minimum an additional eighteen seats in the House and in the Electoral College once the seceding states had been readmitted to Congress. And yet, if the slaveocracy had its way, the freed slaves would remain noncitizens and nonvoters, ensuring that those seats would be controlled by the same slaveholders who had led the recent rebellion. One Southerner who had served in federal office before the war confidently told a Northern journalist that "we'll unite with the opposition up North, and between us we'll make a majority. *Then* we'll show you who's going to govern this country."[21]

As legal historian Garrett Epps has explained, the Republicans in Congress needed to find a way to bring the eleven seceding states back into the Union and into the halls of Congress without enabling the white planter elite to take back up the reins of power. The solution, they concluded, was to grant blacks the full rights of citizenship.[22]

"Slavery is not abolished until the black man has the ballot," social reformer and former slave Frederick Douglass declared after the war. For decades preceding that war, free blacks had claimed their citizenship and had struggled to force whites to recognize the rights that came with that status. During the Civil War, many blacks fought and lost their lives for the Union, further earning their right to call themselves Americans. A member of the Fifty-Fourth Massachusetts Regiment, the acclaimed African American infantry regiment that suffered heavy losses, wrote in 1864 that as a reward for their sacrifice, "all we ask is . . . the rights of citizenship"—including the right to vote.[23]

Republicans wanted to enfranchise blacks for more partisan reasons. If blacks were citizens, and in particular citizens with the right to *vote*, they could prevent the slaveocracy, all Democrats, from returning to power. "We *must* insist on the elevation of the blacks, or submit our own necks to the swords of the [Southern] whites and their allies," opined the *Boston Evening Traveller*, a Republican-affiliated newspaper. If blacks were given the right to vote, they would surely take over in South Carolina, Mississippi, and Louisiana, where they outnumbered whites, and they would also wield significant political power in the rest of the Confederate states, where they averaged about 40 percent of the population. No one doubted that the vast majority of newly enfranchised blacks would vote for Republicans, the "party of Lincoln" that emancipated them. Blacks' political power—and by extension that of the Republican Party—would be even greater if a significant number of whites loyal to the Confederacy were prevented from reclaiming their citizenship rights, as Republicans in Congress argued should be the case.[24]

Radical Republicans were not the only ones who recognized the transformative power of black citizenship. Seeing what might come, shortly after the war Robert E. Lee and twenty-five former Confederate leaders published a manifesto stating that the "people of the South" were "opposed to any system of laws which will place the political power of the country in the hands of the negro race." For Lincoln's assassin, John Wilkes Booth, black suffrage was even more intolerable than emancipation. On April 11, 1865, Booth was among the crowd that heard Lincoln publicly suggest that some African Americans be given the right to vote. "That means nigger citizenship," Booth declared. "Now, by God, I'll put him through. That is the last speech he will ever make." Four days later, Lincoln was dead.[25]

For the residents of the seceding states, the path back to full citizenship required a presidential pardon, which would soon be forthcoming. But for the leaders of the Confederacy such as Lee and Davis, President Andrew Johnson would prove to be less forgiving.

On May 29, 1865, Johnson issued a "Proclamation Granting Amnesty to Participants in the Rebellion with Certain Exceptions," in which he attempted to divide the former confederacy in two. "I say, as to the leaders, *punishment*," he declared, but "I also say leniency, conciliation, and amnesty to the thousands whom they have misled and deceived." Under the proclamation, if the residents of the rebellious states took an oath swearing to "faithfully support, protect, and defend the Constitution of the United States and the Union of the States thereunder," then they would regain rights of citizenship, once again able to call themselves Americans. Once they had executed the oath, they could vote, serve on juries, and hold state or federal office, as well as regain all their confiscated property (aside from their slaves).[26]

But the proclamation contained fourteen exceptions for the leaders of the "pretended Confederate government," as well as for all Southerners who owned property of more than $20,000, the equivalent of about $300,000 today. Tens of thousands of men in this category faced permanent loss of their political and civil rights, as well as their property. Some, like Lee and Davis, were at real risk of criminal punishment, including execution. The sister of one exempted Confederate officer described it as "mortifying" that her brother was "not even recognized as a citizen and had no rights and would have no support from the law," rendering him "perfectly powerless." These men's only hope of regaining their citizenship status, and of safeguarding their life, liberty, and property from the federal government, was to apply personally to Johnson for a pardon.[27]

By the summer of 1865, Walt Whitman had landed a day job as the pardon clerk in the US Attorney General's Office, and he was overwhelmed. There "is a perfect stream of Rebels coming in here in all the time to get pardoned," he wrote to one friend, and explained to another that President Andrew Johnson had recently issued an amnesty proclamation requiring "all the rich men & big officers of the reb army" to plead their case individually with the president if they wanted to win back their citizenship rights along with their confiscated property. The chaos extended to the White House. Upon arriving, one journalist found waiting in Johnson's anteroom "two or three Rebel Generals, as many members of the Rebel Congress, and at least a score of less noted leaders." When the door to the president's office opened, "the crowd rushed in as if scrambling for seats in a railroad car," all pleading their case before Johnson, who presided with a "pile of pardons, a foot high" before him.[28]

But most of these "rich men & big officers" would have to wait. As Whitman wryly observed, President Johnson "is not in any hurry" to grant them amnesty."[29]

Robert E. Lee joined the throngs seeking a pardon, submitting his application to the president shortly after Johnson issued his proclamation. Lee shouldn't have bothered. Although Johnson was no friend of the former slaves—he had owned slaves himself—he also detested the slave-owning planter elites such as Lee, Davis, and the rest of the slaveocracy. Johnson was a self-made man. Born penniless, he never attended a day of school in his life, and he started his career as a tailor. Throughout his life he carried a chip on his shoulder that even becoming president of the United States failed to dislodge.[30]

Johnson particularly detested Lee and Jefferson Davis, both wealthy men born or married into pedigreed families. With Davis it was personal. The two had served together in the Senate, and Johnson had never forgotten a speech Davis had given on the Senate floor in which he made derogatory comments about the sort of people who become "a blacksmith or a tailor"—a slight that

Johnson was sure had been intentional. So Johnson was not about to let Lee, Davis, and the rest of the slaveocracy off the hook so easily. When former Confederate lieutenant James Longstreet met with Johnson to lobby for a pardon, he was flatly denied. "There are three persons in the South who can never receive amnesty," Johnson told him, "Mr. Davis, General Lee, and yourself. You have given the Union too much trouble."[31]

Like tens of thousands of other Confederate elites, Lee and Davis would remain in a paradoxical limbo. They had lost the right to vote, hold government office, or consider themselves full citizens of a newly reunited United States of America. At the same time, they were at serious risk of trial, imprisonment, and execution for betraying the country that now denied they were one of its own.[32]

Even as former Confederates were begging Johnson to restore their citizenship rights, the Republicans in Congress were looking for ways to grant those same rights to the newly freed slaves. They began with legislation, enacting the Civil Rights Act of 1866 over President Johnson's veto. That act established birthright citizenship for all Americans, regardless of race, color, or previous condition of servitude, and attempted to safeguard blacks' civil rights, including the right to make and enforce contracts, sue and be sued, give evidence in court, and convey property.

The problem with ordinary legislation, however, is that it can be repealed by a subsequent Congress. What was needed was a constitutional amendment—a higher law that could not be easily reversed should the political winds shift in the South's favor—granting citizenship to black Americans and at the same time barring the slaveocracy from regaining the citizenship rights they had lost as a result of rebellion. Congress quickly went to work and drafted the Fourteenth Amendment to the Constitution, which did both.

Historian Eric Foner refers to the Fourteenth Amendment as part of the "second founding." In a mere 481 words, the amendment worked profound changes to the structure of governmental power by elevating the federal government over the states and prohibiting states from depriving any person of due process and equal protection of the laws. In addition to these momentous changes, the Fourteenth Amendment served the practical goal of simultaneously bestowing full citizenship on blacks while partially denying it to the slaveocracy.[33]

The first sentence of the Fourteenth Amendment declares, "All persons born or naturalized in the United States, and subject to the jurisdiction thereof, are citizens of the United States and of the state wherein they reside." That one sentence erased the Supreme Court's holding in *Dred Scott v.*

Sandford that blacks were not citizens, guaranteeing citizenship to all persons born in the United States, regardless of their race, religion, or ethnicity.

Recognizing, however, that citizenship alone would not ensure that blacks exercised political power, Section 2 of the Fourteenth Amendment provided that if a state barred any category of its male inhabitants over age twenty-one from voting for any reason aside from participation in the rebellion, then a state's representation in Congress would be reduced proportionately. No longer would the South be able to claim seats in Congress or votes in the Electoral College based on the black residents they disenfranchised. Finally, Section 3 prohibited the leaders of the Rebellion from holding state or federal office unless Congress by a vote by two-thirds of each House removed the disability. In addition, the Reconstruction Acts of 1867, which established the terms for the seceding states' readmission into the Union, temporarily disenfranchised this same group of men.

In one stroke, the Radical Republicans ensured that the former slaves would exercise their full rights of citizenship even as they barred Davis, Lee, and thousands of other Confederate leaders from doing so. The Southern states reluctantly ratified the Fourteenth Amendment as a condition of readmission into the Union, and in July 1868 it officially became constitutional law.[34]

And just in time. President Johnson's animosity toward the slaveocracy had been eclipsed by even greater hatred for the Radical Republicans. He was in open warfare with Congress, which would soon impeach and then come one vote shy of convicting him. Johnson was also vociferously opposed to giving blacks citizenship rights. "If blacks were given the right to vote," Johnson had railed before the war, "that would place every splay-footed, bandy-shanked, hump-backed, thick-lipped, flat-nosed, woolly-headed, ebon-colored negro in the country upon an equality with the poor white man." His views did not change during or after the war. "I am for a white man's government, and in favor of free white qualified voters controlling this country, without regard to negroes," he declared in 1864, and he disparaged blacks' mental capacity to vote in his annual message to Congress on December 3, 1867. During an 1866 visit to the White House by a delegation of black men led by Frederick Douglass, Johnson told Douglass that allowing blacks to vote would be a gross injustice to poor whites. As the delegation left, Johnson sneered "I know that d__d Douglass; he's just like any nigger, & he would sooner cut a white man's throat than not." The Radical Republicans and the blacks seeking their citizenship were now Johnson's enemies; most of the Southern Democrats were his friends.[35]

Johnson began pardoning the slaveocracy as fast as he could. By 1866, he had pardoned thirteen thousand of the fifteen thousand Confederate "rich men & big officers" who applied. Then, on Christmas Day in 1868, Johnson issued a proclamation that purported to give "unconditionally and without reservation . . . full pardon and amnesty" to "every person who, directly or indirectly, participated in the late insurrection or rebellion." Johnson wanted to give back the full rights of citizenship to *every* member of the Confederacy—regardless of their stature or wealth—including Jefferson Davis and Robert E. Lee.

But Johnson's pardons came too late. He could immunize Confederate leaders from criminal trial and give them back their confiscated property, but he could not release them from the Fourteenth Amendment's provision barring them from holding state or federal office, or their disenfranchisement under the Reconstruction Acts. Only Congress could do that, and the Radical Republicans who dominated that institution showed no inclination to make exceptions.[36]

On February 23, 1870, Senator Henry Wilson of Massachusetts rose to address the chamber at the 41st Congress's second session. "I present the credentials of the Hon. H. R. Revels, Senator-elect from Mississippi," he declared, "and I ask that they be read, and that he be sworn in." The occasion was momentous. Just five years after the nation formally abolished slavery, Hiram Rhodes Revels was to be the nation's first black member of Congress.[37]

In a delicious irony, Revels would be taking over a position last occupied by Jefferson Davis, who nine years before had delivered a farewell address to a packed chamber and then, in a dramatic exit, strode up the center aisle and out through the swinging doors. "The great principle of retributive justice has finally presented itself before us here at this moment," declared Senator Jacob Howard, Republican from Michigan, for "the seat in this body once occupied by the leader of the slave-holders' rebellion is now to be taken by a member of that despised race for the perpetual enslavement of which that war was waged." Meanwhile, the same constitutional amendment that had empowered Revels to take his seat barred Davis from serving in any elected office. The Northern press, which could never pass up a chance to humiliate Davis, had a field day. A widely published cartoon by Thomas Nast showed Davis watching bitterly from behind a curtain as Revels took over his place in Congress.[38]

When the day finally came for Revels to join his white colleagues in the domed Capitol building, a mixed-raced crowd packed into the galleries of the Senate Chamber to witness the swearing-in of the nation's first African American member of Congress. Reporters from a dozen papers were also there to record the moment. But all would leave disappointed. As quickly became clear, Democrats were not going to allow Revels to be seated without a fight.

Dressed in a black custom-made suit over a starched white shirt and cravat, Revels sat directly behind the Speaker's desk, forced to listen as one Democrat after another excoriated him and his race. Willard Saulsbury of Delaware spoke for his fellow Democrats when he thundered that the "advent of a negro or mulatto or octoroon in the Senate of the United States . . . [is a] great calamity . . . a great and damning outrage." Senator Garrett Davis of Kentucky chimed in to describe it as a "morbid state of affairs."[39]

But Democrats did more than complain about a "colored" man joining their ranks; they came up with a host of reasons why Revels was ineligible to serve. Most were technical queries about his credentials that were quickly dealt with by the Republicans. But then Senator Davis voiced a serious objection, one that would occupy the Senate and the headlines of newspapers around the country for the next three days. The US Constitution requires that a senator "have been nine years a citizen of the United States" to be eligible to serve. Davis spoke for all of the Democrats when he declared that Revels did not fulfill that condition.[40]

Although the Fourteenth Amendment had overruled the Supreme Court's decision in *Dred Scott v. Sandford* by establishing birthright citizenship for all regardless of race, that amendment was only two years old in 1870 and, according to the Democrats, it did not purport to "reach back to the birth and impart a new political quality to classes and races of men." Accordingly, they argued that Revels "has not been a citizen of the United States for nine years past, as required by the Constitution." In other words, Revels could not take his seat in Congress because he was seven years shy of the requisite nine years of citizenship. Indeed, under that logic, no black person could.[41]

Republicans were outraged by the very premise of the Democrats' argument, and in particular their reliance on the infamous *Dred Scott* decision. Not only had the Fourteenth Amendment rendered it a nullity, Republicans insisted that the Supreme Court's decision had *never* been the law of the land. Senator Charles Sumner of Massachusetts, a leader of the Radical Republicans, thundered that *Dred Scott* was "born a putrid corpse," and lingered only as "a stench in the nostrils," with no lasting effect on the citizenship of blacks. Senator Howard declared himself "nauseated" that its very name would be uttered in the halls of Congress, and Senator John Sherman of Ohio railed that "the *Dred Scott* case was a singular, strange infatuation; a denial of the truth of history; a perversion of the facts upon which it was based." Whatever its legal effect in 1857, Senator James Nye of Nevada exclaimed that *Dred Scott* "has been repealed by the mightiest uprising which the world has ever witnessed." Senator Howard added that *Dred Scott*'s wrongness was conclusively demonstrated by the "dreadful war through which we have passed," the death of hundreds of thousands, and the "emancipation of the entire black race and . . . restoration to their lost rights as citizens of the United States."[42]

In other words, Republicans argued that the Civil War and the Fourteenth Amendment that followed had not merely overturned *Dred Scott*, they had expunged it from the law. Under that view, the Fourteenth Amendment did not *make* blacks citizens; it merely gave them back the citizenship that *Dred Scott* had erroneously revoked with no legal basis.

As the debate wore on, the dispute between Democrats and Republicans went far deeper than the requisite years of citizenship required to be a senator under the Constitution. Just as Republicans denied that the Supreme Court had ever had the authority to declare blacks noncitizens, the Democrats scorned the idea that the Fourteenth Amendment could give it to them. "Revels is not a citizen of the United States" even now, Senator Davis declared, because the "farce" that was the Fourteenth Amendment could not make him one. He agreed with Senator Saulsbury, who insisted that the Fourteenth Amendment is "no more part of the Constitution than anything which you . . . might write upon a piece of paper and fling upon the floor." For the Democrats, no mere words on paper could transform blacks into citizens, and they would never concede a black man's right to serve beside them in Congress.[43]

In contrast, for the Republicans, a black man's admission to the halls of Congress symbolized that the country had finally corrected its greatest mistake—not only racialized slavery, but the presumption of inequality that undergirded it. "All men are created equal, says the great Declaration [of Independence]," Senator Sumner proclaimed in defending Revels's eligibility to be seated in the Senate, "and now a great act attests this verity. Today we make the Declaration a reality. . . . In assuring the equal rights of all we complete the work." The Fourteenth Amendment, together with the Thirteenth Amendment abolishing slavery and the Fifteenth Amendment guaranteeing black men the right to vote, had rectified the Constitution's original sins, enshrining the equality principle of the Declaration of Independence permanently into the Constitution and declaring blacks to be citizens of equal stature with whites. As *Harper's Weekly* described it, "the colored Senator from Mississippi [was] . . . a living symbol of the victory of equal rights."[44]

Finally, on Friday afternoon, the question of Revels's eligibility to serve in Congress was put to a vote. "There was not an inch of standing or sitting room in the galleries, so densely were they packed," the *New York Times* reported, and the atmosphere was "intense." As all knew would be the case, the senators divided strictly along party lines, with the forty-eight Republicans voting for Revels's admission and the eight Democrats against. Having been warned that any outburst would lead to immediate expulsion, the crowd was so silent that a "pin might have been heard to drop" as Revels took the oath. On February 25, 1870, at 4:40 p.m., Revels became the first "colored member" seated in the United States Congress.[45]

In 1854, while still slaves, Dred and Harriet Scott may well have been in the audience when Revels gave a sermon while visiting St. Louis, only to learn that he was subsequently arrested for the crime of "preaching the gospel to Negroes" without a license. Dred died before the war, but Harriet lived until 1876—long enough to see that same man take his seat as a member of the US Senate.[46]

When Revels joined Congress in 1870, more than 700,000 blacks were registered to vote in the former Confederate states, outnumbering the 660,000 whites permitted back on the rolls. The Fourteenth Amendment barred Confederate leaders from holding office. The Reconstruction Acts of 1867 prevented residents of the former Confederate states from registering to vote for delegates to state constitutional conventions unless they could swear that they had never held state or federal office and afterward "engaged in insurrection or rebellion against the United States, or given aid or comfort to the enemies thereof." Some states inserted provisions in their new constitutions disenfranchising former Confederate leaders in future elections as well. In Louisiana, one delegate at the convention spoke for many when he railed, "By what right . . . do those who have plotted treason and fought in rebel armies ask the right to vote?" To be sure, most white residents of the former Confederacy quickly won back their citizenship and their right to vote, despite the objections of some Radical Republicans. But their former leaders did not.[47]

In the decade following the Civil War, politically powerful Confederate leaders such as Lee and Davis—the former "slaveocracy"—were shunted to the side, rendered bystanders in a reunited nation as newly enfranchised blacks began taking part in Southern political institutions. Over six hundred African Americans, most of whom had been former slaves, served as state legislators. Blacks held a majority of seats in the lower house of the South Carolina legislature, where they dominated the legislative process. One Northern journalist marveled, "Sambo . . . is already his own leader in [South Carolina] . . . The Speaker is black, the Clerk is black, the doorkeepers are black, the little pages are black."[48]

Blacks also regularly won statewide positions, such as secretaries of state, speakers of the state houses, district attorneys, and justices on state courts. Three were elected lieutenant governors. At the national level, fourteen blacks served in the US House of Representatives, and two black men, Revels and

Blanche K. Bruce, served as US senators, both representing Mississippi. Black votes also ensured widespread Republican victories throughout the South. As South Carolina's *Marion Star* explained, "the enslaved have not been merely emancipated, but invested with every political right of the ruling race. Thus suddenly elevated, [they] outnumber the whites by an overwhelming majority, and have all the power." In the battle for citizenship, blacks had won and the former leaders of the Confederacy had lost.[49]

Or so it appeared in 1870.

On July 22, 1975, Robert E. Lee IV sat in the gallery of the House of Representatives as the debate unfolded twenty feet below. He was there to watch the House vote on the joint resolution to "restore posthumously full rights of citizenship" to his great-grandfather, General Robert E. Lee.[50]

As Lee's great-grandson looked on, House members heaped praise on the Confederate general. Representatives from both the North and South described him as a "great citizen," a "patriotic American," a man of "great humanity" and "noble character." Gillespie Montgomery of Mississippi declared Lee someone whom "all Americans would be proud to refer to as their fellow citizen." Representative M. Caldwell Butler of Virginia asked, "If Robert E. Lee is not worthy of being a U.S. citizen, then who is?"[51]

Also remarkable was all that was not said. The only time slavery was mentioned was when Congressman Kenneth Hechler of West Virginia incorrectly stated that Lee had "freed the Lee family slaves long before the war began." A search of a newspaper database to gauge contemporary coverage of the event turned up more than three hundred articles on Lee's restored citizenship, not one of which was critical of that choice, and almost none of which used the words "slavery," "traitor," or "treason" when describing Lee.[52]

John Conyers was one of the few members of Congress to oppose giving Lee his citizenship back. Elected in 1964 to represent a predominantly black district that encompassed most of Detroit, Michigan, Conyers had joined a small handful of other black members elected to Congress in the twentieth century. Before his election he had been a prominent member of the civil rights movement, and he argued, unsuccessfully, for reparations for the descendants of slaves. But Conyers did not bother putting up much of a fight against restoring Lee's citizenship—a symbolic gesture he referred to as "bicentennial fluff"—and the resolution went to a vote. General Lee's great-grandson was "beaming" as the electronic tally board lighted up with a final vote of 407 to 10 in favor of its passage.[53]

A few weeks later, on the front porch of General Lee's former home on the grounds of Arlington National Cemetery, President Gerald Ford signed what he described as the "long overdue" joint resolution restoring "full rights of citizenship to General Robert E. Lee." Ford declared: "General Lee's character has been an example to succeeding generations, making the restoration of his citizenship an event in which every American can take pride."[54]

Two years later, it was Jefferson Davis's turn. On January 25, 1977, Senator Mark Hatfield, a Republican from Oregon, introduced a joint resolution to "restore posthumously full rights of citizenship to Jefferson F. Davis," and thereby end "a glaring injustice in the history of the United States."[55]

Unlike Lee, Davis had never sought a pardon. "'Tis been said that I should apply to the United States for a pardon, but repentance must precede the right of pardon, and I have not repented," he proclaimed in a speech to the Mississippi legislature in March 1884. Never doubting that he had supported a "righteous cause," Davis was loudly unapologetic. "Remembering as I must all which has been suffered, all which has been lost, disappointed hopes and crushed aspirations," he declared toward the end of his life, "yet I deliberately say, if it were to do over again, I would again do just as I did in 1861."[56]

By 1977, Davis's lack of remorse no longer posed an obstacle to the return of his citizenship. The congressional resolution emphasized Davis's service in the Mexican War, in Congress, and as secretary of war under President Franklin Pierce. His most famous role—that of president of the Confederate States of America—was mentioned only in passing and was followed by the observation that he had never been convicted of a crime, and so "was never shown to have committed any wrongdoing." Representative Montgomery pronounced it "only right and proper that we should honor this outstanding American by posthumously restoring the full rights of citizenship." The resolution passed unanimously and was signed by President Jimmy Carter on October 17, 1978.[57]

The restoration of Lee's and Davis's citizenship rights was the capstone of the preceding century's repudiation of Reconstruction, which had come to an abrupt and ignominious halt in 1877. In that year, Democrats agreed not to contest the questionable recount that gave the presidency to Republican Rutherford B. Hayes, and in return the Republicans withdrew federal troops from the South and ended the enforcement of laws protecting the freed slaves.[58]

The tide turned swiftly. In 1890, Mississippi held a convention to write a new state constitution that was attended only by whites. "We came here to exclude the negro," declared the convention president. They succeeded. In 1876, 52,705 blacks were registered to vote in Mississippi; in 1898 only 2,832 remained on the voting rolls. In Louisiana, 130,344 blacks were registered in 1896; after a new state constitution was adopted in 1898 establishing a poll tax, that number went down to 5,320 in 1900. In Virginia, Georgia, and Alabama, less than 5 percent of the black population was registered to vote by the early 1900s.[59]

The Fifteenth Amendment prohibited race-based restrictions on voting, but the Southern states accomplished the same goal through a combination of poll taxes, literacy tests, grandfather clauses, and all-white primaries, plus a heavy dose of intimidation—all through laws written in race-neutral terms yet applied to disenfranchise African Americans. Georgia senator Walter F. George explained that although "careful to obey the letter of the Federal Constitution . . . we have been very diligent in violating the spirit of such amendments and such statutes as would have a Negro to believe himself the equal of a white man."[60]

The federal government not only lost the will to protect the citizenship of black Americans, it also lost interest in depriving the Confederate leaders of theirs. In 1872, Congress passed the Amnesty Act, which removed the Fourteenth Amendment's office-holding disqualification for the great majority of former Confederates. On June 6, 1898, Congress eliminated the bar against holding public office in federal or state government for all the former rebels—albeit long after most had passed away—rendering Section 3 of the Fourteenth Amendment a dead letter.[61]

By the beginning of the twentieth century, the citizenship rights of all whites were fully restored, even as blacks were stripped of their newly won citizenship in all but name. The Confederacy's leaders were now celebrated where before they had been reviled. During this same period, hundreds of monuments to the Confederacy were constructed in front of courthouses, state houses, and public parks. Thousands of schools, parks, and highways were named for Confederate leaders, and in particular for Robert E. Lee and Jefferson Davis. Even Captain Henry Wirz, the commandant of Andersonville prison who was executed for murdering and mistreating Union prisoners, has a memorial outside a park in downtown Andersonville. The inscription at its base describes him as the "victim of a misdirected popular clamor."[62]

But there are no statues of Hiram Revels to be found. His life is commemorated only by the small headstone on his grave barely large enough to fit his last name. A few road signs and his name on a boy's dormitory at Alcorn State University in Mississippi, where he served as president for nine years, are the only public acknowledgment of his service to the United States. The same is true for the handful of other black men who served in Congress alongside him during Reconstruction. Even today, their names remain unknown to most of their fellow Americans.

Wong Kim Ark

CHAPTER 3

BIRTHRIGHT CITIZEN

When Wee Lee went into labor with her first child in the fall of 1870, she must have felt both lonely and afraid. She would be giving birth at her home on the second floor of 751 Sacramento Street, above the store her husband owned with his partners in the heart of San Francisco's Chinatown. Most women in nineteenth-century California gave birth at home, but in any case hospitals in San Francisco rarely admitted a person of Chinese ethnicity. White doctors were unwilling to visit a Chinese home, and there were not many Chinese midwives or even many Chinese women nearby to assist her. In 1870, there were fewer than five thousand Chinese women in the United States, amounting to only 7 percent of the total Chinese population and a mere blip in a country of 38 million people. Her child would be an even greater rarity: out of the 63,254 ethnic Chinese listed in the 1870 US census, only 518 were native-born.[1]

Like most of their fellow immigrants, Wee Lee and her husband, Wong Si Ping, were from the Guangdong province in southeastern China, where life had always been hard and had recently gotten harder. In the mid-nineteenth century, the Qing dynasty had fought and lost the Opium Wars against France and Britain, and China was forced to concede commercial privileges and vital territory, including Hong Kong. Internal rebellions, a series of natural disasters, and oppressive taxation had driven farmers off their land, disrupting the rural economy and encouraging mass migration. Wee Lee and Wong Si Ping were among those who fled to Gum Saan, or "Gold Mountain," the Chinese nickname for the United States that had stuck even after the California gold rush had fizzled out by 1860.[2]

They settled in San Francisco's Chinatown, by far the most densely populated neighborhood of the city. Though small, Chinatown thrummed with life. As a visitor in 1895 described it, the air was heavy with the scent of incense and sandalwood mixed with the odor of roast pork and the "sickly sweetness of opium smoke." The streets were a riot of color. Flowered lanterns hung from painted balconies, and the buildings' walls were adorned with scarlet bulletins in Chinese characters. Pedestrians thronged the sidewalks, mostly men in loose, mandarin-collared tunics, their hair in a long queue, or braid, down their backs. Commerce thrived. The storefronts on the first floors of the wooden row houses sold every item imaginable from all over the world, though mostly food from China. Displays to tempt the passerby—from pickled radishes to shark fins to duck's eggs embedded in mud, all the more delicious because they were months old—spilled out onto the sidewalk.[3]

Wong Si Ping would have joined the hustle and bustle every morning, but Wee Lee was forced to remain a perpetual observer, passing her days watching a slice of this scene from her second-story window on Sacramento Street. Respectable Chinese women did not parade along the streets or mingle with strangers in public spaces. And in any case, she couldn't walk far. As a woman of the merchant class, it is likely that the bones of her feet had been crushed and then bound tightly with strips of cloth, so that she was forced to balance her weight on appendages just a few inches in length. Her "lily feet" would have helped Wee Lee prove to immigration inspectors that she was not a slave girl or a prostitute barred from entering the country. But once she had settled in the United States, her immobility only isolated her further.[4]

Yet Wee Lee's life with her husband in California was preferable to that of a *sausaanggwai* (grass widow) who stayed behind in China, firmly under her mother-in-law's thumb and endlessly awaiting her husband's return. As a Cantonese folk rhyme warns:

> *Oh, don't ever marry your daughter to a man from Gold Mountain:*
> *Lonely and sad—*
> *A cooking pot is her only companion. . . .*
> *Out of ten years, he will not be in bed for one.*
> *The spider will spin webs on top of the bedposts,*
> *While dust fully covers one side of the bed.*[5]

Spiders had spun no webs from Wee Lee's bedposts. On October 1, 1870, she safely delivered a baby boy. She named him Wong Kim Ark.[6]

———————

Wee Lee and Wong Si Ping lived legally in the United States for many years before their son's birth. At the time, there was no such thing as an *illegal* immigrant because there were almost no laws barring noncitizens from entering the country. But they likely never considered America their permanent home, and for good reason. "The Chinese must go," was the slogan of one prominent labor leader—a message the family received daily in big ways and small.[7]

The Wong family certainly knew that the Chinese were discouraged from living outside Chinatown and their children from attending San Francisco's public schools, and that all Chinese immigrants were barred by federal law from becoming US citizens. Wong Si Ping would likely have learned from his customers of the special taxes imposed on Chinese fishermen, laundrymen, and miners to limit immigration and encourage the Chinese to leave. He may have heard gossip about the ordinance requiring all prisoners held in the San Francisco County jail to have their hair cut within an inch of their scalp—obviously targeted at Chinese men, most of whom wore their hair in a long queue, as Chinese law required. And he was directly affected by the San Francisco ordinance making it a misdemeanor to carry baskets on a pole across one's shoulders, as Chinese merchants did to transport their goods across town.[8]

Discriminatory laws were not their only concern. In October 1871, when the Wongs' baby was still in diapers, a mob of about five hundred whites swarmed Los Angeles's tiny Chinatown—really nothing more than an alley strung with red banners and lanterns, housing fewer than two hundred Chinese men, women, and children. Over the next few hours, the mob murdered eighteen Chinese men with "fiendish pleasure." They kicked, stabbed, shot, and hanged their victims, resorting to clothesline when they ran out of rope. "Bring me more Chinamen, boys!" shouted a self-appointed hangman from a balcony, who "danc[ed] a quick step" while he awaited delivery of the next victim. Stores up and down the alley were looted and destroyed, and the pockets of men dangling by their broken necks were emptied. One victim hung naked from the waist down, his pants stolen and one of his fingers cut off to get at his diamond ring.[9]

The massacre was widely reported in the national press, so Wee Lee and Wong Si Ping surely heard about it. And yet they remained on Gold Mountain with their new baby. In the age-old rationalization of so many ethnic minorities before them, did they think, *But it couldn't happen here*? Did they assume that the violence that beset the handful of Chinese immigrants in the backwaters of Southern California could never repeat itself on the modern, cosmopolitan streets of San Francisco?

If so, they were wrong.

On the evening of July 24, 1877, hundreds of men, many newly out of work as a result of the deepening economic depression, gathered at a sandlot behind San Francisco's City Hall to listen to an "incendiary harangue against the Chinese" by a "well-dressed man . . . evidently under the influence of liquor." That was the spark that set the men aflame. With shouts of "Chinatown!" the crowd of "hoodlums" lurched toward the Chinese quarter, "rend[ing] the air with . . . demoniacal yells" as they went. They ripped up the slats of the wooden sidewalks to use as weapons and battering rams, breaking into Chinese laundries and businesses along the way to steal money, then tipping over the coal lamps to set them on fire as they left. They marched toward Chinatown, "resolved to exterminate every Mongolian and wipe out the hated race." Fearing for their lives, "not a Chinaman was to be seen on the streets" and "every door and shutter" in the Chinese quarter was "closed fast." Even so, when the night was over, four Chinese men lay dead, one shot and then burned to death after the mob torched his home.[10]

We can't be sure that the San Francisco pogrom was the reason that Wee Lee and Wong Si Ping chose to return to China. But we know that shortly afterward, the family packed their bags and left the United States with eight-year-old Wong Kim Ark and his five-year-old younger brother, giving up their home and store at 751 Sacramento Street. As the steamship pulled out of San Francisco harbor, it was the last time that Wee Lee would ever set sight on the United States.

But her eldest son would be back.

As the steamship SS *Coptic* approached the port of San Francisco in August 1895, Wong Kim Ark, now twenty-four years old, must have breathed a sigh of relief. The journey between China and San Francisco took about a month, and for those crammed into steerage it was an ordeal. As the *Coptic* sailed into port, Wong likely joined his fellow passengers on the bow, breathing the fresh sea air and watching the hills above San Francisco Bay materialize from the wreath of morning fog. He was finally home.[11]

This was the third time Wong Kim Ark had enjoyed the view of San Francisco harbor from the deck of a steamship. After leaving for China at age eight with his parents, Wong returned several years later to the United States with an uncle. Although still a child, his formal education was over, and he began work first as a dishwasher and then as a cook, living in a mining camp in the Sierras. Eight years later, in 1889, Wong left for China again. His father had died the year before, and as the eldest son, Wong likely made the trip to pay his respects at his father's grave and help his newly widowed mother put the family's affairs in order.[12]

Wong's return to China in 1889 had a happier purpose as well. At age nineteen, it was high time that he was married. Wong's parents would never have left it up to him to find a spouse, and in any case there were few women to choose from in California. In recent years, it had only become harder for Chinese women to immigrate to the United States. California's antipathy to the Chinese had swept the country, inspiring Congress to pass the Chinese

Exclusion Act of 1882, which barred all but select groups of Chinese men, and most Chinese women, from immigrating to the United States. By 1890, there were fewer than four Chinese women in the United States for every one hundred Chinese men, and a significant portion of these were prostitutes or servant girls—neither of whom were a suitable match for a merchant's son. Marriage to a white woman was simply unthinkable, both culturally and legally under California's anti-miscegenation law.[13]

Even had he been able to find a prospective bride on his own in the United States, Wong did not appear to be the type of young man to rebel against filial obligations. In an 1894 photo, he is the model a dutiful Chinese son. Despite having lived in the United States for twenty of his twenty-four years, his hair is braided in the traditional Chinese queue and he is wearing a high-necked mandarin tunic rather than a Western shirt and jacket. With his broad, open features and baby-smooth skin, he could pass as a child, though at five foot seven he was likely taller than both his parents.[14]

Young as he appeared, Wong not only found a wife on his 1889 sojourn to China, he also conceived his first child. His bride, Yee Shee, was no more than seventeen, with bound feet like her mother-in-law. Together with Wong's younger brother and his mother, Wong and his new wife took up residence in a sturdy five-room house with brick walls and a dirt floor in Ong Sing village in Guangdong province, awaiting the arrival of the family's first grandchild.[15]

But Gold Mountain called, and Wong would not stay in China long enough to meet his son. On July 26, 1890, just a few months shy of his twentieth birthday, Wong returned by himself to the United States, where he rented a room and went back to work as a cook, sending whatever money he could save back to his mother and wife in Ong Sing village. Wong would not return to China again until December 1894, when he would meet for the first time his eldest child, a boy named Wong Yook Fun, and conceive a second child with the wife he had not seen for four years.[16]

Before he left for the United States once again in 1894, did Wong worry about his ability to reenter his own country? The Chinese Exclusion Act of 1882 barred Chinese laborers from entering the United States, though Chinese merchants, teachers, students, and diplomats could still do so if they could prove their status to immigration officials' satisfaction. The law was the first significant barrier to immigration, and the first explicitly to target a group on the basis of race and class. Congress's intent was clear. As one US senator explained, the law was enacted to "protect . . . white people of the Pacific States . . . against a degrading and destructive association with the inferior race now threatening to overrun them." The Chinese Exclusion Act was also responsible for creating the immigration bureaucracy and its attendant paperwork that took root and is still with us today—the forms, photos, stamps, seals, and signatures, as well as the officials needed to process all this paperwork and detain and deport those who could not satisfy the law's requirements.[17]

But the Chinese Exclusion Act was of no concern to Wong Kim Ark. After all, he was no immigrant. The first sentence of the Fourteenth Amendment to the US Constitution, ratified two years before he was born, provides: "All persons born or naturalized in the United States, and subject to the jurisdiction thereof, are citizens of the United States and the State wherein they reside." By virtue of his birth on US soil, Wong Kim Ark was an American.

In the words of legal historian Garrett Epps, the Fourteenth Amendment's birthright citizenship guarantee is the "key to the egalitarian, democratic Constitution that emerged from the slaughter of the Civil War." This provision of the Fourteenth Amendment, ratified in 1868, overruled *Dred Scott* by guaranteeing citizenship status to the newly freed slaves. But the Fourteenth Amendment was intended to do far more than overturn a single Supreme Court decision. Its birthright citizenship clause was the great equalizer, ensuring that the United States is "one nation, with one class of citizens, and that citizenship extends to everyone born" on US soil. No group who made their home in the United States could be perpetually excluded because of their race, ethnicity, religion, social class, or former condition of servitude. Whatever the status of one's parents, birth in the United States was the cleansing act from which all emerged as caste-less equals.[18]

Under the Fourteenth Amendment, Wong Kim Ark was a US citizen. To reenter his country, he need only prove the location of his birth. But it was Wong's misfortune that his return coincided with the US government's conclusion that citizenship by "mere accident of birth" created an unacceptable loophole in the Chinese Exclusion Act.[19] Remarkably, the question of who qualified for birthright citizenship remained unsettled almost thirty years after that provision had been added to the Constitution. A few lower courts had held that the Fourteenth Amendment's birthright citizenship guarantee applied to children born to immigrant parents who had never naturalized, including Chinese immigrants who were barred from doing so under federal law. But in previous opinions the Supreme Court had expressed "doubts" on the matter—fertile ground on which to plant a ruling for the government. So as the SS *Coptic* sailed into San Francisco Bay in August 1895, the US government began the search for a test case to bring that question of "vast importance" before the nation's highest court.[20]

It chose Wong Kim Ark.

Today, the nation has dozens of immigrant detention facilities housing forty thousand would-be immigrants for the months it can take to resolve their cases. But in 1895 the United States had only just begun to exclude immigrants, so California had no place to put them while they awaited word of their fate. When Wong was denied entry into the United States, he was forced to remain under guard on the ship he had arrived on, the SS *Coptic*. When that boat was ready to depart, he was transferred to the SS *Gaelic*, and then finally to the SS *Peking* as these boats sat in the San Francisco Bay harbor. The food and water he had received during his month-long journey had been poor and minimal, and it could only have gotten worse as the captains of these ships were forced to host an unwanted third-class passenger for weeks on end.[21]

At least Wong was not fighting alone. A consortium of Chinese interest groups known in the mainstream press as the "Chinese Six Companies" quickly hired a lawyer to represent Wong, as eager to defend the first case to test birthright citizenship as the government was to bring it. Within a few days, the lawyer had filed a habeas corpus petition on Wong's behalf. The ancient writ of habeas corpus—a Latin term roughly equivalent to "you shall have the body"—allows anyone in the United States, whatever their race, creed, religion, or citizenship, to challenge their unlawful detention in court. The petition was slapdash, at least by today's lawyerly standards. Essential dates and names were added in cursive squeezed between the typewritten boilerplate. But it was good enough to get Wong a court date.[22]

Enlisting the courts to protect a persecuted minority's civil rights is a strategy most closely associated with the National Association for the Advancement of Colored People (NAACP) on behalf of African Americans. But the Chinese did it first. The Chinese Six Companies kept a handful of white, establishment lawyers on retainer, paying them to bring cases on their behalf, and they did so at a relentless pace. In the decade that followed the enactment of the Chinese Exclusion Act of 1882, recent arrivals from China filed over seven thousand cases challenging exclusion, deportation, and discriminatory laws and practices. It is an extraordinary number, especially considering that there were only about 110,000 people of Chinese descent living in the United States at the time. Roughly 7 percent of the Chinese population went to court.[23]

Although the Chinese won with some frequency in front of the lower courts, their track record in the US Supreme Court was abysmal. The nine justices had often ruled unanimously against Chinese plaintiffs in cases challenging exclusion and deportation, citing Congress's clear intent to prevent an "Oriental invasion" that posed a "menace to our civilization." As everyone involved in the case knew, Wong Kim Ark was sure to end up in front of that tribunal before the case was done.[24]

The stakes in Wong's case were momentous. At issue was the future of birthright citizenship not just for those of Chinese ancestry, but for every child of an immigrant who had yet to naturalize by the date of the child's birth. As Wong's lawyer explained to a journalist: "Think of all the people in this country who have been born of parents who owed allegiance to either Great Britain, Germany, Italy or some other European Power. Are all these people to be declared not citizens?" Wong's best chance, the lawyer knew, was to tie his claim to citizenship to that of hundreds of thousands of children of *white* immigrants, ensuring that they would all stand or fall together.[25]

But the government and its supporters countered that to grant the Chinese birthright citizenship would be disastrous. If the children of Chinese immigrants were considered US citizens, then they "may go and come whenever and wherever they please," and would also have the right to hold public office and "exercise the elective franchise." An editorial in the *San Francisco Call* stated that it would be "the height of absurdity" to give such rights to an "unassimilable race" who "wear a foreign dress, speak a foreign tongue," and whose native-born children remain as "distinctively alien as the rawest recruit from the cooly hordes of Canton."[26]

Now it would be up to the Supreme Court to decide.

———————

On the afternoon of Friday, March 5, 1897, US solicitor general Holmes Conrad rose to his feet as the nine justices filed into the Old Senate Chamber in the US Capitol, ready to begin the oral argument in *United States v. Wong Kim Ark*. In 1860, the court had moved upstairs from its original, more cramped quarters in the basement of the Capitol, and in 1935 it would move again to its own building—the hulking, Greek Revival–style temple at One First Street, just a block away. But for now, the Old Senate Chamber suited the nine justices well. The half-domed ceiling, green marble pillars, and marble busts of the previous chief justices gave the room grandeur befitting the stature of the tribunal that presided within it. Nine upholstered chairs were arranged behind a raised bench, separated from counsel and audience by a decorative iron railing. Chief Justice Melville Fuller sat in the middle, four colleagues on either side, all dressed in robes of black silk. (Fuller, who was under five and a half feet tall, had arranged for his chair to be raised, putting him on the same plane as his taller colleagues but forcing him to rest his feet on a hassock.)[27]

The chief justice was likely worn out from performing his important role the day before, when he had sworn in William McKinley to serve as the twenty-fifth president of the United States. The post-election timing of the oral argument in Wong Kim Ark's case was no accident. Neither the government nor Wong's team of lawyers wanted the case to become entangled in election politics, especially because the Supreme Court's decision could jeopardize the voting eligibility of hundreds of thousands who had always thought themselves US citizens.[28]

Solicitor General Conrad, a tall man with prematurely graying hair and an "erect military bearing," invariably made a good impression on the justices. Conrad was a Democrat from a prominent Virginian family of former slave owners, and he had served as a Confederate cavalry officer during the Civil War. Although Conrad would not have appreciated the comparison, he shared with Wong Kim Ark the experience of having his citizenship questioned. Like all those who fought for secession, Conrad lost his citizenship rights during the Civil War and for at least a time was unable to vote or to hold public office. After the war he studied law in his father's office in Winchester, Virginia, and became an active member of the Democratic Party, eventually winning a seat in the Virginia legislature in 1878 before being appointed solicitor general by Grover Cleveland, a Democrat, in 1895.[29]

Sitting just a few feet away were Supreme Court veterans William Evarts and Joseph Hubley Ashton, who had been hired by the Chinese Six Companies to handle the argument for Wong. As they sat waiting their turn to argue, Evarts and Ashton may have experienced an uncomfortable sense of déjà vu. Only a few years before they had teamed up to argue another high-profile case before the Supreme Court on behalf of a Chinese litigant but had lost in an opinion shot through with anti-Chinese animus. They had every reason to fear they would lose again.[30]

Speaking first, Solicitor General Conrad made the only legal argument available to him in light of the clear language of the first sentence of the Fourteenth Amendment. Seizing upon that amendment's qualification that birthright citizenship applied only to those "subject to the jurisdiction" of the United States on the date of their birth, Conrad argued that the term "jurisdiction" referred to *political* as well as territorial jurisdiction, and argued that children of aliens, though born in the United States, were under the political jurisdiction of their parents' home country. Because Wong's parents were citizens of China at the time of his birth, Conrad claimed they were "subject to the jurisdiction of the Emperor of China." As their child, Wong was therefore also the subject of a foreign power because, in Conrad's words, the "domicile of the parent is the domicile of the child. Their people are his people."[31]

But Conrad did not limit himself to this textual argument. Halfway through his brief he dropped a bombshell worthy of a former officer in the Confederate Army, declaring that the Fourteenth Amendment is of "doubtful validity" so "far as the ten Southern States were concerned." Why? Because the Southern states' admission back into the Union after the Civil War was conditioned on their ratification of that amendment—a process Conrad considered "coerc[ive]" and amounting to "a blot on our constitutional history."[32]

In other words, the solicitor general of the United States was defending a federal governmental policy against constitutional challenge on the ground that the provision of the Constitution was . . . well . . . unconstitutional. The claim was as audacious then as it would be now. In 1870, Democratic senators Willard Saulsbury and Garrett Davis had argued that Hiram Revels could not take his seat in Congress because the Fourteenth Amendment purporting to make him a citizen was illegal and unconstitutional, but they had decisively lost that argument. Now, twenty-eight years later, Solicitor General Conrad had resurrected it while speaking on behalf of the US government. Nor did Conrad stop there. He took aim at the entire Reconstruction era, which he colorfully described as "that unhappy period of rabid rage and malevolent zeal when corrupt ignorance and debauched patriotism held high carnival in the halls of Congress." The Confederacy may have lost the Civil War, but Conrad intended it should win the peace.[33]

Conrad was strangely silent, however, on the practical consequences of the government's position. The race-neutral language of the Fourteenth Amendment made it impossible for the government to distinguish children born to Chinese immigrants from those born to Europeans who had yet to naturalize. If Wong was not a US citizen at birth because his parents were noncitizens, then the same was true for every person born on US soil to foreign parents, whatever that person's race. If the government won, Conrad's legal argument could unravel the status of millions, including those whose families had been in the United States for many generations. After all, if the child of an alien is himself an alien, then that person's children are also aliens, and the children of that person's children are aliens . . . and so on.

Conrad turned this awkward policy question over to George D. Collins, a private San Francisco attorney who had played a key role in getting the case before the Supreme Court. While still a law student, Collins wrote a celebrated law review article questioning birthright citizenship and arguing that the Chinese were "utterly unfit [and] wholly incompetent, to exercise the important privileges of an American citizen." Collins's harangues on the issue had helped to spur the government to bring its test case.[34]

Not satisfied to stay on the sidelines, Collins had lobbied the attorney general to make him "special counsel" in the *Wong Kim Ark* case so that he could take over the litigation from Solicitor General Conrad. But Collins's reputation was equal parts brilliant lawyer and nasty human being. "I would not employ [him] in any matter whatsoever," declared US attorney Henry S. Foote in private correspondence with the attorney general, explaining that Collins "has rather a bad reputation as regards professional ethics." (Foote's assessment of Collins's character was validated a few years later, when Collins was convicted of bigamy and perjury.)[35]

Wisely, the government refused to hand over the momentous *Wong Kim Ark* case to Collins. But Conrad did ask Collins to prepare an *amicus curiae* brief, playing the role of "friend" to the court, in which Collins was to take the lead in raising policy arguments against birthright citizenship for those of Chinese descent. Collins took on the task with gusto, though he appeared to spend as much time litigating his case in the press as he did briefing it in court. The *San Francisco Examiner* quoted Collins extensively. "For the most cogent reasons we have refused citizenship to Chinese subjects," Collins declared in the pages of that publication, referring to the bar against Chinese naturalization, "and yet as to their offspring who are just as obnoxious, and to whom the same reasons apply with equal force, we are told that we must accept them as fellow citizens and that, too, because of the mere accident of birth!"[36]

In the racist logic of his era, Collins had a point. With the passage of the Chinese Exclusion Act of 1882, Congress had expressly barred the Chinese from naturalizing after a Joint Special Committee to Investigate Chinese Immigration concluded that they were "a class of people wholly unworthy to be entrusted with the right of American citizenship"—a prohibition that remained in place until 1943. The consensus in Congress was that unlike the "Aryan or European race," the Chinese lacked "sufficient brain capacity . . . to furnish motive power for self-government," and had "no comprehension of any form of government but despotism." If Congress had the constitutional authority to prevent the "unworthy" Chinese from acquiring citizenship—and in the 1890s, most assumed it did—then Collins argued that surely the Constitution did not force the nation to give citizenship status to their equally "obnoxious" children simply because they were born on US soil.[37]

Collins began his brief to the Supreme Court with a sermon. The "honor and dignity in American citizenship" was "sacred," he proclaimed, and must be protected from the "foul and corrupting taint of a debasing alienage." Are "Chinese children," he asked, "born in this country to share with the descendants of the patriots of the American Revolution the exalted qualification of being eligible to the Presidency of the nation, conferred by the Constitution in recognition of the importance and dignity of citizenship by birth?"

He answered his own question, "If so, then . . . American citizenship is not worth having."[38]

Unlike Solicitor General Conrad, Collins did not shy away from the consequences of his argument. He acknowledged that the government's interpretation of the Fourteenth Amendment would overnight strip citizenship from hundreds of thousands of children of immigrants—children who had come of age and now voted in federal and state elections, held political office, served in the military, traveled abroad under the protection of the US flag, and who had always considered themselves to be Americans. Collins airily dismissed the disruption such a ruling might cause. But he also suggested a neat solution: all the *white* individuals affected could acquire citizenship through naturalization, leaving as perpetual aliens only the children of Chinese, Japanese, Indians, Arabs, and other racial groups "unworthy" of citizenship.[39]

When it was finally Wong's attorneys' turn to speak, they made short shrift of the government's "extraordinary proposition" to eliminate birthright citizenship for the children of aliens. The government's position would replace citizenship based on birth on US soil, known by the Latin term *jus soli* (right of the soil), with citizenship based on birth to a US citizen, known as *jus sanguinis* (right of the blood). Such a reading of the Constitution would strip citizenship from hundreds of thousands, possibly millions, born to immigrant parents. Included would be the very group the Reconstruction Congress most clearly sought to protect—the former slaves and their children. Worse, it would defeat the Fourteenth Amendment's overarching purpose to rid the country of "Caste" and "Oligarchy of the skin," as Senator Charles Sumner put it in 1869— the scourges over which, they argued, the Civil War had been fought.[40]

Wong's lawyers then walked the justices through the legislative history of the Fourteenth Amendment. The limiting phrase "subject to the jurisdiction" was meant to exclude from citizenship only the "children born in the United States of foreign diplomatic agents" and "Indians . . . who maintain their tribal relationships," because neither group was subject to the jurisdiction of US civil and criminal laws. Children of diplomats were long excluded from citizenship by custom. The US Constitution of 1787 excluded Native Americans from citizenship and taxation in recognition that the tribes were separate sovereigns, and the framers of the Fourteenth Amendment maintained that rule for the same reason. (Today, however, all Native Americans are citizens at birth under the Indian Citizenship Act of 1924.) But the children of immigrants, whatever their race, were included in the birthright citizenship guarantee.[41]

Congressional debates in 1866 preceding the amendment's ratification had addressed the very question at issue in Wong's case. When Pennsylvania senator Edgar Cowan asked, "Is the child of the Chinese immigrant in California a citizen?" the answer was a clear yes. "We are entirely ready to accept the provision proposed in this Constitutional Amendment," declared California senator John Conness on the floor of the US Senate, "that the children begotten of Chinese parents in California . . . shall be citizens."[42]

For Wong Kim Ark and his attorneys, as for Solicitor General Conrad and the US government, the Civil War itself was on trial. Evarts and Ashton decried the solicitor general's suggestion that the Fourteenth Amendment "is not a valid part of the Constitution of the United States," and accused the government of having "disdain" for the amendment's framers. In the aftermath of the Civil War, the country established birthright citizenship "irrespective of the nationality, or color, or race, or previous political condition of their parents," they explained. Yet under the government's reading of the Constitution, "the war has not terminated" and antebellum views excluding certain races from citizenship still held sway. If the government's position prevailed, Evarts and Ashton argued on Wong's behalf, it would eliminate the constitutional changes for "which the country had paid so dearly in costly treasure and still more costly blood."[43]

The court did not issue its opinion for a little over a year—an unusually lengthy delay suggesting disagreement among the justices. The case had become such a thorn in the justices' side that when the court finally issued its decision, Justice David Brewer privately circulated among his brethren a poem in mock celebration:

> At last the end of Wong!
> We've studied, written long,
> And may be wholly wrong;
> Yet join the happy song,
> Goodby, goodby to Wong.[44]

Out on $250 bail, Wong continued to work as a chef and live in a rented room in San Francisco, surely wondering every day whether the court would declare that he was an alien without permission to remain in the United States. Then, on Monday, March 28, 1898, the news arrived. In a rare Supreme Court victory for a "Chinaman," Wong had won. Not only was he now safely an American citizen entitled to remain in the United States for the rest of his life, he had won that right for every child born on US soil, regardless of their race, color, or ancestry.

In his opinion for the court, Justice Horace Gray explained that the majority had reached the "irresistibl[e] . . . conclusion" that the "fourteenth amendment affirms the ancient and fundamental rule of citizenship by birth within the territory." (Wisely, the court ignored the government's argument that the Fourteenth Amendment was invalid because Southern states had been "coerced" into ratifying it.)[45] The majority agreed with Wong's lawyers that the Fourteenth Amendment's qualifying language "and subject to the jurisdiction thereof" was intended merely to exclude members of Indian tribes and children of diplomatic representatives, as well as children of foreign enemies born during a hostile occupation—long-standing exceptions to the common-law rule of birthright citizenship. In those cases, the parents (and thus their children) were *not* within the full jurisdiction of the United States, in that they were not subject to the full range of civil and legal sanctions that could be imposed on all other residents. This put them in marked contrast to the children of aliens, such as Wong. Whatever the immigration status of Wong's parents, they and he were subject to all the same criminal and civil laws as any resident.

The court's strongest argument for granting Wong Kim Ark birthright citizenship was also the most pragmatic. To hold otherwise "would be to deny citizenship to thousands of persons of English, Scotch, Irish, German, or other European parentage who have always been considered and treated as citizens of the United States." However tempting it might be to deny birthright citizenship to the Chinese, the race-neutral language of the Fourteenth Amendment would require excluding children of European immigrants from citizenship as well, and the court was unwilling to disrupt the status of so many.[46]

Chief Justice Fuller penned a lengthy dissent. The mere "accident of birth" in the United States did not automatically subject the child to the jurisdiction of the United States, Fuller argued, and repeated Collins's arguments that it made no sense to grant birthright citizenship to a race that was barred from naturalizing. But of the eight justices who voted on the case, Fuller could convince only Justice John Marshall Harlan to join him. In the words of Fuller's biographer, the *Wong Kim Ark* case "was perhaps his worst defeat on the Court."[47]

Justice Harlan's decision to join in the dissent in the *Wong Kim Ark* case is startling, complicating his legacy as an advocate for racial equality. His stance in favor of civil rights for blacks had led Frederick Douglass to declare him "a moral hero." In 1896, just a year before Wong's case reached the court, Harlan had written an angry dissent in *Plessy v. Ferguson*—the case establishing "separate but equal" accommodations for whites and blacks, cementing Jim Crow racial segregation into US law until the Supreme Court's 1954 decision in *Brown v. Board of Education* finally began to dismantle it. The court's lone dissenter in that case, Harlan had passionately argued that "our constitution is color-blind." He condemned his colleagues in highly personal terms, declaring "the judgment this day rendered will, in time, prove to be quite as pernicious as the decision made by this tribunal in the *Dred Scott* case"—a pronouncement that eventually earned him the title of "racial prophet."[48]

But it seems that Harlan also had his racial blind spots. For Harlan, the Constitution's principle of racial equality stopped just short of the Chinese.

The US government had lost the battle to eliminate birthright citizenship. Native-born children of Chinese immigrants were now free to come and go from the United States, to vote, hold office, and exercise all the other rights of citizenship.

That was not all. Under federal statute, children born to US citizen fathers anywhere in the world were also automatically US citizens at birth, entitled to all those same rights. Like Wong, many native-born men of Chinese ancestry had little choice but to return to China to find a spouse. These Chinese wives frequently remained behind in China; they were visited, at most, once every few years by their absent spouses, who dusted off the "webs on top of the bedposts" for long enough to conceive another child before going back to their jobs on Gold Mountain. Eventually, these children grew up and sought to come to the United States for the same economic reasons that compelled their fathers' parents to arrive before them. The Supreme Court's decision in *United States v. Wong Kim Ark* meant that they were citizens at birth too.[49]

But federal immigration officials were not going to give up so easily. With no basis in law, they adopted the presumption that all persons of Chinese ancestry seeking to enter the country were excludable noncitizens, placing the onus on the "alleged citizen" to demonstrate otherwise. The secretary of Treasury, who at the end of the nineteenth century was responsible for overseeing immigration enforcement, endorsed the view expressed by Treasury officials that the "Chinese are an undesirable addition to our society," and so "every presumption, every technicality and every intendment should be held against their admission, and their testimony should have little or no weight when standing alone."[50]

The paperwork required to prove citizenship upon reentry to the United States was overwhelming. Hearings on the question could take days and were scheduled only after the individual claiming citizenship had endured weeks of detention. Lengthy interrogations were coupled with invasive physical examinations requiring that applicants strip naked to be measured, poked, and prodded in an effort to determine their age and relationship to claimed relatives. As one examiner's notes attest, the ordeal required scrutiny of the applicant's "hair, (caputal, axillary, facial, and pubic), condition of skin, eruption and development of teeth, development of sexual organs, facial expression, and general attitude." And officials concluded that because no witness of Chinese ancestry could be trusted, anyone claiming birthright citizenship must produce at least two white witnesses attesting to that fact, which created a nearly insurmountable obstacle for many.[51]

At every step of the way, the immigration officials treated claimed citizens with contempt. A Chinese spokesman complained that the immigration service viewed "every Chinese applicant . . . as a cheat, a liar, a rogue and a criminal." As sociologist Mary Roberts Coolidge observed in 1909, "all Chinese are treated as suspects, if not as criminals," by the immigration officers charged with determining their citizenship.[52] One detained immigrant scrawled on the walls of his prison cell:

America has power, but not justice.
In prison, we were victimized as if we were guilty.
Given no opportunity to explain, it was really brutal.
I bow my head in reflection but there is
nothing I can do.[53]

At times, high-level government officials were so bold as to ignore the Supreme Court's decision in *Wong Kim Ark*'s favor, making up new exceptions to birthright citizenship that were nowhere in the text of the Fourteenth Amendment or the court's precedent. In 1904, the San Francisco newspapers praised Victor H. Metcalf, secretary of the Department of Commerce and Labor, for refusing to allow the admission of native-born citizen Yee Ching Ton. Yee had spent most of his twenty-six years in China, but upon his arrival in San Francisco he produced witnesses attesting that he had been born in that city. Without a shred of legal support, Metcalf declared that a person who "waits until he is 26 years of age . . . before he attempts to claim his birthright is not within the reasoning upon which the Supreme Court reached its decision in the *Wong Kim Ark* case."[54]

Wong Kim Ark was well aware of the limits of his judicial victory. After winning his Supreme Court case, he did not return to Ong Sing village to see his wife and children for another seven years, perhaps because the months of detention were too painful to risk reliving. But desire to see his family finally drew him back in 1905, and then again in 1913.

Each time Wong returned, he had to produce the documents attesting to his citizenship. He was even required to prove that he was himself—a hard task in a world before fingerprinting and DNA testing, and in which immigration officials insisted that all Chinese looked alike.[55] And like many other Chinese Americans, Wong was forced to prove his citizenship even when he was not trying to enter the United States. In 1910, an advocacy group for birthright citizens of Chinese descent complained to the secretary of commerce and labor that Chinese Americans were "liable to arrest at any time and place by zealous immigration officials upon the charge of being unlawfully in the country." Wong experienced the problem firsthand.[56]

In October 1901, while living in El Paso, Texas, Wong was arrested on the grounds that he was a "Chinese person" living illegally in the United States. He was taken into custody and freed only after he posted $300 bail. Wong must have despaired to find himself once again behind bars on account of his Chinese ancestry, despite being the named plaintiff in the Supreme Court case establishing that all persons born in the United States were US citizens. It was not until February 18, 1902, that US commissioner Walter D. Howe declared, once again, that Wong was a citizen entitled to remain in his own country.[57]

But it was far worse for Wong's children.

On October 28, 1910, Wong Kim Ark's eldest son, Wong Yook Fun, arrived on the steamship SS *Korea*. Yook Fun had been conceived during Wong's first year of marriage in 1890 and was now twenty years old. It took at least a week to travel from Ong Sing village to Hong Kong by a combination of horse-drawn wagons and boat, and then another month in steerage on a steamship before he arrived in San Francisco.

Like all new arrivals of Chinese ancestry, Yook Fun was taken by a US government ferry from the SS *Korea* to the new immigration detention facility on Angel Island in the center of San Francisco Bay. Angel Island had opened its doors only a few months before, and the press had quickly dubbed it the "Ellis Island of the West." But the two immigration facilities were nothing alike. Ellis Island was a processing center primarily for European immigrants, most of whom were allowed to enter and, if they chose, eventually become American citizens. Angel Island primarily served as a detention center for Asian immigrants, many of whom would be turned away under US immigration law, and all of whom were barred from becoming US citizens. Ellis Island welcomed future Americans; Angel Island excluded unwanted aliens.[58]

Like all the detainees at Angel Island, Yook Fun was not permitted visitors and his written communication was closely monitored. On December 4, 1910, after being imprisoned for more than a month, he wrote a letter to his father that was translated and included in the record by immigration officials on the lookout for fraud:

Dear Father,

Now I am in the detention shed. I am well. Please do not worry and buy me more clothes, ½ doz. socks and a cap, also some money.

Your son, Yook Fun.

One wonders what US immigration officials thought of Yook Fun's plea for money and socks—requests that, at least to the modern reader, epitomize a father-son relationship.

Immigration officials questioned Wong for two days in an attempt to determine whether Yook Fun was really his son. The interrogation must have brought back for Wong all the terrible memories of the months of captivity he endured on a steamship as he tried to demonstrate his own citizenship. He was asked about his parents, his younger brother and his family, his sons, and his own travel back and forth between China and the United States. And he was asked in mind-numbing detail about the placement of houses and their occupants in Ong Sing village—answers he sometimes stumbled over, likely because it had been five years since his last visit.

Finally, on Christmas Eve, 1910, Acting Commissioner Luther Steward issued his verdict. The evidence "shows conclusively that the applicant's claims are fraudulent," he declared, because "material" differences between Wong Kim Ark and Yook Fun's testimony proved that they were not actually father and son. Yook Fun was deported to China on January 9, 1911, never to return.[59]

For many years after, Wong's three other sons made no effort to enter the United States. Perhaps their spirit had been broken by Yook Fun's detention and deportation, by the hostility of the immigration inspectors, or by Wong's own reluctance to put himself and his children through that process again.

But then thirteen years later, in 1924, Wong's third son, Wong Yook Sue, sailed across the Pacific Ocean in the hope of joining his father in the United States. At first, he had no better luck than his older brother. As before, both Wong and his son were interrogated at length. As before, a three-member commission of immigration officials unanimously denied Yook Sue's admission to the United States.

But Yook Sue fought back, choosing to appeal rather than to be deported on the next steamship to China. He got lucky. The decision was reversed and Yook Sue entered the United States as an American citizen. Heartened by this success, Wong's second son, Yook Thue, came a year later and was admitted to the United States in March 1925. And then his youngest child, Wong Yook Jim, was last to be admitted as a US citizen the following year, but only after spending three weeks in detention on Angel Island. He was a tiny boy of eleven, standing only four foot two, who had traveled all the way from China by himself to live with a father he had never met. Wong must have felt enormously relieved—the family's citizenship battles were finally over.[60]

The Wong family's experience was typical. Immigration inspectors assumed that all the "cunning" Chinese were liars and cheats, and put the presumption on US citizens from China to prove their status as birthright citizens or the children of birthright citizens. Undoubtedly, many Americans were forever barred from entering their country, as happened to Wong Kim Ark's eldest son.

But the story is complicated, because at least some of the time, the immigration inspectors were right.

Between 1894 and 1940, 97,143 Chinese claiming to be citizens were admitted into the United States, amounting to nearly half of the total number of individuals of Chinese descent who entered the country. According to historian Erika Lee, a "large majority of these cases were likely fraudulent." A government program in the 1950s that encouraged confessions of fraud in return for immigration status found that about 25 percent of Chinese in the United States in 1950 had entered on the basis of false claims of citizenship by themselves or another family member—and that number was likely significantly lower than the actual percentage of fraudulent claims.[61]

False claims of citizenship were a common method used by Chinese trying to enter the United States after the Chinese Exclusion Act barred most from other avenues of immigration. Creating false paperwork to support a claim of citizenship was easier than attempting to fool immigration officials into believing that a Chinese laborer was really a merchant or teacher. It was also big business. Because the children of birthright citizens were themselves automatically citizens, a birthright citizen like Wong Kim Ark returning from China could report to immigration inspectors that he had fathered another child, then sell the slot of a "paper son" to another family, providing an affidavit and testimony to support the claim. Joseph Swing, the immigration commissioner during the Eisenhower Administration, complained, "Ever since the first Chinese came over here . . . the male Chinese went back . . . and he'd come back with a man child, and that went on, until there were ten, eleven children, all male, over the years. Well of course, it was a big fraud. . . . Going way back, the whole gang's illegal. They just had us spinning our wheels, trying to track these things down."[62]

The numbers are striking. A 1925 study of 256 Chinese American men arriving in San Francisco found that they claimed a total of 719 children born in China, a whopping 670 of whom were male while only 49 were female—in the words of immigration officials, an "absurd" proportion. In a 1925 report, the commissioner general of immigration observed that the "foundation has been laid in the records for the coming of thousands of foreign-born alleged children of citizens of the Chinese race." The "situation is not peculiar to San Francisco," he added, "as the Chinese entering the United States at the other ports of entry for Chinese are, as a rule, claiming about all the children they could possibly have in China and most of them deny having any girls."[63]

An improbable number also claimed birthright citizenship. Immigration officials could not help but notice that after the 1906 San Francisco earthquake and fire destroyed all of San Francisco's birth records, claims of birthright citizenship soared since now there was no way to disprove birth on US soil. Immigration officials joked that every Chinese woman in the United States must have given birth to eight hundred sons to account for the thousands now claiming to be native-born citizens.[64]

Ironically, immigration officials' obsessive documentation of the Chinese created more opportunities for fraud even as they barred legitimate US citizens from entering their own country. Services to assist immigrants attempting to enter illegally became a cottage industry, supported by the many corrupt immigration officials willing to share application questions or look the other way in return for payment. Would-be immigrants could purchase "coaching books" that included hundreds of questions applicants should prepare for in advance of their interviews. Witnesses to US births were easy to find for the right price. Coaches found inventive ways to communicate with clients detained on Angel Island to alert them to dates, names, and other facts they would need to know to verify their status as a paper son. Immigration officials confiscated notes hidden inside the shells of peanuts, which had been pried apart and then carefully glued back together before being sent as part of a care package. In one case, important dates and names had been cooked inside pork buns. In another, a note had been wrapped around an orange whose rind had been removed and then pasted back together.[65]

The system penalized the real citizens even as it aided those seeking to defraud it. Actual citizens, unprepared to run the gauntlet, could easily stumble over the detailed questions about the location of houses in their home village or the exact names and birthdates of neighbors and children, even as the well-coached imposter would sail through. Fraudulent claimants competed with legitimate ones, all in a battle with immigration officials seeking to keep the Chinese out of the United States.[66]

On Tuesday, October 18, 1960, Wong Hang Juen, also known as Ernest J. Wong, submitted an application to become a permanent resident of the United States. He lived at 579 Pacific Street, on the edge of San Francisco's Chinatown. A photo accompanying his application reveals a middle-aged man with thick, black-rimmed glasses. Under his sports coat he is wearing a checked shirt that screams the 1960s. Wong Hang Juen worked as a cook at the boutique Drake Hotel at the corner of Powell and Sutter Streets on Union Square, and his employer submitted a letter attesting that he was "of good character and an A1 employee." A check of his fingerprint records found he had no criminal record, and the Bank of America stated he had $3,021.30 in his savings account. He stated under oath that he was not now, and had never been, a member of the Communist Party.[67]

Still, Wong Hang Juen's application for permission to remain in the United States was risky. As he stated in his affidavit, "I last entered the United States claiming to be WONG YOOK SUE, the citizen son of WONG KIM ARK. I now admit that I am a citizen of China and that I have never been a citizen of the United States. . . . I am not related to my immigration father, WONG KIM ARK, in any way."[68]

It seemed that Wong Kim Ark, too, was the father of a paper son.

Hang Juen had come forward to confess the fraud as part of the Immigration and Naturalization Service's Chinese Confession Program, which operated from 1957 until about 1965. The program arose from Cold War fears that Communist China would use its "paper sons" in the United States to infiltrate the government and undermine democracy. The US government encouraged the Chinese living in the United States to come clean about their fraudulent claims of citizenship, typically in return for permission to remain in the country as green card holders under their real name, and eventually qualify for legitimate citizenship. It was a chance to wipe the slate clean, to give families a fresh start in the United States without the convoluted layers of fake documents and lies to weigh them down. The process would also enable them to sponsor their real family members living in China for visas to come to the United States. For the US government, it was a chance to root out Communist influences. Men like Hang Juen were routinely approved for permanent residence despite having committed fraud, but left-leaning labor leaders were often deported.[69]

The Chinese Confession Program required those seeking to remain in the United States to reveal the names of family members and friends who had also entered the country on false pretenses.[70] Hang Juen had been flagged by another confessor in an unrelated case, and he surely felt he had no choice but to admit that his real father had paid for him to pretend to be Wong Kim Ark's son. In his one-page typed confession, he took pains to note, "I believe that WONG KIM ARK was actually born in the United States as he claimed," and also that "the third son, YOOK JIM, is a true son of WONG KIM ARK."

By the time Hang Juen confessed that he was Wong Kim Ark's paper son, Wong Kim Ark had passed away. We cannot know what Wong would have said in his own defense. But others have explained that the Chinese saw no reason to obey racist laws and policies that barred the Chinese—and *only* the Chinese—from entering the United States. One Chinese immigrant explained, "If we told the truth, it didn't work. And so we had to take the crooked path."[71]

Wong, in particular, had little reason to respect US immigration laws. He spent four months imprisoned on a steamship by a government that conceded he was native-born but wanted to deny him citizenship anyway. His eldest son, Wong Yook Fun, was barred from entering the United States after weeks of travel and months of detention on Angel Island. The evidence strongly suggests that Yook Fun was Wong's actual son—he remained intimately involved in the family's day-to-day life more than a decade after he was denied entry into the United States, helping Wong's youngest son (and his brother), Yook Jim, emigrate to the United States. Wong may have decided that in a system in which legitimate claims of citizenship are routinely attacked or ignored, he had nothing to lose by claiming a paper son as his own.

From the perspective of a century later, the morality of paper sons and their citizen fathers is complicated. Are they criminals, or are they the victims of a racist and inhumane system? Did they help or harm the United States? Does the United States regret the presence of a group of immigrants who mined the gold and built the transcontinental railroad at extraordinary speed and under harsh conditions? Or those, like Wong and his children, who took jobs that white American men refused to do, laundering the clothes and cooking the meals to be enjoyed by the "real" citizens? In the words of Stanford professors Gordon H. Chang and Shelley Fisher Fishkin, Chinese immigrants and their children, both legal and illegal, in big ways and small, "helped build America."[72] And yet the United States continually told them: *You are not American.*

As Wong's life drew to a close, he chose to leave the United States permanently. Like his parents, he preferred his bones to rest in China, not the country in which he had spent the bulk of his life. So at age sixty-two he returned to Ong Sing village. He left the teeming streets of San Francisco for a patch of earth with twenty-two single-story houses, to live in a brick home with a dirt floor where he could hear the shouts of the children flying their kites along the nearby river. He spent his old age with a long-neglected wife who raised their children by herself on bound feet. In 1932, when Wong left the United States for good, he had spent less than a sixth of his life in China. His name would be added to the history books as the man who had established birthright citizenship for all Americans. And yet it seemed that China, and not the United States, was his home.

But Wong Kim Ark's youngest son, Wong Yook Jim, came of age in a different America. Yook Jim arrived in the United States in 1926, at age eleven, and he made the United States his home. At first he worked as a waiter in Chinese restaurants in Minneapolis, Chicago, and Sacramento. During World War II he joined the army, then spent twenty-five years in the Merchant Marine. He married a Japanese American woman who had been imprisoned in an internment camp during World War II, and they raised their children together in San Francisco, some of whom still live there today.

Yook Jim had known vaguely that his father was involved in a case that reached the Supreme Court, but he "didn't know it was important" to anyone outside of his family.[73] Then one day in 1998, when he was in his mid-eighties, he read in a Chinese language newspaper about the celebration of the hundredth anniversary of the Supreme Court's decision in his father's case, held at the San Francisco headquarters of the Chinese Six Companies.

The event made him want to learn more about the father he had hardly known. His granddaughter, Alice Wong, then a college student, went to the National Archives and Records Administration near San Francisco to review Wong Kim Ark's extensive files—files that told the story of his father's long battle to be recognized by the country in which he had been born. Shortly after, Yook Jim and Alice went to Angel Island to attend the ceremony marking its designation as a National Historical Landmark and Park. It was the first time that he had been back to the site where he had been held in detention as a small child, when his father had come to prove, one last time, that they were all US citizens.[74]

BECAUSE SUFFRAGE LEADER CAN'T
VOTE SHE WILL START A ROW

Ethel Coope Mackenzie

CHAPTER 4

CITIZEN SUFFRAGIST

I t was the social event of the month; some would say the year. The crowd that surged through the gates of Oakland's Idora Park on a damp Saturday night in March 1911 was a slice of upper-crust California. "Well-gowned" women on the arms of "intelligent men of standing" made their way up the grassy slope of the twenty-acre walled-in park toward Idora's amphitheater. Among the attendees were civic leaders, government officials, renowned artists, and eminent professors. They were all there to hear words of wisdom from Sylvia Pankhurst, a "slip of a girl" fighting one of the great civil rights battles of the new century.[1]

Pankhurst was the young, beautiful, militant British suffragist from the famous family, now on a whirlwind tour of the United States to tell tales of her battles on the front lines for women's suffrage in England. California was on her itinerary for good reason. In a special election in October, just seven months away, the state would vote on Proposition 4—a proposal to amend California's constitution to grant its one million women the right to vote.

If Proposition 4 passed, California would become the sixth state in the nation whose women could vote, and San Francisco the largest city in the world to allow the other half of its population to have a say in its governance. The women of California would help decide not just whom to send to state government in Sacramento, but also who should represent them in Congress and serve as their president. Leaders of the national suffrage movement intended that California would be the keystone supporting the ultimate goal: an amendment to the US Constitution guaranteeing women the right to vote.[2]

But first they had to convince the men of California to give their women the vote—a hurdle they had already tried and failed to clear in 1896 in a devastating loss that set the women's suffrage movement back more than a decade. When the prominent citizens of San Francisco gathered at the Idora Theater to hear Pankhurst in March 1911, they knew they were at the start of a long battle with no guarantee of success.[3]

Ethel Coope Mackenzie was surely eager to learn all that Pankhurst could teach her. At twenty-six, she was roughly the same age as the famous English suffragist, but Ethel was a relative newcomer to the battle for women's suffrage, and an unlikely recruit to the cause. She was the only child of wealthy vintner John Frederick Coope, the owner of the Ben Lomond vineyard in Santa Cruz, whose pinot noirs had won top prizes at the World's Fairs in Paris and Chicago. The San Francisco papers treated Ethel as a minor celebrity. The family lived a comfortable life, splitting their time between the family mansion in Santa Cruz and a three-story Victorian on tony Nob Hill in San Francisco. The society pages of the local papers adored her, describing her as "possessed of beauty and charm of manner that have won her much admiration." Flattering photos and sketches accompanying these articles reveal a young woman with soft, pleasant features, her hair worn in a loose bun as was the style of the day.[4]

As the sole inheritor of a world-renowned vineyard, Ethel had at first shown little interest in the burgeoning labor and progressive movements, and she was certainly not on the warpath against "demon alcohol," as were many suffragists. No one who knew her in 1911 would have predicted that four years later she would be the named plaintiff in one of the most important Supreme Court cases of the decade.

A few years before, when she was barely out of her teens, Ethel had joined the Club Women's Franchise League of San Francisco, known as the club for wealthy and socially prominent women interested in dabbling in the suffrage moment. To her surprise, Ethel caught suffrage fever. Despite being one of the younger members, she led committees, organized speakers, and was entrusted with the delicate task of persuading San Francisco's "men of leisure and men of affairs" to support the cause. Her warmth and affability, coupled with her stature as the daughter of a prominent vintner, gave her the social standing and the confidence to convince men in San Francisco's high society that California's women deserved the vote.[5]

Not that she found the task easy. Even the more enlightened men seemed to view the idea of women voting with amusement, as if they were being asked to give the franchise to a particularly adorable golden retriever. Ethel reported that some of these men exclaimed "they would be glad to grant [women] the ballot" if women "could introduce their angelic characteristics into politics." She suppressed the urge to roll her eyes in the interest of gaining their votes.

But she preferred such patronizing responses to the man who told her he would "rather his sister would lose a leg than gain a vote"—though as Ethel observed, "the preference was entertained without consulting the sister."[6]

At Idora Park on that March evening, Pankhurst concluded her speech with a call to action. "Why do we want the vote?" she asked, before answering the question herself. "For the same reason men do, and for several reasons in addition." Men had "organized the world in which we live," and their laws "press hard upon the women." She reminded the audience that "even here in California" married women did not have control of their wages or property, or a right to remain the guardians of their children. California's women were underpaid, overworked, and were required to follow the laws just like the men, even though they had no say in making them.[7]

As Pankhurst neared the conclusion of her remarks, her refined audience interrupted frequently with applause, at times beating their feet against the floor. Raising her voice, Pankhurst cried out, "I want to see every woman in this state asking for suffrage and I want to see every man clamoring for her to have it!" The crowd rose to their feet to applaud her. The club women of San Francisco left Idora Park newly resolved to win the right to vote for themselves and their fellow Californians.[8]

In 1911, the city of San Francisco was a bustling commercial metropolis, wealthy and thriving. Only five years earlier, in 1906, the great earthquake and subsequent fire had killed three thousand and left half of the city's population of four hundred thousand homeless. But San Francisco rebounded quickly. The tragedy's silver lining was that it allowed the city to shed the last remnants of its scruffy pioneer origins, emerging as a gleaming, modern twentieth-century metropolis.[9]

No man, woman, or child who walked the streets of San Francisco in 1911 could claim ignorance of the upcoming vote for women's suffrage. Dotting the city's thoroughfares were three hundred billboards proclaiming the message in foot-high letters. The official "Votes for Women" posters, featuring a young woman in a long yellow dress unfurling a pennant with that slogan, were pasted by the dozens along fences and walls up and down the streets of San Francisco. The suffragists had convinced some of San Francisco's most prominent department stores to host suffrage displays in their windows. (The stores didn't have much of a choice, rightly fearing their mostly female clientele would stage a boycott if they refused.) A large, permanent electric sign at Market and Fourth Streets blared the same message into the night, and the streetcars running along Market Street bore placards calling for the voters to "Give your girl the same chance as your boy."[10]

The club women of San Francisco were to thank for all this publicity. Ethel and her fellow club members devoted the seven months between Pankhurst's speech in March and the special election in October to persuading California's men to give them political power. Now it would all come down to how the men of California voted on Tuesday, March 10, 1911.

Despite her young age, Ethel was charged with the enormous task of organizing the "watchers"—the thousands of men and women sent out to monitor the San Francisco polls on election day to ensure all went smoothly. She knew that many of the men of San Francisco opposed the idea of women's suffrage. One poll watcher happily reported that a man told her "he was going to vote for us . . . on the same theory that he would use in having a bad tooth pulled—it had to be done some time, and he might as well get over it now." But another voter told the suffrage supporters handing out literature in front of the polls, "If my wife did that I'd beat her." To which they responded, "That is just why we want the ballot so badly—to protect women from men like you."

Ethel and her fellow club women were confident that Proposition 4 would prevail statewide, putting an end to a battle they had lost fifteen years before.[11] But then the first returns began to tell a different story. By eight o'clock in the evening, the atmosphere at the women's headquarters became "increasingly gloomy" as polls showed women's suffrage losing by large margins.

At eleven on election night, Harry Dean, the field manager for the anti-suffrage movement, declared Proposition 4 had lost. He congratulated the state's voters for "leav[ing] the political pool for men to wade in," adding "it is the sweet women we all want." On Wednesday, October 11, the front page of the *San Francisco Chronicle* made the bad news official. A headline in bold, all caps print spanning the width of the paper declared: "Woman Suffrage Amendment Defeated by 5000." The *Los Angeles Times* and the *Los Angeles Express* also gave prominent space to the defeat.[12]

Like her sisters in arms, Ethel tried to appear positive. "We shall start again tomorrow with new vim and greater hopefulness than ever," she told one reporter. But the loss must have been a crushing blow. At their headquarters, women sank their head into their hands, unable to face the terrible news. It is "awful hard to work this hard for a losing cause," said one woman, unable to maintain the upbeat front. She must have spoken for Ethel and them all.[13]

But then, incredibly, it turned out the papers had got it wrong; the "anti" voters had celebrated too soon. When the final vote was tallied later in the afternoon on Wednesday, the women of California learned they had won the franchise after all, albeit by the slimmest of margins. "From Defeat Women Seize Victory," blared the headline of the *Santa Cruz News* the next morning. Proposition 4 had passed by only 3,587 votes, an average of one vote in each precinct in the state. Overnight, the number of women with full suffrage in the United States doubled; the floodgates had opened.

Photos from that evening show women in full-length dresses with fitted sleeves, bodies bound by corsets, hair piled elaborately atop their heads. They are grinning from ear to ear, their arms raised. These women know they have just surmounted the single greatest barrier to their fight for equality, that they are at the threshold of a freedom and autonomy that they could hardly imagine before this day. And the savvier women among them realized that this win was not just about California; it was a step in the direction of a constitutional amendment that would grant all American women the right to vote in all elections nationwide.

The suffrage movement was not Ethel's only preoccupation. She also took weekly voice lessons with Gordon Mackenzie, a celebrated Scottish tenor known for his soulful ballads sung in his native Scottish burr.

Mackenzie had a colorful past—perhaps more colorful than Ethel's mother may have realized when she hired him to guide her daughter's musical education. He was christened Peter Gordon Mackenzie and raised in the rugged mountains of the Scottish Hebrides, where Gaelic was his first language. His father intended that his son would join his business trading jute, a vegetable fiber used to make a course cloth for chair seats, sacks, curtains, and rugs, which earned the family a steady if meager living. It was a hard life in a hard climate, but it was the only life the Mackenzies had ever known.[14]

Young Gordon Mackenzie had other ideas, however, and did what others only dream of: he ran away. He landed in genteel Savannah, Georgia, and soon won a coveted position as a tenor at one of Savannah's most popular churches. His talent got him invited to sing at the World's Fair in Chicago in 1893. In a stroke of luck that would forever change his life, among the audience was Cornelius Vanderbilt, the patriarch of one of the wealthiest families in America. Impressed, Vanderbilt brought Mackenzie to New York and helped him land a position as the tenor at St. Bartholomew's Church, where Mackenzie secured a contract for $1,200 a year—among the highest paid tenors in the city.[15]

In the years that followed, Mackenzie became a household name among the New York elite and a beloved entertainer of the middle and upper classes. He regularly sold out concert halls holding thousands. One critic gushed that his "voice of velvet" is "pure and clear," "vibrant and soul-stirring." Another declared him to be a "magneti[c] . . . personality" whose charisma animated his performances. Mackenzie was a social as well as a musical success. Thick, wavy hair kept slightly longer than the fashion, full lips, and a penetrating gaze suggest that his looks as well as his beautiful voice contributed to his overall charm. Socially prominent women regularly invited him to sing a few songs when they entertained at home, for which he was well compensated, and then they inevitably asked him to stay on for drinks and dinner with their guests. A perpetual bachelor, his name popped up with some frequency in the society pages of the New York papers. Effortlessly, it seemed, Peter Gordon Mackenzie had propelled himself from a jute trader on a gloomy island in the Outer Hebrides to a life of Gatsbyesque splendor at the height of the Gilded Age.[16]

But Mackenzie's luck ran out in 1904 when he was diagnosed with tuberculosis, a moment described as "the greatest shock and most severe blow" of his life. At the turn of the century, tuberculosis was often a death sentence. By the early 1900s, it killed one in seven people living in the United States and Europe, and the death rate for those diagnosed with the illness was over 50 percent. The disease took a terrifying toll on its victims. It was known colloquially as consumption because it appeared to devour its victims, who coughed up blood and dwindled into pale wraiths lacking the strength even to sit up in their beds. Before the discovery of antibiotics, the only known treatment was a change of climate and exposure to lots of fresh air. But these "cures" were more often than not ineffective, and the sanatoriums that sprang up to house patients were known as "waiting rooms for death."[17]

Terrified, Mackenzie immediately moved to Arizona for the warm, dry climate. And there he got lucky again, beating the odds, regaining his health and his voice. In June of the next year he moved to San Francisco, where he took on voice students and returned to giving regular concerts. But the experience forever changed him, and the bachelor life had seemingly lost its luster.[18]

Ethel was his adoring student. She was a little more than half his age when they met, and she had spent her entire life within the protective fold of her small and close-knit family. The couple epitomized the maxim that opposites attract: Ethel fell for Mackenzie's worldly sophistication, while Mackenzie was drawn to Ethel's rooted stability. But they may also have been brought together by their shared iconoclasm: neither was willing to accept the fate that their era had dictated for them. Nor could it have hurt that they were both exceptionally attractive, or that Ethel was the sole heir to a large fortune. Whatever the reasons, the two were engaged within a year of Ethel's first voice lesson.[19]

Ethel Coope and Peter Gordon Mackenzie were married at 4 p.m. on August 14, 1909, at Ethel's Nob Hill home. The papers reported that their wedding was a surprisingly "simple affair" for such a high-profile couple. Ethel was given away by her grandfather, S. W. Billing, who took her deceased father's place, in a ceremony before only a few close friends. The couple exchanged their vows under a floral bell, the bride wearing a gown of "white messaline satin . . . ornamented with silver and pearl trimmings" and carrying a bouquet of lilies of the valley with a wreath of the same in her dark hair. According to the local papers, the couple "dispensed with every detail that might add ostentation to the simple service"—though they did not forget to invite the press to report on the event. They planned to live together with Ethel's mother on Leavenworth Street after they returned from their honeymoon.[20]

Ethel and Gordon Mackenzie's romance would have quickly faded from history had Ethel not decided to exercise the right to vote for which she had fought so hard. A little more than a year after she celebrated Californian women's victory at the polls, on January 22, 1913, Ethel left her Nob Hill home, heading to the county registrar's office to register to vote in the upcoming election.

In preparation for this outing, Ethel would have donned a high-necked white blouse and dark, A-line skirt reaching to her ankles—the typical outerwear of upper-class women in San Francisco in that era. But she would have had to forgo the usual whalebone corset, for Ethel was seven months' pregnant with the couple's first child when she left her home that January morning for her appointment with San Francisco registrar Harry Zemansky. Over the past four years, she had met her husband, seen a victorious end to the fight for women's suffrage, and was on the verge of starting a family. Adding her own name to the registry of Californian voters would have been the final, satisfying flourish to mark the major achievements of her twenty-seven years.

But when she arrived at the registrar's office, Zemansky flatly refused to place her name on the rolls. As he explained, pursuant to a federal law known as the Expatriation Act of 1907, Ethel's widely reported marriage to a noncitizen had disenfranchised her. Indeed, the registrar informed her that not only was she barred by law from voting, she was no longer an American citizen.[21]

When they wed, Ethel may not have known the legal consequences of marrying her dashing Scotsman. She was only twenty-four then, and the Expatriation Act of 1907 that had taken her citizenship, and so also her vote, was only two years old. In any case, on her wedding day in 1909, she had no vote to lose.

But by the time she marched into the registrar's office and demanded to add her name to the voting rolls, Ethel already knew what the answer would be.

Just the year before, on February 14, 1912—four months after California's women had won the right to vote—Ethel had led a committee of seven women charged with transforming a date typically devoted to flowers and romance into a voting registration day for women. Ethel and her fellow club women helped 875 women register that day, clearing the final hurdle between these women and the vote. Even the clerks didn't seem to mind the extra work. "We like to see the ladies here," said one. "It makes it more cheerful for us."[22]

The day was not joyful for all, however. As Ethel observed, several of the women were barred from registering because they were married to foreigners. As a result of their choice of marriage partner, they had lost citizenship and by extension their right to vote. If Ethel had not known of the consequences of marrying her handsome Scotsman before Valentine's Day 1912, she certainly knew it after.[23]

The Expatriation Act of 1907 was to blame for the women's disenfranchisement. Section 3 of that act provided that "any American woman who marries a foreigner shall take the nationality of her husband," simultaneously losing her US citizenship in the process. She would be allowed to "resume her American citizenship" only upon "termination of the marital relationship." The *Congressional Record* is nearly silent as to why Congress chose to pass such a law, but the era in which it was enacted allows us to guess at the reasons.[24]

Under the legal doctrine known as "coverture," upon marriage "man and wife were one, and the man is that one." In its purest form, coverture meant that married women had no legal personhood separate from their husbands. If she was owed a debt or worked for wages, her husband had the right to collect the money. Married women could not own, inherit, or bequeath property; could not open a bank account or borrow money; could not sue or be sued, sign contracts or a will; and could not work or even travel without their husband's permission. A married couple was typically issued only one passport, which would be in the husband's name. Although coverture was fading by the early 1900s, it was far from dead, and it surely affected Congress's view that a family should have one, and only one, citizenship—that of the husband.[25]

The law was also a nativist response to the massive influx of immigrants into the United States at the start of the twentieth century, peaking at a record high of 1,285,349 in 1907. New arrivals from that year alone amounted to 1.3 percent of the total US population. (In contrast, in 2017, the United States accepted approximately 1 million new immigrants into a population of 320 million, and the majority of those new immigrants were already in living in the United States on temporary visas.) Many of these newcomers were from eastern or southern Europe, and experts warned that the country would be overwhelmed by "vast throngs of ignorant and brutalized peasantry" from these regions. One mayor complained that his city attracted "the worst classes of Europe . . . the most idle, vicious and worthless people among us." When the governor of Louisiana, John M. Parker, declared in 1911 that Italian immigrants were "just a little worse than the Negro, being if anything filthier in [their] habits, lawless, and treacherous," he was articulating the widely held views of his day.[26]

Parker had been elected in spite of, or perhaps owing to, his role in organizing a mob in 1891 that had lynched eleven Italians who had been suspected of murdering the New Orleans police chief. On the whole, the nation shrugged. A *New York Times* editorial concluded that the "lynchers of New Orleans were 'law abiding' men" compelled to respond to the "menace" posed by New Orleans's large Italian population. Theodore Roosevelt, then serving on the United States Civil Service Commission, wrote to his sister, "Personally, I think it rather a good thing, and said so." In 1911, a bipartisan commission led by Senator William Dillingham concluded that immigrants from southern and eastern Europe posed a "serious threat to American society and culture," and the Dillingham Commission Report became the basis for subsequent legislation restricting immigration by race and national origin in the years to come.[27]

In this atmosphere, American women who married foreigners were perceived as tainting the nation's purity, of undermining its white, Anglo-Saxon identity, so it was more preferable to expel them from the citizenry than to accept their mixed marriages. But gender played a role here too. The nation only felt threatened by foreign men marrying American women; when American men took foreign wives, the law automatically gave these women American citizenship.[28]

The law may also have been a product of the bruised American male ego. "I felt hurt because these rich women in the East did not . . . marry some of those good boys" but instead married foreigners, a representative complained at a congressional hearing on the subject. Some members of Congress appeared obsessed with the idea that American women of fortune were marrying penniless aristocratic foreigners, selling themselves for the title of "Countess So-and-So." That such women were the equivalent of whores was not just hinted at but declared outright. "Women who go and sell themselves for a title might sell themselves even cheaper if you tempt them," one congressman remarked. No matter that less than 1 percent of marriages between US citizen women and foreigners were to men of nobility. America had eschewed titles of nobility as antithetical to the nation's values, and so women who chose to marry aristocratic foreigners were considered un-patriotic and un-American.[29]

Nor did Congress contemplate the possibility that the new law would strip American women of the right to vote, likely because in 1907 the vast majority of American women had no such right. But that was changing quickly. Between 1907, when the Expatriation Act became law, and 1920, when the states ratified the Nineteenth Amendment to the US Constitution giving all American women the right to vote, eleven states (including California) voted to enfranchise their women. Almost every year after 1909, thousands or millions of American women joined the ranks of voters—save for the women married to foreigners.[30]

For Ethel, the loss of her right to vote was so painful because she had been instrumental in making that change. "It was something of a shock," she told reporters, "to learn that after two years of hard work to bring suffrage to California I could not enjoy the right I had helped to give other women." And she knew better than anyone that the wrong that befell her was shared by many. "It is not merely my own citizenship that is involved," she explained. "There are 4,000,000 women in the equal suffrage states, and many of these are doubtless in the same predicament as myself."[31]

For many women, the consequences of losing their citizenship were far worse than losing the vote. In 1915, as today, loss of citizenship had devastating results. Access to many professions was limited to citizens. Inez Milholland Boissevain risked losing her license to practice law when her marriage to a foreigner terminated her citizenship, and Florence Bain Gual was fired from her job as a public school teacher, which she had held for fifteen years, for the same reason. If these women's foreign husbands abandoned them and their children, they were left destitute. Under federal law, as well as the laws of many states, aliens were barred from owning real property, and so women who married noncitizens were at risk of forfeiting their land and their homes and were unable to inherit such property from their parents. Women who lived abroad with their husbands could not get a US passport, or protection from the US Consulate. The consequences could be far-reaching, at times even bizarre. A Pennsylvania woman who married a noncitizen was subsequently criminally prosecuted under a state law that barred noncitizens from owning dogs.[32]

Worst of all, noncitizens have no right to remain in the United States, as native-born American Lillian Larch would learn. Larch married a Canadian who later died. When she applied for welfare on behalf of herself and their four children, she was threatened with deportation to Canada on the grounds that she was an alien pauper who had no right to remain in the United States. Women's groups tried to help her regain her citizenship by challenging the legality of her marriage—a challenge that, if successful, would have restored her citizenship but permanently stigmatized her and their children by declaring them to have been born out of wedlock. "I don't know what to do," she said. "All the fight has gone out of me—I am ill, penniless and weary." She told a *New York Times* reporter, "I am American-born and reared in America and I want my citizenship, but it is such a terrible price to pay." The effort to restore her citizenship failed, and Larch was deported with her children to Canada on May 2, 1931, with no source of support, at the height of the Great Depression. No one knows what became of her.[33]

In a few sensational cases, the consequences of the laws expatriating women made it onto the front pages of the nation's newspapers and into the halls of Congress. Augusta Louise de Haven-Alten's case was one example. Haven-Alten came as close as one could get to being American aristocracy. She was born in New York City to a family who could trace its pedigree back to the colonial days. Her ancestors had served as high-ranking officers in the military, and more than one relative had been appointed an ambassador to a European country. Her father was a naval commander who had served with distinction in the Civil War. As a teenager, Augusta fell in love with a German baron, and they married in Berlin in 1886, on her nineteenth birthday. (Hers is among the tiny percentage of such marriages involving European royalty; the prominence of her case may have contributed to the misperception that American woman married foreigners primarily to obtain a title.)[34]

The match was a poor one from the start. Haven-Alten's husband took charge of her large trust fund and spent it all, and he was serially unfaithful to her. She brought divorce proceedings against him in 1912, but the German courts refused to allow her out of the marriage. In 1917, the United States declared war on Germany, and overnight Haven-Alten, who was still a German citizen, became an "enemy alien." Her remaining assets were immediately seized by the US government, leaving her destitute.[35]

As the daughter of a politically and socially connected family, Haven-Alten had the wherewithal to petition Congress for a private bill to restore her citizenship. Members of Congress knew her family and vouched for her. As one declared: "This woman's Americanism has never been questioned." But individual members grumbled. Representative John Edward Raker, a Democrat from California, complained that Congress was being used as a "divorce court." Expounding from the floor of the House of Representatives, he objected to an "American woman marrying a foreigner and then, just the moment things do not go right, she commences to squeal and jumps back to the United States and asks for protection."[36]

Representative Raker was generally unsympathetic to the plight of American women whose citizenship was revoked. Nonetheless, he had a point about the problematic precedent set by passing private bills to give women like Haven-Alten her citizenship back. Nellie Grant Sartoris, the daughter of President Ulysses S. Grant, lost her citizenship when she married an Englishman. She, too, benefited from a private bill when she sought to regain her citizenship after divorcing her husband. As Raker observed, women connected to wealthy or politically powerful families could occasionally wring from Congress legislation allowing them to be returned to the fold, but the vast majority of American women in their situation could not.[37]

It was no secret, then, that American women lost their citizenship upon marriage to a foreigner, and that the consequences could be severe for the women involved. Ethel was outraged that the law treated her as if she had no identity outside of her husband's. "Pickpockets, murderers, embezzlers and ex-convicts of all kinds are deprived of the right of suffrage, but I have done nothing criminal unless it be a crime to marry a foreigner," she complained. So she decided to do something about it, not just for herself, but for everyone in her situation. She told one reporter that it was "just another fight for suffrage that I am making alone."[38]

Ethel had a simple way to regain her citizenship, and thus her right to vote. Her husband could naturalize, and under federal law she would then automatically become a US citizen once again—not because she was born in the United States or had lived in the country all her life, but because the man she married was now himself a US citizen and the law declared that her citizenship automatically followed his. But that solution offended Ethel. She refused to accept the law's implicit message that she had no legal identity separate from her husband, and she "resented the fact that a mere episode like marriage to the man of her choice should disenfranchise her." Most important, she wanted to help the other women in her situation by challenging the statute that expatriated her.[39]

So Ethel took action. On that January morning in 1913, she traveled from her Nob Hill home to the Registrar's Office knowing full well that her attempt to register would be rejected—which is why she made sure that newspaper reporters would be there to record the event.

The journalists who had enjoyed reporting on her every social engagement did not let her down, giving her story prominent coverage. San Francisco registrar Harry Zemansky, they reported, stated "firmly but calmly that Mrs. [Mackenzie] could not enroll . . . on the ground that her husband . . . is an Englishman." And they ran her picture with the story—a classical profile showing a clear-eyed young woman staring hopefully up into the distance, a few tendrils of hair escaping its loose coil to curl softly around her neck and forehead. The subsequent coverage from other news outlets made much of the irony of a suffragist being denied her newly won right to vote. The *Wisconsin State Journal* lamented that this "prominent" suffragist and "energetic" and "tireless" recruit of new women voters could not herself "participa[te] in the fruits of the suffrage victory"—indeed, could not even count herself an American citizen.[40]

A few months later, on Friday, April 4, 1913, Ethel gave birth to the couple's first child. The baby boy, named after his father, weighed a healthy nine pounds. Again, the story was too good for the newspapers to ignore. "At last there is a citizen in the family," the *Los Angeles Times* exclaimed under the headline "Child May Vote, Mother Cannot."[41]

But Ethel could not leave the story there. So she did what all red-blooded Americans do when the government violates their constitutional rights: she filed a lawsuit. "I filed this petition with the supreme court," she explained, "because I know that there are thousands of women in California who, because they are married to men of other countries . . . are deprived of the right to vote."[42]

Ethel was not fighting alone. Milton T. U'Ren, a thirty-six-year-old lawyer and leader of the Progressive movement, took on her case, filing suit on her behalf against John P. Hare and the rest of the members of the San Francisco Board of Election Commissioners. U'Ren argued that the Expatriation Act of 1907 violated the Fourteenth Amendment to the US Constitution, and so must be struck down as invalid.

Section 1 of the Fourteenth Amendment guaranteeing citizenship to "all persons born or naturalized in the United States" had been added to the Constitution in 1868 to overrule *Dred Scott* and ensure that the citizenship of former slaves, free blacks, and their descendants could never be questioned again. But the Fourteenth Amendment was written without reference to race or gender, and Wong Kim Ark's case had confirmed that its sweeping language applied to everyone. The US Constitution had made Ethel Mackenzie a citizen at birth, and so U'Ren argued that Congress had no authority to take her citizenship away.

Now that the case was before the US Supreme Court, it captured the whole nation's attention. As one paper put it, *Mackenzie v. Hare* was "a test case that has become internationally famous in suffrage circles." From the *Pittsburgh Press* to the *Ottawa Citizen* to Utah's *Ogden Standard* to Davenport, Iowa's *Daily Times*, Ethel's story shared the front page with updates from the carnage wrought by the Great War in Europe—often alongside pictures of Ethel together with her infant son in her lap. An old hand by now, Ethel knew exactly how to generate the public's sympathy for the plight of women who had lost their citizenship under an archaic law. Papers across the country published outraged letters by readers commenting on the injustice of a law that expatriated American women married to foreign men, even as it automatically granted the foreign wives of American men US citizenship.[43]

But not all the coverage was positive. One newspaper argued that "not even a California woman can have her cake and eat it too." Tongue in cheek, the editors quipped, "We do not know whether a Scotch husband is worth more than a vote, or a vote is worth more than a Scotch husband." Either way, the "choice has to be made," and "Mrs. Mackenzie . . . has chosen to be a Scotchwoman, and a British subject" rather than an American entitled to vote. Some letters to the editor voiced the same sentiment, and members of Congress did not appear interested in rescinding the law on their own. For Ethel and women in her position, her citizenship was now in the hands of the nine men sitting on the US Supreme Court.[44]

On the morning of November 11, 1915, U'Ren headed for the semicircular Old Senate Chamber in the US Capitol, the same courtroom in which Wong Kim Ark's lawyers had successfully argued that the Constitution protected birthright citizenship less than twenty years before.

U'Ren was surely nervous as he sat waiting for the marshal of the court to lead the justices from the robing room in the north corridor of the Capitol into the wood-paneled court room. Then as now, the marshal wore the traditional double-breasted black frock coat that trailed down to mid-knee. In 1913, U'Ren, like all lawyers arguing before the court, was expected to appear in the same outdated attire, a throwback to the Victorian era that lingered on at the Supreme Court despite the modern preference for the more casual sack suit. (In the 1890s, future senator George Wharton Pepper of Pennsylvania made the mistake of arriving to argue his client's case in "street clothes," only to overhear Justice Horace Gray whisper to a colleague, "Who is that beast who dares to come in here with a grey coat?" After that, the court's staff took to keeping frock coats of various sizes on hand in case counsel arrived unprepared.)[45]

As the justices entered the courtroom, the marshal cried out: "Oyez! Oyez! Oyez! All persons having business before the Honorable, the Supreme Court of the United States, are now admonished to draw near and give their attention, for the Court is now sitting. God save the United States and this Honorable Court!" At these words, the low murmur of chatter ended abruptly, and with a scraping of chair legs on the wooden floor everyone in the small courtroom rose in unison and remained standing until the nine justices had settled themselves on the bench. U'Ren moved toward the lectern, as he was scheduled to speak first. He must have hesitated for a moment, staring down at the stack of papers on which he had written out his argument in longhand, polished on the long train ride from San Francisco to Union Station in Washington, DC. He had never addressed so many jurists at once and had never argued a case of such importance. This moment was the pinnacle of his young but already impressive career.

In 1915, oral argument before the US Supreme Court was neither recorded nor transcribed. Few reporters bothered to attend these sessions and report on them, as is routine today. So we do not know exactly what questions the justices asked, or how U'Ren and his opposing counsel responded. But we do know that the case was presented over two days, on November 11 and 12, 1915, suggesting that the court, like the nation's newspapers, had taken a particular interest in the matter.

We also know that U'Ren did not limit his argument to pure questions of law. Like advocates today, he drew upon the justices' emotions, using the Great War ravaging Europe to drive home how much was at stake for Ethel and women like her. In his brief to the court, he explained that Ethel's loss of citizenship did not only take away her identity as an American and her right to vote; it also jeopardized her physical safety during a world war. "The decree of this Court will determine not merely whether [Mackenzie] is a citizen of the United States or of England," he wrote, "but will decide also whether she is a citizen of a neutral country or an enemy of the three great world powers of Germany, Austria-Hungary and Turkey, and as such, subject to detention, capture and death at the hands of these powers."[46]

In truth, Ethel was not at risk as long as she remained comfortably ensconced at Nob Hill with her husband and baby. But she had brought this fight on behalf of all women married to noncitizens, some of whom *were* in real danger. The justices of the Supreme Court would have known the threat was real, even if the named plaintiff was herself relatively safe.

After the argument, U'Ren almost certainly returned to San Francisco by the transcontinental express, a trip taking over three days. There was no reason to stay in Washington, DC, any longer, and certainly no reason to miss the Thanksgiving holiday at home with his family. The court never announced in advance when it would issue its opinions, so he would have to wait at home for the telegram that would inform him whether Ethel had the right to call herself an American.

The decision came surprisingly quickly. Only three weeks later, on December 6, 1915, the court issued a thirteen-page opinion in which all nine justices were unanimous in their ruling. The court held that Ethel Coope Mackenzie had lost her citizenship under the Expatriation Act of 1907, and that nothing in the Constitution barred Congress from taking it from her.

The majority opinion was authored by Justice Joseph McKenna, a slight man with snowy white hair, usually sporting a bow tie beneath a neatly trimmed beard. McKenna was the only justice appointed by President William McKinley during his four years in office and is generally viewed as a poor choice. Although he served on the court for just a few days shy of twenty-seven years, the historical consensus is that he "made no significant contributions to legal interpretation." Scholars of the court described him as a "political hack." McKenna's contemporaries were even less kind. Chief Justice William Howard Taft said flatly "he was not a useful member of the Court." Writing to a friend, Taft expressed his frustration that McKenna somehow "wrote an opinion deciding the case one way when there had been a unanimous vote the other, including his own." In keeping with this consensus, McKenna's opinion for the court in *Mackenzie v. Hare* is a jumble of mostly unrelated thoughts and ideas that, strung together, gave Congress enormous power to revoke citizenship.[47]

McKenna began by noting that the "identity of husband and wife is an ancient principle of our jurisprudence" and that "to merge their identity, and give dominance to the husband . . . has purpose." In short, he seemed to be declaring that marital expatriation is good policy—though that was not the question the court had been asked to decide.[48]

McKenna then turned to the heart of the matter—whether the US Constitution gave Congress the power to revoke women's citizenship. He conceded both that the Fourteenth Amendment to the Constitution conferred citizenship on Ethel and that nothing in the Constitution expressly gave Congress the power to take it away. But that was irrelevant, according to McKenna, because he concluded that Congress did not *force* Ethel to give up her citizenship, rather she had *chosen* to do so. Marriage is "a condition voluntarily entered into," he observed, and Ethel had "notice of the consequences." Although he claimed the court "sympathize[d] with plaintiff in her desire to retain [her citizenship] and in her earnest assertion of it," he put the blame for its loss squarely at her feet. "The marriage of an American woman with a foreigner has consequences" and brings "national complications," he wrote, so "as long as the [marital] relation lasts, it is made tantamount to expatriation."[49]

Although the reasoning is muddled, McKenna seems to be saying that the Expatriation Act of 1907 did not revoke Ethel's citizenship against her will because Ethel voluntarily chose to marry a foreigner. As even Justice McKenna must have realized, that reasoning gave Congress extraordinary power to take away citizenship not only from women who married foreigners but from just about any American for almost any reason. At least theoretically, the rationale underlying the court's decision in *Mackenzie v. Hare* empowered Congress to enact legislation expatriating its citizens for living abroad, or joining a new political party, or criticizing the government, because, like marriage, these are all "voluntary" activities, and individuals would have had "notice of the consequences." Over the next few decades, Congress would do its best to put that theory into practice.

The Supreme Court's decision came as a blow for Ethel and her husband. They had lived charmed lives. Neither had been willing to settle for the hand they had been dealt, and they had successfully fought against the conventions that constrained them. Mackenzie had escaped a hardscrabble home in rural Scotland. For her part, Ethel had played a vital role in the enfranchisement of California's women, and could see that a constitutional amendment guaranteeing all women the right to vote was on the horizon. They had expected to win *Mackenzie v. Hare*, just as they had won most of the major battles of their lives so far.

But for Ethel Mackenzie, all was not lost. She was the wealthy wife of a celebrated and socially prominent entertainer. She and her husband were both white, and so they were both permitted to naturalize under federal law—a privilege denied to Asians and other racial minorities. Her husband had the time and money to navigate the complex process of petitioning for citizenship and was willing to do so to please his wife.

Yet even for this privileged couple, it was not easy. Mackenzie was awarded his citizenship more than five years later—years in which Ethel was barred from voting even after the Nineteenth Amendment supposedly guaranteed that right for all American women. Finally, on Thursday, January 6, 1921, a federal court issued him his naturalization papers—an event that revived interest in Ethel's struggle to regain her rights. "Santa Cruz Girl Restored to Citizenship," one headline announced.[50]

The moment was bittersweet. As a result of her husband's naturalization, Ethel automatically became a US citizen again and regained the civic rights she had lost upon her marriage. But she did not obtain that status because she had been born in the United States and was entitled to it under the Constitution, or because the law should never have taken it from her in the first place. As she told the *San Francisco Chronicle*, her husband's naturalization "means that I will be received back into the fold, but only because I am his wife."[51]

US representative Ruth Bryan Owen

CHAPTER 5

CITIZEN STATESWOMAN

In 1928, the Fourth of July in Lake Worth, Florida, dawned bright and hot. The scene that unfolded over the course of that day is easy to imagine. In the town's main square, the band shell is a sea of red, white, and blue bunting. Dozens of American flags droop along Main Street, now littered with the detritus of the parade an hour before—abandoned ice cream cones, a riot of confetti, the welcome spray from the fire engine's hose long since dried to a memory on the steaming pavement. On stage a brass band launches into yet another rendition of "Dixie," stalling for a guest of honor who has yet to arrive. Little children and dogs thread their way through the crowd, caught up in the adult's buzz of anticipation. Hundreds have already taken their seats in the folding chairs that fan outward onto the grassy square. Others remain clustered in loose knots under the shade of stately maples, delaying the moment when they will take their seats in the blazing sun. But no one is leaving anytime soon. The crowd of a thousand had been waiting in the smothering Florida heat for this moment, the highlight of the day's festivities.[1]

The guest of honor's Ford Coupe pulls up with its horn honking. Christened the "Spirit of Florida," it is ferrying Ruth Bryan Owen, the Democratic nominee to represent the Fourth District of Florida in the US House of Representatives. The arrival of any political candidate is an event in this sleepy town, but particularly when that candidate is the first woman to make a serious run for Congress in Florida. Owen had won the Democratic primary the month before, ousting the longtime incumbent. In 1928, only ten women have ever served in Congress. If Owen is elected, she will be the first and only woman in Congress from the American South. She is considered a celebrity for another reason as well—she is the daughter of William Jennings Bryan, "the Great Commoner," who was three times the Democratic nominee for president, though he never managed to attain that office.[2]

Owen emerges from the car looking "fresh as a daisy" despite the heat and her hectic schedule. Tidy and handsome, her steel gray hair cut short and styled in tight waves around her ears, she is wearing her trademark black silk, pearls, and a black cloche hat. She smiles and waves as she makes her way to the stage. To look at her, you could never guess that she was near to accomplishing her goal of visiting every precinct in the Fourth District of Florida—home to over half a million people, and larger than many states in terms of both geography and population. One newspaper editor exclaimed that despite her grueling schedule she was "full of pep," her "voice going as strong as ever." He concluded: "This weaker sex stuff is exploded for me forever."[3]

Owen is not alone on this hot July day. She has brought her secretary, whose job it is to keep the candidate on schedule—an impossible task when the candidate is Ruth Bryan Owen. Owen was particularly unwilling to leave any event before greeting the women who had come to support her, knowing that her candidacy was an inspiration in a state whose men had recently voted against enfranchising them. (Florida would not ratify the Nineteenth Amendment giving women the right to vote until 1969.)[4]

The entourage usually included eight-year-old Helen Rudd as well, Owen's fourth and youngest child. Owen had concluded that the best way to avoid charges that she had abandoned her children for politics was to bring her youngest with her. This last child was a surprise—an unwelcome one, Helen realized years later. Helen's impending arrival forced her mother to cut short a lucrative tour on the Chautauqua lecture circuit, where Owen was the highest-paid female speaker. Owen had bargained hard for that honor, in part because she was the sole source of support for her family after her husband returned from World War I an invalid. So, in an era when a married, upper-middle-class mother of four children was expected to keep house and socialize—usually with considerable hired help—Owen toured the country for months on end, speaking to hundreds of thousands to earn the money needed to pay their bills.[5]

Helen would hold her mother's hand as they mounted the stage, then take a seat beside her on the platform as they waited for the local dignitary to complete a long-winded introduction. "It is truly a great honor for me to introduce our speaker," the speaker would begin, before inevitably pivoting to talk about Owen's famous father. Owen was endlessly being cornered by men and women over sixty, who pumped her hand with tears in their eyes as they expressed their love for her recently deceased father. (It was a joke among Owen's family that if all the men who told her they had voted for him had actually done so, "the old bird would have won at a walk.") A parent's celebrity is a hazard for any child who goes into the same profession, but it was a particular problem for Owen, who had many reasons to want to distance herself from the man who for a good twenty years owned the Democratic Party. But if Owen was vexed at such moments, she was seasoned enough not to show it. With a final flourish of welcome, the master of ceremonies would wrap up his remarks and turn the stage over to the woman who was taking Florida by storm.[6]

Owen announced her first run for office in 1910, when she was only twenty-four years old—a bold move considering it was a full ten years before American women won a constitutionally protected right to vote. But later that same year she married Reginald Altham Owen, an Englishman and an officer in the Royal Engineer Corps, and she put her political aspirations aside to move with him to his post in Jamaica. Like Ethel Mackenzie and thousands of others, Owen automatically lost her American citizenship upon her marriage to a foreigner. Also like most others, she had no idea of the consequences when she entered into the union.[7]

In 1915, when Ethel Mackenzie was challenging the Expatriation Act of 1907 in the US Supreme Court, Owen was thousands of miles away serving as a surgical nurse in Egypt. When the war broke out in August 1914, the family had moved back to England and then Reginald had left for the front lines as part of the Dardanelles campaign. But Owen couldn't stand to remain isolated in safety in London. So she talked her way onto the last ship carrying civilians to Cairo, bringing her toddler son with her, with the hope of occasionally seeing her husband when he was on leave. Once she arrived, she learned that nurses were in short supply and she quickly volunteered. Her goal, she explained in a letter to a friend, was to be "absolutely as near the war as I could be without being myself a soldier."[8]

As *Mackenzie v. Hare* wound its way through the judicial system, Owen was arriving at the hospital each morning, donning her starched white nursing bib and turban, then scrubbing her arms and hands with disinfectant before entering the operating theaters. Her days began by cutting blood-soaked clothing off mangled limbs, irrigating wounds, and changing dressings. She tended men whose injuries were terrifying to behold, their skin puckered by burns and their eyes weeping from gas. One million British soldiers died in World War I, and double that number came home wounded—their bodies and faces horribly mangled from shrapnel, artillery, machine guns, gas, and, most of all, by the disease that ran rampant through the bodies packed together in muddy trenches. The experience turned her into a lifelong pacifist. Years later, she would describe her despair as she watched trains full of troops arrive at the Cairo train station, fresh-faced young soldiers pouring out of the front carriages even as hundreds of new coffins were carried out the back.[9]

The Great War that devastated Europe also shattered Reginald Owen's health. He fell ill and was diagnosed with Bright's disease, also known as "trench nephritis," an acute and chronic inflammation of the kidneys. Owen convinced the authorities to transfer him to the hospital where she worked, and she nursed him from the brink of death back to moderate health. Still, the doctors told Owen that he had less than a decade to live.[10]

In 1918, Owen was thirty-three years old, the mother of three young children with a fourth soon on the way, and the wife of an invalid. With nowhere else to turn, Owen took the family to Coral Gables, Florida, where her parents had settled. Once there, she quickly took on a role that she had watched her father occupy for decades: lecturer on the Chautauqua circuit. By all accounts, Owen was as mesmerizing as her father, both in content and style. Born with a broad chest and strong vocal chords, which was useful in an era without microphones, she could project her voice so that she could easily be heard by thousands. For years, she toured the country, joining luminaries such as former president Theodore Roosevelt, social activist Jane Addams, and educator Booker T. Washington, to entertain and educate crowds. In an era before television, Chautauqua events regularly sold out. During her time on the circuit, Owen spoke to over a million people on a wide variety of topics, from art history to her world travels to pacifism. All in preparation for this moment when she, too, would seek elected office.[11]

But Ruth Bryan Owen first had to surmount one major obstacle: she was not a US citizen.

Under the US Constitution, to be eligible to serve in Congress Owen was required to be a US citizen—a status that, despite her pedigree as the daughter of an American political icon, she had lost upon her marriage to an Englishman.

———————

Luckily for Owen, women refused to give up the fight for independent citizenship even after Ethel Mackenzie lost her case in the US Supreme Court. This time, however, they focused their efforts on Congress. Every year between 1913 and 1922, women lobbied to introduce a bill ending marital expatriation. In 1917, Jeannette Rankin, the first female member of the House of Representatives, finally persuaded the House Committee on Immigration and Naturalization to hold a hearing on the subject. (The newspapers expressed surprise that Representative Rankin would "come to the aid of cupid" considering that she herself was a "spinster.")[12]

But Rankin's male colleagues were hostile, turning the long-awaited hearing into a disaster. Throughout the proceedings, the congressmen derided women who chose to marry foreigners as disloyal and unpatriotic, and seemed obsessed with the idea that rich American women were marrying penniless foreign aristocrats for their titles. Representative Harold Knutson complained that if Rankin's bill passed, then such a woman "becomes 'Countess So-and-So'" while remaining an American, which "is not my conception of democracy." The congressmen were undisturbed by the double standard under which American women who married noncitizens immediately lost their citizenship, while the foreign wives of American men immediately became US citizens. "Under the tutelage of her kind American citizen husband," one representative explained, such a woman was sure to "become an American and a patriot at heart." Apparently the congressmen did not have such faith in American women's powers to similarly transform their foreign husbands.[13]

Even those congressmen who were not outraged by the idea of American women marrying foreign men treated the whole matter as nothing more than a joke at their female constituents' expense—perhaps because in 1917, those constituents still couldn't vote.

In frustration, one female witness declared: "Every question you asked this morning has been from . . . the standpoint of the man who is safe in his citizenship. . . . You have your citizenship; we love ours." Her outburst was met by stony silence. The women left that hearing convinced of what they already knew—they would not be treated seriously by their representatives in Congress until they had the power to vote them out of office.[14]

That moment came a mere three years later, on August 18, 1920, when Tennessee became the thirty-sixth state to ratify the Nineteenth Amendment and American women across the nation gained the constitutional right to vote. After that, the movement for independent citizenship quickly gathered speed, and both the Republican and Democratic parties vowed to end marital expatriation for American women who resided in the United States. Suddenly, members of Congress were quick to agree that marital expatriation was "as archaic as the doctrine of ordeal by fire."[15]

The hearings and subsequent debates profiled the women who had suffered serious harm as a result of their sudden loss of their citizenship. Helen Papanastasion, who had married a Greek citizen in 1917 while working at the American consulate in Greece, also lost her job pursuant to federal regulations barring the employment of noncitizens. Shortly thereafter, food became scarce in Greece, but she was barred from buying her bread at the US legation because she was no longer an American. The United States' entry into the Great War had a devastating effect on women whose husbands were citizens of the Central Powers. In the words of US Representative John L. Cable, these women "awakened to find that they were alien enemies, merely because they happened to have married a resident foreigner whose country was at war" with the United States. The government seized these women's property, threatened them with deportation, and subjected them to "humiliating sur-veillance" for the duration of the war.[16]

This time the men in Congress did not laugh or joke upon hearing these stories, but instead vowed to do something about it. Two years later, they did.

In 1922, Representative Cable introduced a new bill officially entitled the Married Women's Independent Citizenship Act but universally referred to as the Cable Act. The new law ended automatic expatriation of most, though not all, American women who married foreign men, as long as they continued to reside in the United States. It also attempted to rectify the damage done by the Expatriation Act of 1907 by permitting women who had lost their citizen-ship under that act to naturalize through an abbreviated process. The women's groups that had fought hard for this moment celebrated their victory.[17]

But it was only a partial victory. In a pattern that was often to be repeated, women's progress toward equality came at the expense of racial minorities. For the Cable Act did nothing to prevent American women from losing their citizenship on the basis of their race or the race of their noncitizen husbands. Congress had made it clear that it would no longer punish white American women for marrying white foreign men, but it showed no such compassion for people of color.

Section 3 of the Cable Act provided that "a woman citizen of the United States shall not cease to be a citizen of the United States by reason of her mar-riage." But then it went on to create a significant exception to that general rule for "any woman citizen who marries an alien ineligible to citizenship." From its inception, the United States permitted the naturalization only of "free white persons." The law was amended in 1870 to allow naturalization of "persons of African nativity, or African descent," but it continued to bar all other nonwhite aliens from becoming Americans. Policing the racial boundaries of citizenship was left to the courts, who denied citizenship, and also denaturalized, immi-grants from countries such as Burma, India, Syria, and the Philippines on the ground that they were not "white" within the meaning of the law. As a result of these judicial decisions, even after the Cable Act became law, American women who married noncitizens of Asian, Arab, or South Asian descent im-mediately lost their citizenship and could not regain it until the termination of their marriage. For the same reason, American women who fell into those same racial categories themselves and had lost their citizenship under the 1907 Expatriation Act were unable to regain it through naturalization.[18]

As a white woman married to a white man, the 1922 Cable Act enabled Ruth Bryan Owen to regain her lost citizenship. But she had to undertake the bu-reaucratic hassle of completing the forms and then scheduling a court date at which a judge would grant her naturalization petition—a task that she found difficult and possibly demeaning, so she did not complete the process until April 27, 1925. And just in time. The following year, she announced her candidacy for the US House of Representatives, fifteen years after her first campaign for that office had been derailed by her marriage.[19]

Owen faced an uphill battle. No woman had ever been elected to Congress from the American South. The Florida Democratic Party endorsed her opponent, an eleven-year incumbent. The *New York Times*, which consistently referred to her in its headlines as "Bryan's daughter" rather than by her own name, was pessimistic about her chances, observing that "the voters of Florida are notably opposed to accepting women in politics."[20]

As predicted, Owen lost the 1926 Democratic primary. But to everyone's surprise she came within a hairsbreadth of victory, losing by only 776 votes in a district of over half a million people. Her defeat was declared only after a "suspense[ful]" day of vote counting in which Owen and her opponent traded the lead several times. Many of her political supporters urged her to challenge the election results and demand a recount, particularly after discovering that the ballot boxes in Key West had been stuffed with votes under the names of deceased residents. Owen refused to do so, but she did issue a tongue-in-cheek statement congratulating Key West for its civic engagement. As summarized by her daughter years later, Owen observed that in "most communities that she knew of, people lost all interest in public affairs when they died," adding that it must be "hard to keep up to date on the issues after one was dead and buried." Nonetheless, Owen continued, she felt sure that if those deceased voters had "really understood the issues in the election just past," they "would have voted for her." The next time Owen visited Key West, the local leaders welcomed her with a smile and told her that they believed that *all* the residents of Key West, both above and below ground, would be inclined to vote for her were she to run again.[21]

In 1927, Owen's husband died after a long illness. Characteristically, Owen dealt with her grief by throwing herself into a frenzy of activity, which included international travel, another round of speeches on the Chautauqua circuit and, as everyone had expected, another run for Congress in 1928. To overcome the "handicap" of her gender, she decided it was essential to "meet the voters personally and let them see and hear what I had to say." For many politicians in the 1920s—an era without a 24/7 news cycle or easy means of transportation—campaigning was a part-time activity. Not for Owen. Over eight months, she met with ninety newspaper editors, gave over five hundred speeches, and visited every precinct in her district.[22]

Owen's hard work paid off. She won the Democratic primary, beating the incumbent by over fourteen thousand votes and breaking records for voter turnout. Although the general election was never in doubt, she campaigned with the same fervor, defeating her Republican opponent William C. Lawson by a two-to-one margin on November 6, 1928. She would be one of only seven women elected to the 71st Congress. Upon her victory, Owen referred humorously to her father's three unsuccessful bids for president: "There! I am the first Bryan who ran for anything and got it!" The local papers celebrated with her, dubbing her the "First Lady of the South."[23]

But Owen's fight for her seat in Congress was not over. After being trounced at the polls, William Lawson now argued that Owen was constitutionally ineligible to serve in Congress. Article I, Section 2 of the US Constitution provides that "no person shall be a Representative who shall not have . . . been seven years a citizen of the United States." Owen had lost her US citizenship in 1910 upon her marriage to a British citizen and had not regained it until 1925—only three years before she was elected to Congress. Because Owen had not been "seven years a citizen of the United States," Lawson argued she was not eligible to be seated in Congress and her seat should go to him.

Lawson's challenge could not have come as a complete surprise. During the campaign, he had distributed thousands of pamphlets quoting the relevant constitutional provision and then asking voters to "draw their own conclusions" about Owen's eligibility to serve. Owen herself had addressed the citizenship issue many times during the campaign, to the obvious satisfaction of voters. But voters do not get to decide whether a candidate is qualified to serve; the Constitution leaves that determination solely in the hands of the House of Representatives.[24]

Lawson was aggressive. After failing to convince Florida's governor to withhold her certificate of election, he filed a formal challenge with the House of Representatives. He also hired a team of lawyers who briefed the question and insisted that the House hold a hearing.[25]

At least publicly, Owen was sanguine. At one event, she described Lawson's challenge as a "joke" and an "absurdity," and she laughed when the subject was raised during an interview in December of that year. A newspaper headline declared, "Mrs. Owen Pokes Fun at Election Contest."

Nonetheless, Lawson's challenge to her eligibility must have been a thorn in her side during what should have been a moment of triumph. And his legal arguments could not be laughed off. The Constitution clearly requires that members of the House of Representatives have been "seven years a citizen of the United States," and Owen could not be certain that her fellow members of the House, almost all men and a sizable majority Republicans, would adopt her more flexible interpretation of that provision. A sympathetic article in the

Fort Myers News-Press criticized Lawson for bringing the challenge, but then observed, "Technically [he] may be correct."[26]

Nine months after Owen had been sworn in as the Fourth District's congress-woman, the House Election Committee finally convened for its hearing on the question. Owen had served more than a third of her two-year term in office, and by all reports she was a success. She had won rave reviews from the local Florida papers and the *New York Times* alike. Remarkably, when she asked to be on the House Foreign Affairs Committee, the Republicans created a new seat for her. Through some combination of her gender, her famous father, her intelligence, and her remarkable charm, she was in demand both profes-sionally and socially from the day she arrived in the nation's capital. She "cap-tivated Washington completely," one observer reported. And yet it was still unclear whether she was constitutionally eligible to serve as one of Florida's representatives in Congress.[27]

On Friday, January 17, 1930, at ten in the morning, the committee gath-ered in a "stuffy little" room in the Capitol building to hear argument from Lawson's attorneys. In attendance were eight of the nine House Election Com-mittee members, as well as Lawson's two attorneys and several witnesses. The audience consisted of a gaggle of journalists from papers around the country who had been following this story closely, as well as many women who had come in a show of support. Owen sat alone at the table reserved for her.

At least outwardly, Owen appeared confident. She wrote her own brief and appeared on her own behalf, forgoing a lawyer because, she explained, the issues were "so simple that they do not require any legal presentation." Lawson's lawyer requested an hour to make his case; Owen told the chairman, "I do not propose to take more than five minutes myself." Still, a hearing at which her new col-leagues decided whether she would be replaced by her Republican challenger, a man she had trounced at the polls, surely rankled. Her occasional outbursts during Lawson's presentation, as well as her fiery speeches when it was her turn to speak, suggest she took this hearing more seriously than she claimed.[28]

Lawson, dubbed a "poor loser" by the Florida papers, chose not to ap-pear in person at the hearing, sending his lawyers, Noah Bainum and H. B. Morrow, in his place. In his opening remarks, Bainum stated that Lawson's efforts to remove Owen from office were neither "personal" nor "political." "Mr. Lawson wants the dignity and solemnity of this constitutional provi-sion maintained," Bainum declared, and nothing more. (This claim was hard to swallow, considering that Lawson was arguing not only that Owen should lose her seat in Congress but that it should be awarded to him.) "I have the highest regard for [Mrs. Owen], as I had for her father," Bainum declared, and then added that both his wife and wife's sister had voted for her. Wisely, Bainum was trying to shift the focus from Owen personally to the legal question about whether she had attained the seven years of citizenship required by the Constitution. But his comments may have inadvertently reminded the committee that Owen was a role model for newly enfranchised women everywhere—women who might punish the committee members at the polls were they to decide she was not eligible to serve.[29]

Bainum's argument was straightforward: the eligibility clause in Article I, Section 2 of the Constitution required that members of the House of Representatives be "seven Years a Citizen," and Owen failed to meet that standard. She had "expatriated herself by marriage with a British subject," he explained, and she "remained a British subject" until her naturalization on April 27, 1925, less than three years before she took office.[30]

The committee was not convinced. "Do you think . . . we should overlook altogether the fact that she was a native-born citizen and had been such for 24 years [before her marriage]?" Representative Charles Kading asked Bainum. To which Bainum, unwavering, responded yes. Kading pressed the point further, arguing that the Framers of the Constitution included the seven-year citizenship requirement to prevent a "foreigner coming over here" from serving in Congress shortly thereafter. He then inquired of Bainum, "Do you think that it would be good reasoning to conclude that Mrs. Owen had lost all the qualities of good citizenship by reason of her first 24 years' residence here because of the mere fact that she married a foreigner?" In his response, Bainum sought to avoid impugning Owen's patriotism directly, noting that she "is an exceptional woman." But he supported the point in principle. "Ordinarily, I think that an American woman marrying a foreigner acquires so many bad habits that the [seven-year citizenship] limitation ought to be absolute."[31]

This exchange was too much for Owen, who could not remain silent even though she had previously been admonished for speaking up during Bainum's presentation. "May I inquire whether you consider a man marrying a foreigner subject to exactly the same sweeping denunciation?" she interjected. This time, the committee did not object to her interruption, and Bainum was forced to answer. "No," he responded, "because a man does not lose his citizenship by marrying a foreigner." While a legal truism, that was beside the point, as he and everyone in the room knew. Owen had been making a moral argument, not a legal one. As her question made clear, if the United States did not fear that an American man would gain "bad habits" by marrying a foreign wife, then it would be unfair and unjust to assume that an American woman would.[32]

It was 1 p.m. and after three hours of presentation, Lawson's attorneys still had more to say. The hearing was adjourned to the following day—a Saturday. The House Election Committee appeared to be taking this challenge to Owen's eligibility seriously, even if Owen claimed not to.

That Saturday morning Owen again arrived at the hearing room alone. She would be the sole person to speak in her own defense. She brought no lawyers, no staff members, not even a friend or family member to sit beside her. Better than most, Owen knew how to manipulate an event to her advantage. She must have liked the image she presented: a woman alone against a bevy of lawyers who were trying to deprive her of the office bestowed on her by the voters of the Fourth District of Florida. But she took a risk in adopting this David versus Goliath approach. The legal questions underlying Lawson's challenge were significant and untested. Owen was relying perhaps too heavily on the assumption that her male colleagues would not want to risk angering their newly enfranchised female constituents by refusing to seat her.

Owen stood to present her case, tucking her hands behind her back and bracing herself against a bookshelf. She was unusually tall, and from that position she commanded the room. The journalists in attendance were awed by her, describing her as "striking" and possessing "exceptional . . . mental qualities" and "native eloquence" that reminded observers of her famous father.[33]

Owen began by once again insisting that hers was an easy case. Contrasting herself to her opponent, who had paid for several lawyers to argue on his behalf, she explained that she was representing herself "not . . . because I place any reliance in my own ability" but rather because the case is "so simple."[34]

To be sure, Owen did have legal arguments—two of them. First, she asserted that the 1922 Cable Act not only restored her US citizenship, it also erased the fifteen years in which she had been stripped of that status. Section 4 of that act provides, "After her naturalization she shall have the same citizenship status as if her marriage had taken place after the passage of this act." Owen read that phrase to retroactively give her back the years of citizenship the 1907 Expatriation Act had taken from her.[35]

Second, she argued that, in any case, the constitutional requirement that she be "seven years a citizen" required only a *cumulative* period of seven years of citizenship, not a *consecutive* period directly preceding the election. Because at the time of her election she had been a citizen of the United States for twenty-four years before her citizenship had been revoked, and another three years after she had naturalized, she easily met that requirement.[36]

But Owen spent little time discussing the law. She had laid out the legal arguments in her written brief, and the committee members clearly understood the issues. She was there to convince her colleagues that stripping her of her seat in Congress was as unjust, immoral, and unfair as the Expatriation Act of 1907 had been to strip her of her citizenship in the first place.

And she made clear to them that their vote was not only about her political future, but also theirs. She implied, without ever saying it, that American women might punish at the polls any member of Congress who voted against her. Her presentation—which was more akin to a political speech than a legal argument—was aimed not only at the members of Congress who sat on the committee, but also at the press who had crowded into the room to hear her speak, and by extension all the constituents who would read the coverage of the hearing. When it came to the court of public opinion, no one was more capable than the queen of the Chautauqua circuit. She planned to win not only the battle for her seat in Congress, but also the war of public opinion.

Her theme, striking for its time, was that men and women must be treated as equals. "No man ever lost his citizenship through his marriage," she told the committee. Likewise, "no American man has ever been called before a committee of this sort to explain his marriage." She declared that American women have the "right to the same consideration at the hands of her Government as is enjoyed by the male citizen." Although the facts of her particular case were unusual, she emphasized that the committee's decision would "affect . . . millions of American women," because it concerned the "recognition of the right of an American woman . . . to exactly the same treatment that is meted out to a man." Again and again, she reminded the committee of the inherent injustice embodied in the Expatriation Act of 1907, declaring:

> The last thing that is done to a man who has disqualified himself in the eyes of his Government as a citizen, the last punishment that is ever inflicted on a man is the deprivation of citizenship. The traitor, the felon, the lowest criminal, is deprived of his citizenship, and yet by the enactment of my country I was deprived of my citizenship for no fault of my own, for no lack of loyalty to my country, but because I was a woman.[37]

She claimed that the Cable Act of 1922 put an end to this, not only changing the law going forward but also eliminating the discrimination of the past. That act "is designed to right an injustice done to . . . all American women," she told the committee, and it "had as its intent the giving to the American woman the same dignity and individuality of citizenship which is enjoyed by the male citizen."[38]

In fact, the Cable Act fell far short of that ideal. It perpetuated the long-standing common law rule that a woman who moved abroad with her foreign husband, as Owen had done, lost her citizenship unless she affirmatively petitioned to keep it. Like so many other supporters of the Cable Act, Owen also overlooked its blatant discrimination against women who married noncitizens who belonged to racial minorities, as well as all the nonwhite American women who had lost their citizenship under the Expatriation Act but were barred by racially discriminatory naturalization laws from getting it back, as Owen had done in 1925. But the Cable Act did rectify the injustice done to many white women who married white men and remained in the United States—the only voters that were likely to have influence in Congress anytime soon.

Owen concluded by throwing down the gauntlet, placing at the committee's feet the task of interpreting the act to ensure justice for women. "I think there is no better time and place for that act to be interpreted than before this committee of Congress," she declared. When doing so, she urged the committee to consider the "spirit of this act as well as the letter." Her message was clear. Whatever ambiguities remained in the text, the committee had the power to interpret that law to ensure that she—and by implication all women—were treated as equals to men.[39]

Owen then pivoted to the personal. She reminded the committee that Lawson's lawyer, Bainum, had claimed that women who marry foreigners and move abroad bring back "vicious habits" when they return to the United States. To rebut these arguments, she felt compelled to reveal "personal facts" that she "regret[ted] very much inserting in a public record." Her "voice dropped to almost a whisper" as she recounted her war work, first as the founder of a hospital for injured Americans in England, then as a surgical nurse in Egypt, and finally as a resident back in Florida, where she was the sole breadwinner for her family during her husband's long illness. The atmosphere in the packed committee room was intense during Owen's "dramatic plea" for her seat in Congress. "Tears rolled down the . . . cheeks" of some in the audience, who "sniffed audibly" as Owen spoke of her personal sacrifices.[40]

Now it was Bainum's turn to interrupt. He interjected that had never intended to criticize Owen personally, noting once again that "Mrs. Owen was quite an exception." He had meant only to point out that there were "very undesirable people" who should be kept from serving in Congress. Owen took full advantage of this interruption. She readily agreed that Bainum had not targeted her personally, but rather had made a "general statement as to the vicious habits which American women might bring back." Owen used that moment to press home her point that Bainum's comments impugned *all* American women. By implication, if the committee sided with him, they were adopting his assumptions of the morals and loyalty of the female half of their constituency—and would surely reap the consequences at the polls now that those women could vote.[41]

Once the hearing was over, the decision was left to the Elections Committee to issue a report recommending a decision to the House of Representatives, which would then vote on her case. It is impossible to know whether Owen was worried about the outcome. The press coverage had been universally positive, and the House Election Committee members appeared to be sympathetic. Nonetheless, her case raised novel legal issues, and the legal arguments were far from clear. The Election Committee's silence for several months after the hearing could only have heightened her anxiety.

Finally, on March 1, 1930, more than two months after the hearing concluded, the Election Committee announced the result. Although Owen must have been deeply relieved to read that the committee unanimously found that she was eligible to take her seat in Congress, she was likely taken aback by the committee's report, which acknowledged that it "is to be regretted that the committee is not in harmony upon the constitutional question involved." The members were deeply divided on the legal basis for its decision. A bare majority of five members of the committee concluded that the Constitution's requirement that a member of the House be "seven years a citizen" allowed for cumulative citizenship. According to the majority, Owen's three years of citizenship after her 1925 naturalization, when added to her twenty-four years of citizenship before her marriage in 1910, meant she easily met the seven years of citizenship required by the Constitution.[42]

The other four members of the committee disagreed. On the constitutional question, they sided with Lawson, concluding that the Constitution required that the seven years of citizenship immediately precede the election. Indeed, these four asserted that permitting cumulative citizenship was "dangerous," pointing out that the majority's reasoning would allow a man born in the United States to Russian-citizen parents to return to Russia on his seventh birthday, and then come back to the United States after decades in Russia and immediately take a seat in Congress. Such a man would be the Framers of the Constitution's worst fear, for he would surely not have "purged himself of foreign influences and become imbued with the spirit of our institutions," as the Framers intended.[43]

Nonetheless, these four members of the Election Committee also found that Owen was eligible to take her seat in Congress after concluding that the Cable Act "obliterated" Owen's fifteen years of expatriation, restoring her citizenship as if it had never been taken from her. Their reading of the statute was heavily influenced by the newest addition to the Constitution—the Nineteenth Amendment. They argued that the Cable Act, "passed subsequent to the adoption of the nineteenth amendment . . . should be viewed in the light of that amendment in extending the rights and privileges of American women."

In an extraordinary act of constitutional interpretation, these four congress-men stated that the Nineteenth Amendment not only gave women access to the ballot, it "place[d] her upon an equality with American men."[44]

Placed her upon an equality with American men. These words jump out of the page to the modern reader. This was the same declaration of equality that Owen had made in her own defense, albeit without specific reference to the Nineteenth Amendment. But Owen's vision of political and civic equal-ity for women—a vision shared by at least these four members of the House of Representatives and likely many others who subsequently voted to seat her on the same grounds—was not one that prevailed in the decades that fol-lowed. For many years to come, women were explicitly denied equal status in the nation's political and civic life. In 1930, when the Elections Committee issued its report, thousands of state laws discriminated against women: these laws enabled their husbands to take their wages; barred women from inherit-ing property, serving as trustees to their family's estates, or obtaining custody of their children upon divorce; prohibited women from entering a variety of professions; and excluded them from serving on juries or being witnesses in court. Federal law also discriminated against women in numerous ways, such as by denying women access to certain federal jobs and equal treatment under the nation's immigration and citizenship laws.

Ruth Bryan Owen won from the House Elections Committee not only a unanimous ruling in favor of her eligibility to serve in Congress, but also a declaration of equality for women that was far before its time.

On June 6, 1930, the full House of Representatives finally voted on the ques-tion. Members of the committee gave long speeches on the floor of the House attesting to Owen's "patriot[ism]" and her "Americanism," listing her family's pedigree in the War of Independence and before and making constant ref-erences to her famous father. Representative Judson Newhall, a Republican from Kentucky, asked: "Does anyone here present doubt that this daughter of the great commoner, this daughter of a long line of American patriots, has a sufficient background of Americanism? I dare say not one." Finally, a voice vote was called on House Resolution 241, declaring that Democrat Ruth Bryan Owen, "duly elected Representative" from Florida, was "entitled to re-tain her seat." The House of Representatives—a majority Republicans, almost all men—stood to cry out a unanimous "Aye!" Owen's place in Congress was finally secure.[45]

Also worth noting was all that was not said. During the months of debate over Ruth Bryan Owen's eligibility to serve, no one mentioned that Senator Hiram Rhodes Revels's eligibility to serve in the Senate had been challenged on nearly identical grounds sixty years before. Owen's and Revels's eligibility battles share striking similarities. Both saw their citizenship challenged by those who refused to accept their claims to full membership. And both cases raised fundamental constitutional questions about the power of constitutional amendments to alter the very nature of the constitutional compact, widening the circle of those considered to be full-fledged members of the polity and granting that new group all the civil, political, and social rights of citizenship.

In his defense, Revels's supporters argued not only the technical point that the Fourteenth Amendment's birthright citizenship provision retroactively granted him citizenship from birth, but also that the abolition of slavery and the Reconstruction Amendments to the Constitution—including but not limited to the Fourteenth Amendment—had incorporated the equality principles of the Declaration of Independence into the Constitution and the nation as a whole. Likewise, Owen and her supporters claimed not just that her years as a US citizen added up to the requisite number of years, but also that the Nineteenth Amendment, by giving women the right to vote, had transformed them into citizens with equal status to men—a sea change that, they argued, should inform the interpretation of all laws and practices going forward.

Battles over congressional qualifications are rare, and Owen's and Revels's fight shared common questions about citizenship, equality, and the transformative power of constitutional amendments. So at first blush it seems remarkable that neither Owen nor her supporters mentioned Revels's favorable precedent in the many months during which the House considered her eligibility to serve.

Perhaps the details of Revels's case had been forgotten, the sixty years between them obscuring the many similarities. Or perhaps Owen and her supporters preferred not to draw the comparison. True, Revels won the battle over his citizenship and eventually took his Senate seat in 1870. But those who questioned African Americans' claims to equal status as US citizens won the war. In 1930, Owen was one of eight women in Congress, a number that would only grow—albeit slowly—over the next ninety years. That same year, only one African American sat in Congress, the very first to be elected in the twentieth century. The experience of African Americans such as Revels demonstrated that the constitutional right to full citizenship and even the right to vote would not be enough to ensure equality for any group if the nation refused to view them as equal citizens.

The Cable Act of 1922 was further evidence—if any was needed—that racial minorities were not yet securely citizens of the United States, either culturally or legally. As a result of that law, white women married to white men—women like Ruth Bryan Owen and Ethel Mackenzie—were now safely in possession of their citizenship along with their right to vote. But even as Owen benefited from that change in law—regaining her citizenship, winning an election with the support of Florida's female voters, and then the battle to take her seat in Congress—women continued to lose their citizenship for marrying men in certain racial categories. Nor could women regain their lost citizenship if found to be in those same categories.

To her credit, Owen decided to use her political power to change that even before her own position in Congress was secure. On March 6, 1930, she was a witness at a hearing before the House Committee on Immigration and Naturalization considering legislation that would end the race-based vestiges of marital expatriation. She began her testimony by acknowledging that although "no one has greater cause than I to recognize the value" of the 1922 Cable Act, it had not gone far enough. Perhaps wisely in light of the times, Owen chose to frame her complaints about the act in terms of gender, not race. She argued that the Cable Act perpetuated "discrimination . . . against women" by stripping only American women, and not American men, of their citizenship for marrying foreigners who were also racial minorities. Because "the only equitable view that can be taken is that men and women are entitled to exactly the same consideration from their government," she was firmly in favor of amending the law to eliminate the disparity in treatment. Although she did not mention race, the effect of her advocacy was to ensure that *all* American women, regardless of their race or the race of their husbands, retained their US citizenship. As the *Tampa Tribune* put it, "Mrs. Owen realized its injustice to many other women, now and in the future," so she worked to "save the citizenship" of fellow American women.[46]

The bill passed both houses of Congress, and on March 3, 1931, President Hoover signed it into law. The papers gave Ruth Bryan Owen all the credit. "Congresswoman Owen . . . got into the very front lines and led the charge" against the discriminatory provisions of the Cable Act, declared the *Cincinnati Enquirer*. The *New York World-Telegram* affirmed: Congresswoman Owen "has won the most important battle women have carried on since the suffrage campaign." Another journalist observed, the "ghosts of Susan B. Anthony and Lucretia Mott must rest . . . in peace" now that the "last vestige of discrimination against woman's citizenship is removed."[47]

In June of 1930, Owen did not have a moment to savor the House of Representatives' confirmation of her election eighteen months before, or to worry
about whether the law closing the loopholes in the Cable Act would pass. She
was busy touring her district as she campaigned for the Democratic primary,
held only a few days before the House vote. "Mrs. Ruth Bryan Owen Wins
Election Fight," exclaimed the *Tallahassee Democrat*, a headline that captured
both the "aye" vote on the floor of the House confirming her eligibility to serve
and the news that she had trounced her male Democratic opponent in the
primaries by a four-to-one majority. Alongside the headline ran a photo of a
regal Representative Owen, a small smile playing at the corner of her lips, in
her trademark pearls and a cloche hat.[48]

Joseph Yoshisuke Kurihara

Fritz Julius Kuhn

CHAPTER 6

BLUT CITIZEN

By 6 p.m. on Monday, February 20, 1939, the four square blocks surrounding New York's Madison Square Garden were a madhouse, teeming with angry demonstrators watched over by at least a thousand police. They were there to protest the Amerikadeutscher Volksbund, known in the American press as the German American Bund, which was holding a rally inside. The audience numbered twenty thousand, double the size of the protestors outside and, according to the Bund's leaders, only a small fraction of those Americans who supported Nazi Germany and its leader, Adolf Hitler.[1]

Those who made it through the gauntlet of rowdy protestors on Eighth Avenue and into the Garden were transported from the streets of a diverse and chaotic American metropolis to a rally much like those occurring regularly in Germany. At 8 p.m. sharp, the event opened with a parade of uniformed storm troopers carrying red flags emblazoned with black swastikas, followed by a smaller group hoisting American flags. The parade of speakers that followed condemned the "international Marxist Jews" and the "Jewish financiers," whom they blamed both for America's involvement in the First World War and the Great Depression. References to Supreme Court Justice Felix Frankfurter and Treasury Secretary Henry Morgenthau, both Jews, drew hisses. Speaker after speaker harangued "President Frank Rosenfeld" and his "Jew Deal." One speaker drew wild applause when he called on the audience to "join with us in the battle for a . . . Jew-free America!," and many in the crowd stretched their right arm into the air, palm flattened, in the Sieg Heil salute.[2]

Fritz Kuhn, leader of the Bund and the self-proclaimed "American *führer*," was the last to take the stage that night. He appeared in full uniform, his trademark Sam Browne belt straddling his considerable girth, his jackboots pushing him a few inches above his six feet. He wore a black arm band stamped with a swastika, as well as the iron cross he had earned while fighting in the

German infantry during the Great War. Grasping the podium and rock-ing back and forth as he spoke, he blamed the "Jewish communists" for the world's ills. "The Bund is fighting shoulder to shoulder with patriotic Ameri-cans to protect America from a race that is not the American race, that is not even a white race," Kuhn thundered, then declared, "Jews are enemies of the United States." The crowd rose to its feet and cheered.[3]

Despite the chaos on the streets outside, Kuhn considered the evening a great success. The size of the rally and the news coverage that followed would, he was sure, draw more German Americans to recognize that their first alle-giance was to the Aryan race, not the United States of America. For Kuhn, citizenship was a matter of blood, not legal documentation. "We are, first of all, Germans by race, in blood, in language," Kuhn explained in a speech in October 1936. "By obtaining other citizenship papers we have not lost our German character," he insisted, for "we belong to the great commonwealth of all German peoples on this earth."[4]

Kuhn's words echoed those of the Nazi Party. The National Socialist *Welt-anschaung*, or worldview, perceived German citizenship as a matter of *blut* rather than place of birth, country of residence, or legal status. Ethnic Ger-mans anywhere in the world—be it Vienna, Prague, Strasbourg, or Cincin-nati—were *Deutschtum*, or "racial comrades," and so their natural loyalties lay with Germany. Under that principle, Germany had annexed Austria in March 1938 and marched into the Sudetenland in Czechoslovakia six months later, cheered on by the ethnic Germans who lived there. And from that logic, it followed that racially "impure" residents of Germany, that is German Jews, were *not* German citizens—a view enshrined in the 1935 Nuremburg laws that stripped German Jews of their citizenship and forbade marriage and sexual relations between Jews and non-Jewish Germans.[5]

In the Nazi's racialized view of citizenship, 15 percent of the population of the United States—that is, about twenty million people who were either im-migrants from Germany or the descendants of German immigrants—were as much or more members of the German *volk* as they were American citizens. Nazi leadership shared Kuhn's hope that these millions of German Amer-icans—or "Germans in America," as Kuhn preferred to call them—would be Germany's allies in the inevitable race war to come. But they feared that Kuhn was more of a liability than an asset in the recruitment effort, and for good reason.[6]

Born in Munich in 1896, Kuhn served as a machine gunner in World War I. He later joined the Nazi Party and claimed to have participated in the 1923 "Beer Hall Putsch"—Hitler's failed attempt to take over the government in Bavaria. Kuhn emigrated to the United States in 1928 to work as an X-ray technician, became a naturalized US citizen in 1934, and then took over the leadership of the Bund two years later. But despite his respectable Nazi credentials, Kuhn was ill suited to serve as standard-bearer for their cause. He seemed to enjoy ruffling feathers, often alienating the German Americans he was trying to woo on behalf of the Bund. A beefy man, he had a habit of standing with his legs apart and his thumbs tucked into his belt as he harangued crowds in his Bavarian-accented English. And he had an unhealthy attraction to alcohol and women, often using Bund funds to obtain both while his wife and children waited for him at home. To his critics, Kuhn embodied the Charlie Chaplin-esque caricature of Nazis as comical buffoons, to be laughed at more than feared.[7]

And yet Kuhn inspired a cultish loyalty, and his followers saw in their American *führer* many of the same qualities they admired in the German one. Sinclair Lewis's satirical 1935 novel *It Can't Happen Here* suggested that America could fall under the sway of a fanatical fascist leader, just as Germany had succumbed to Hitler only a few years before. Shortly after the Madison Square Garden rally, an editorial in the *New York Times* warned: "We need be in no doubt as to what the Bund would do to and in this country if it had the opportunity . . . it would set up an American Hitler."

Kuhn intended to be that man.[8]

Almost three years later, on December 7, 1941, forty-six-year-old Joseph Kurihara was serving as a navigator on a tuna fishing boat off the coast of the Galapagos Islands. Along with the rest of the world, he would soon learn that Pearl Harbor in his native state of Hawai'i had been attacked by the Japanese that day, killing 2,300 and destroying most of America's warships. Within a week, the United States had declared war on Japan and its allies, Germany and Italy. Like everyone else, Kurihara had "felt th[at] war was in the air," yet he still found it hard to believe that his country would fight in yet another world war.[9]

Joseph Kurihara was born Yoshisuke Kurihara on New Year's Day, 1895, in the village of Hanamaulu in Kaua'i, Hawai'i. He changed his first name when he moved to California at age twenty—a small example of the many ways in which he forged his own path. Kurihara's parents were Japanese immigrants who had come to Hawai'i as agricultural workers and then stayed to raise a family. Like all Issei, or first-generation Japanese immigrants, Kurihara's parents were barred from becoming US citizens under a federal law that prohibited Asians from naturalizing. But their US-born children, known as Nisei, were US citizens by virtue of the Fourteenth Amendment's birthright citizenship guarantee—a status confirmed by the US Supreme Court's 1898 decision in *Wong Kim Ark v. United States*. When Hawai'i became a US territory in 1900, Kurihara automatically became a US citizen by virtue of his birth there.[10]

"Hey! You Jap, I want some information," a government official yelled as Kurihara's fishing boat pulled into San Diego, California, a few weeks after the Japanese attacked Pearl Harbor. "You better tell me everything, or I'll kick you in the ____." In describing the moment a few years later, Kurihara demurely omitted the kick's intended location, but the speaker's sentiment was clear. Kurihara, who had initially been "happy to be back in sight of America," felt his "blood boil." Now well into middle age, Kurihara was a stocky five feet two with rapidly thinning hair, but age had not diminished his finely tuned sense of justice, and he was never one to shy from a fight. Kurihara nonetheless managed to remain calm as he told the man to address him with respect, and he agreed to go with him to the local immigration office.[11]

After waiting for hours, one of the officers finally called him over for questioning.

"What do you think of the war?" he asked Kurihara.

"Terrible," Kurihara responded.

The officer quizzed him about his experience as a navigator, and then asked, "Have you been a good American citizen?"

"I was and I am."

"Will you fight for this country?"

"If I am needed, I am ready," Kurihara replied, adding that he was a veteran of the First World War. Only then was he released from custody and permitted to enter the United States.[12]

In the weeks that followed, Kurihara tried to find a job assisting in the war effort but was repeatedly rejected. Only later did Kurihara realize that his applications were turned down on account of his race.[13]

By 1941, Kurihara had become accustomed to the pervasive prejudice against Americans of Japanese descent, though it never ceased to enrage him. He had left Hawai'i for San Francisco at age twenty to further his education and was shocked by the overt and sometimes violent racism he experienced in California on a near-daily basis. Children threw rocks at him, adults spat on him, and once he was kicked in the stomach by a well-dressed man for no reason. Wherever he went he was called "Jap"—a derogatory term that never failed to cut him to the bone.[14] On a train to San Pedro, California, he sat down next to a woman who told him, "Why don't you take some other seat? I don't want a Jap to s[it] next to me." Kurihara refused, responding: "Sorry madam, I paid my fare. If you don't like my looks, why don't you move?" She did.[15]

Discrimination against the Japanese was government sanctioned. In 1924, Congress amended federal law to bar immigration from Japan, formalizing the Gentlemen's Agreement of 1907, under which Japan agreed to deny passports to Japanese laborers seeking to emigrate to the United States. Also under federal law, all Asian immigrants were prohibited from naturalizing—a racial restriction that would not be completely eradicated from federal law until 1952. In 1913, the California legislature passed a law barring "aliens ineligible to citizenship"—that is, all Asian immigrants—from owning agricultural land, and prohibited leasing land to such aliens for longer than three years. And in a number of states, these immigrants could never become doctors, lawyers, architects, dentists, or teachers, or work for the municipal or state government—all jobs that some states made off-limits to noncitizens.[16]

All of these laws, along with the racial slurs and daily humiliations, infuriated Kurihara and left him "homesick" for Hawai'i—a place he perceived as free from such discrimination, perhaps because Japanese and Japanese Americans constituted more than a third of a diverse Hawaiian population. Nonetheless, he chose to "weather it through" on the mainland for the sake of his education and employment.[17]

As Kurihara was seeking to aid the war effort, America's military and civilian leaders were deciding what to do with the 126,948 people of Japanese ancestry in the contiguous United States—a tiny group that amounted to less than one-tenth of 1 percent of the US population. The great majority—close to 90 percent—lived along the Pacific Coast, often in segregated neighborhoods known as "Japantown" or "Little Tokyo," where street names and shop signs were in Japanese and the local stores sold kimonos and dried seaweed. About one-third of this group were noncitizen immigrant Issei, many of whom did not speak English well. The remaining two-thirds were the second-generation Nisei who were born in the United States and so, like Kurihara, were US citizens.[18]

In the fall of 1941, as the threat of war with Japan loomed on the horizon, the Roosevelt administration sent officials to investigate the "Japanese situation" on the West Coast. The report back was that the vast majority of both Issei and Nisei "are pathetically eager to show [their] loyalty" to the United States. A separate FBI study found the same.[19]

But in the days following the Pearl Harbor attack, newspapers reported that Hawaiian residents of Japanese ancestry assisted the Japanese military by deploying "flashing lights," exchanging gunfire with American soldiers, and carving arrows into their sugar cane fields to guide Japanese pilots. Although these rumors were later proven false, US Navy secretary Frank Knox appeared

to confirm them when he declared a few days later that the attack was the result of "a great deal of active fifth column work going on both from the shores
and from the sampans." Hysteria increased over the next few months as the
Japanese military won a swift series of victories against US and British forces
in the Pacific. The public clamored for protection from those residents who
could trace their lineage to Japan.[20]

On February 19, 1942, President Franklin Delano Roosevelt responded
by signing into law Executive Order 9066, which gave the secretary of war
the authority to remove "any or all persons" from locations he designated as
"military areas." On its face the executive order did not specify either that the
Pacific Coast of the United States was a particularly vulnerable "military area"
or that the "persons" to be removed were of Japanese ancestry. The United
States was at war with Germany and Italy as well as Japan, transforming the
nationals of all three countries into "enemy aliens" and putting both coasts at
risk of attack or invasion.

After the attack on Pearl Harbor, Roosevelt asked Attorney General Francis Biddle to come up with a plan to protect the country from *all* threats from
within, and particularly from the Germans living in the United States. "I don't
care so much about the Italians. They are a lot of opera singers," he told Biddle,
"but the Germans are different: they may be dangerous."[21]

Members of Congress were also concerned about Germans—or at least, one
particular German. A few years earlier, on a muggy August morning in 1939,
the US House of Representative's Special Committee on Un-American Activities called Bundesführer Fritz Julius Kuhn to testify about his role as leader
of the German American Bund. The chamber's double-high ceilings and Corinthian columns added gravitas to the proceedings, as did the phalanx of
photographers snapping pictures as Kuhn raised his right hand and swore to
tell the truth.[22]

The man who came before the committee was surly and unapologetic, but
he had dropped the swagger of his Madison Square Garden appearance only
a few months before and had wisely exchanged his military uniform for a suit
and tie. Earlier that summer Kuhn had been arrested in New York for pro-
fanity and drunkenness—a minor, if humiliating, matter. Then in July he was
arrested again, this time for grand larceny and forgery for embezzling Bund
funds. Although free on bail, the charges against him were serious.[23]

The House's Special Committee on Un-American Activities suspected
that the Bund was controlled by Nazi Germany and tried to get Kuhn to admit it under oath. But Kuhn refused to bite, stubbornly repeating that there
was "not any connection at all" between the Bund and Nazi leadership.[24]

Frustrated, committee members tried to force Kuhn to concede that the Bund adopted the goals and symbols of the Nazi Party, describing through witnesses and other evidence all the ways in which Bundists aped the Nazis. All Bund members were required to take an oath attesting, "I am of Aryan descent, free of Jewish or colored racial traces," and acknowledging the "Leadership Principle," which required members to offer total submission to the decisions of the *Bundesführer*. Bund events were awash in swastikas, and Bund meetings opened with a declaration to seek "a free, Gentile-ruled United States and . . . [a] fighting movement of awakened Aryan Americans," followed by a chant, in unison, of "Free America! Free America! Free America!" The Bund's groups for children—*Jugendschaft* for boys and *Mädchenschaft* for girls—resembled Nazi youth groups and taught the children they were all members of a "pure" German race. Bund strongmen would "maintain order" at Bund meetings, and wore uniforms bearing a striking similarity to those of Nazi SS storm troopers.[25]

Yet Kuhn denied every attempt to connect the Bund to Nazi Germany. Often pounding the table and shouting in anger, Kuhn insisted the Bund was nothing more than a group of patriotic Americans expressing nostalgic attachment to the land of their birth, claiming it was "just as you . . . [do] if you are Irish."[26]

Kuhn made no effort, however, to shy away from the Bund's well-documented vilification of the Jews and prohibition against racial mixing. He readily agreed that membership was limited to "Aryans," which he defined as the "Nordic race." When Kuhn was asked by an irate Representative Joe Starnes if he was anti-Semitic, Kuhn replied yes, then added, "Aren't you?"[27]

Kuhn had a point.

High-level government officials in Congress and the executive branch referred to Jews using the term "kikes" and other slurs. In a 1938 public opinion poll, 71 percent of Americans disapproved of a proposal to allow "more Jewish exiles from Germany to come to the United States," and a year later, 10 percent of the respondents said that "we should make it a policy to deport Jews from this country"—attitudes that explain why the United States admitted so few Jewish refugees before and during the Second World War. Distrust of Jews remained high throughout the war. In a 1942 poll, 44 percent of Americans responded that Jews in the United States had "too much power," and in 1945, 19 percent of Americans considered Jews to be "a threat to America." Racial segregation was also the norm in 1939. The US military maintained separate divisions for black and white soldiers; dozens of states mandated racial segregation in schools, housing, jobs, and public accommodations; and more than half the states barred racial intermarriage and miscegenation. US laws denying and revoking citizenship based on race were cited as models by Nazi lawyers.[28]

As Kuhn surely knew, these were all practices that Representative Starnes, a Democrat from Alabama, loudly supported. In 1944, the NAACP described Starnes as "one of the most vicious of the anti-Negro congressmen from the Deep South," and who "probably more than any other one man . . . was responsible . . . for segregation" in public housing.[29]

Although Kuhn was being investigated by the Special Committee on Un-American Activities, his answers reminded Starnes and the rest of the committee that the Bund's racialized views of citizenship were as American as apple pie. In the coming years, a comparison of the US government's treatment of Bund members like Kuhn to Japanese Americans like Joseph Kurihara—men, women, and children who, unlike Kuhn, had never done anything to suggest disloyalty to the country of their birth—would prove Kuhn's point.

The German American Bund's raucous Madison Square Garden rally, followed by Kuhn's questionable testimony before the Special Committee on Un-American Activities, all suggested that at least a few residents of the United States with close ties to Nazi Germany deserved closer scrutiny. Yet from the beginning, Executive Order 9066 had only one target: those of Japanese descent. Within a few months, Lieutenant General John L. DeWitt, head of the Western Defense Command, had arranged for the removal and incarceration of 112,000 persons of Japanese ancestry living on the Pacific Coast of the United States, including 70,000 American citizens. Neither he nor any other public official ordered mass removal or incarceration of Americans of German or Italian descent living on either coast, or even of German and Italian nationals.

For DeWitt and other military and civilian leaders, allegiance to the United States was governed by race, not place of birth, length of residence in the United States, or citizenship status. "In the war in which we are now engaged," DeWitt explained, "racial affinities are not severed by migration. The Japanese race is an enemy race and while many second and third generation Japanese born on United States soil, possessed of United States citizenship, have become 'Americanized,' the racial strains are undiluted." Although DeWitt acknowledged that there had been no sign of disloyalty by Japanese Americans, he reached the confounding conclusion that the "very fact that no sabotage has taken place to date is a disturbing and confirming indication that such action will be taken." A year later, DeWitt put it even more plainly, stating: "A Jap's a Jap—it makes no difference whether he is an American citizen or not."[30]

DeWitt's views were shared by many. In his diary, Secretary of War Henry L. Stimson claimed as a "fact" that "their racial characteristics are such that we cannot understand or trust even the citizen Japanese." On January 16, 1942, Congressman Leland Ford, who represented Los Angeles, demanded that "all Japanese, whether citizens or not, be placed in inland concentration camps," describing it as a "small sacrifice" to ensure the safety of the West Coast. The entire congressional delegation from the Pacific states joined him, calling for "the immediate evacuation of all persons of Japanese lineage . . . aliens and citizens alike."[31]

These national leaders echoed the widely expressed sentiment of civic groups, local officials, and the general public that *all* Japanese, whatever their citizenship status, posed a "menace" to the Pacific Coast. A March 1942 national public opinion poll revealed that 93 percent of Americans favored removing Japanese nationals from the Pacific Coast, and 59 percent favored displacing US citizens of Japanese ancestry as well.[32]

DeWitt needed no urging. Starting in February 1942, he implemented President Roosevelt's executive order by directing the removal of all persons of Japanese heritage, regardless of citizenship status, from wide swaths of the Pacific Coast. (The government's official order of removal referred to these Americans as "non-aliens.") The order encompassed orphans, foster children living with white parents, the elderly in nursing homes, and American citizens "with as little as one-sixteenth Japanese blood."[33] Tens of thousands were given a few days' or weeks' notice to leave their homes, businesses, or farms, and were forced to sell or abandon most of their possessions. They were herded first into assembly centers, and then assigned to one of ten camps located through the United States.[34]

Joseph Kurihara was one of the first to arrive at Camp Manzanar in March of 1942. Located on a flat, arid plain at the base of the Sierra Nevada mountains in eastern California, Camp Manzanar was isolated and desolate. Although the land around it had once been fertile, the city of Los Angeles had diverted water supply to the area years before, transforming it into a desert subject to extreme temperatures and gale-force winds. Kurihara described "wind [that] blew with such ferocity, at times I thought the building was going to be carried away," and frequent sandstorms that "obscured the sun." "Dust [was] everywhere," he reported. "We . . . slept in the dust; breathed the dust; and ate the dust."[35]

Manzanar would eventually house ten thousand men, women, and children in 575 wooden barracks, all surrounded by barbed wire and guard towers manned by soldiers carrying rifles and sidearms. The barracks were constructed from prefabricated plywood covered with black tarpaper, which Kurihara and other early arrivals built themselves. Each family was given a single room of twenty feet square. Single men like Kurihara were assigned to bunk together, with no barriers between beds or changing areas. The buildings were uninsulated. Cracks between the planks made the barracks unbearably hot in summer and freezing in winter and allowed dust and dirt to permeate every nook and cranny of the living spaces. Furniture was minimal, and mattresses were sacks that the prisoners were instructed to stuff with straw. There was no running water in the barracks, and separate buildings contained the communal showers and latrines, all in open rooms with no barriers for privacy.

The all-white employees and guards running the facility also lived at Camp Manzanar. As Kurihara could not help but notice, they had separate apartments with showers, toilets, stoves, and refrigerators. The guards and other employees also earned "prevailing wages" of approximately 150 dollars a month for their work at the camp, although the Issei and Nisei working alongside them earned only about sixteen dollars a month. Looking around, Kurihara concluded, "Our rights as . . . American citizens were shattered."[36]

———

Just a few months after the US government incarcerated Kurihara along with the rest of the Japanese American population living on the West Coast, a government official stumbled upon a new threat. Near midnight on June 13, 1942, twenty-one-year-old Coast Guard rookie John Cullen was walking his usual six-mile circuit of the Atlantic Coast near Amagansett, Long Island, when a man emerged out of the mist, one of several shadowy shapes in the dark.

"We're fishermen from Southampton and ran aground here," the lead man offered—a reasonable explanation. But then another man in the group shouted in a foreign language that Cullen thought might be German. The first man yelled at him, "Shut up, you damn fool!"[37]

Cullen gathered his courage and told the men they would have to come with him to the Coast Guard station a quarter mile away for questioning. But even as he said it, he knew the order was futile. He had no weapon other than a flare gun, and he was outnumbered four to one.

"I don't want to kill you," the lead man told him, and he offered Cullen three hundred dollars in cash to "forget what he had seen." Cullen took the money and ran for help.[38]

When Cullen returned with three other Coast Guard officers, the men were long gone. But he could see the top half of a U-202, a German submarine, sitting just a few hundred feet offshore, the waves slapping against its metal skin as it dipped back under the water and slid away. Buried in the beach nearby were four soggy German marine uniforms and multiple boxes of explosives. Cullen knew then that he had witnessed a German military operation on US soil.

"I still feel lucky I got out of it alive," he said in an interview twenty-six years later.[39]

Cullen's narrow escape initiated a nationwide manhunt. Two of the men turned themselves in, and the FBI eventually took all eight of the German saboteurs into custody: the four who had landed on the Atlantic Coast near New York City and another four who had simultaneously come ashore in Florida. The FBI also seized their extensive supplies, which included boxes of explosives, bomb-timing mechanisms, incendiary weapons disguised as "pen-and-pencil sets," and $180,000 in cash—the equivalent of about $2.8 million today.

Under FBI questioning, the men confessed that they had been recruited and trained for this mission by the Abwehr, Germany's intelligence agency, under Hitler's orders to send saboteurs into the United States to destroy factories and communications infrastructure.[40]

For the eight saboteurs, justice was swift. After a closed-door military trial that lasted less than a month, they were all sentenced to death. President Roosevelt commuted to life imprisonment the sentences of two men who had cooperated with the FBI. The other six were executed in swift succession by electric chair—the first man seated at 12:01 p.m. on August 8, 1942, and the last pronounced dead a little more than an hour later. They were buried in Potter's Field in the District of Columbia, their headstones unpainted boards numbered 276 to 281.[41]

Only after the war did the public learn key details about the identity of the eight men. Although born in Germany, all had lived in the United States for many years before returning home a few years before the start of the war. Two were naturalized US citizens. They had been selected and trained for this mission in Germany by Nazi intelligence officer Walter Kappe, who had lived in the United States from 1925 through 1937, where he had worked closely with Fritz Kuhn as the German American Bund's press chief. Seven of the eight saboteurs had one significant fact in common: while living in the United States, they had been dues-paying members of the German American Bund.[42]

On a freezing December evening in 1942, Kurihara joined the crowd of about five hundred angry prisoners who had gathered outside the administrative buildings in Camp Manzanar. The men were there to protest the camp administrator's decision to place one of their fellow inmates in the camp jail. Trying to keep warm in the frigid wind, the men swung their arms and stamped their feet as they sang Japanese marching songs, including the

Japanese national anthem.[43] Watching over them were the camp's military police, young men themselves. A witness observed that the MPs were "shaking and scared," perhaps because many "had never seen Japanese people before in their lives," and because they were far outnumbered by the crowd they were supposed to control. Unlike the prisoners, however, the military police had guns.[44]

Kurihara was already well known as a vocal critic of the camps. A few months before, he had stood up at one of the camp's community meetings and asked, "Those of you who claim yourselves as American citizens . . . what are you doing here? . . . Why didn't the government give us the chance to prove our loyalty instead of herding us into camps?" He went on to answer his own questions. "It is not because we are unloyal. It is because we are what we are, Japs!" His outrage palpable, he declared that the US government had decided that "we are no longer American citizens" and so is treating us "like aliens instead of American[s]." In a statement that would prove prescient, he wondered aloud why any of the incarcerated Japanese would "seek to remain as citizens of a country that denies our rights, the rights which we've inherited through our birth."[45]

Kurihara felt the situation at the camp had been "getting ugly" since the fall of 1942, so when the angry crowd gathered in front of the Manzanar jail on that December night, he feared the worst. As the evening wore on, the "wind whipped up," and dust and pebbles flew, adding to the confusion. Kurihara overheard a sergeant "going from soldier to soldier, [telling] them 'Remember Pearl Harbor'"—that is, intentionally provoking the soldiers to use violence against the prisoners milling around the administrative buildings. An empty truck rolled forward—whether intentionally pushed or by accident was never clear—and slammed into one of administrative buildings nearby, unnerving the military police standing guard. The frightened MPs launched canisters of tear gas in an effort to disperse the protestors, and the "smoke was . . . whipped up with the wind," obscuring the soldiers' view. Although there had been no order to shoot, in the panic that followed several soldiers fired their submachine guns into the fleeing crowd, the rapid bursts of semi-automatic gunfire followed by shouts and screams.[46]

When the smoke cleared, seventeen-year-old James Ito and twenty-one-year-old Jim Kanagawa were dead, and ten others injured. A hospital worker who treated the wounded described how they had all been shot in the back, apparently while trying to run away.[47]

For the rest of his life, Kurihara would blame the US government for these young men's deaths, calling it "murder in the first degree, unpardonable and unforgivable." The "bitterness which dominated my feelings for months after the killing of those two innocent boys at Manzanar was so great," Kurihara wrote years later, "I could have murdered any white man as if he were an animal."⁴⁸

Kurihara's response to the deaths at Manzanar was to retreat from the world. He told a friend that he would "retire to my apartment here and read my Bible . . . and study the Japanese language," and he avoided mixing even with his fellow prisoners. He had come to the conclusion that he would never "be able to act and feel freely as an American." He felt his only choice now was to become "100 percent Jap[anese]."⁴⁹

Massive granite steps lead to the grand portico at the front entrance of the Foley Square Courthouse in lower Manhattan, adorned with ten four-story Corinthian columns topped by a floral frieze. But on Tuesday, January 5, 1943, Fritz Kuhn entered through the building's basement entrance—the one reserved for prisoners. He had already spent two years in Clinton Prison in upstate New York for embezzling $14,000 from the German American Bund, and his sentence was not yet over. He had been brought in shackles to New York federal district court as a defendant in the government's first mass denaturalization case in US history.⁵⁰

A few months before, Attorney General Francis Biddle announced an initiative to denaturalize hundreds, perhaps thousands, of Americans who joined pro-German organizations. Under federal law, to become a naturalized citizen the applicant had to swear to "renounce all allegiance" to their home countries and to "support and defend" the US Constitution "without mental reservation." To the government, a naturalized citizen's membership in the German American Bund and similar organizations was proof that they had lied when taking that oath. "This is a matter of loyalty," Biddle explained, and "membership in such societies makes loyalty to any other country impossible."⁵¹

The government's position was aggressive, seeking to denaturalize not just the leadership of the Bund but anyone even loosely affiliated with that and other organizations viewed as falling under fascist or Communist influences. Biddle may have been trying to give the appearance of treating the Japanese and Germans similarly. After all, the government had chosen to incarcerate seventy thousand Japanese Americans who had expressed no disloyalty to the United States. How could it allow German Americans who had loudly proclaimed their loyalty to Germany to remain free—especially after former members of that group had attempted a military operation on US soil?

As legal historian Patrick Weil explains, however, the government's response to these two groups of Americans "was in fact completely unequal." In contrast to its treatment of Japanese Americans, the denaturalization proceedings brought against Bund members such as Fritz Kuhn turned on each individual's acts and words, not ancestry alone. Every person the government sought to denaturalize had their day in court—a level of individualized due process that was denied to the incarcerated Japanese Americans.[52]

That distinction may not have meant much to Kuhn, however. After two years in prison, he was a broken man. He was destitute and in poor health. His daughter had already returned to Germany, and his wife and son would soon follow. He asked to be excused from attending his own trial, telling the judge, "I want to let my case rest in your honor's hands." So Kuhn was not present when multiple witnesses testified about his 1936 meeting with Hitler, financial contributions to the Nazi Party, and repeated statements of loyalty to Germany—all evidence, according to the government, that he had committed fraud when he had sworn allegiance to the United States at his naturalization ceremony.[53]

The ruling in Kuhn's case came swiftly. Judge John Bright agreed with the government that the "German American Bund w[as] formed for German purposes and controlled in thought, and in large part in action, by Germany." The judge cited "practically uncontradicted" evidence that the "Bund taught the so-called blood philosophy that anyone of German blood, regardless of nationality, will remain a German as long as he shall live, and is bound by the ties of blood to remain such regardless of citizenship."[54]

But Judge Bright differed with the government on the issue of revoking Kuhn's citizenship *solely* on the basis of his Bund membership, which was in tension with First Amendment rights to freedom of speech and association. Instead, he rested his decision on Kuhn's individual statements and actions, concluding that Kuhn "did not entirely renounce his allegiance and fidelity to the German Reich, and he has not borne true faith and allegiance to the Constitution and laws of this country, and did not intend so to do at the time of his naturalization."[55]

On March 18, 1943, Kuhn officially lost his US citizenship, making him once again a citizen solely of the German Reich. The ruling transformed Kuhn into an "enemy alien" who could be interned or deported to Nazi Germany.[56]

By the spring of 1944, Kurihara and his fellow prisoners had spent two years in camps. Although the war in the Pacific would not be over for another year, the Allies were clearly winning. The government had to decide what to do with over one hundred thousand prisoners at the war's end.[57]

America didn't want them back. Representative Richard Harless of Arizona explained on the House floor, "We have approximately 25,000 Japanese interned in our State, and . . . are very much concerned that some of these people may be left there to mingle with our people when this war has been completed." A public opinion poll taken in December 1942 found that less than a quarter of Americans supported allowing the incarcerated Japanese Americans to return to their homes at the end of the war. A majority thought that all the prisoners, regardless of their citizenship, should be "sent back" to Japan—though most Japanese Americans had never lived in or even visited that country.[58]

Legally, that was impossible. The Constitution barred the government from deporting US citizens or detaining them indefinitely during peacetime. So the government came up with a clever solution. It would enable Japanese Americans currently in the camps to renounce their citizenship, after which they could be deported to Japan—perhaps even exchanged for Americans held prisoner there. The "good Japs"—that is, those prisoners who had proven their loyalty to the United States by their willingness to serve in the military or their declarations of support to the United States—could then be released into the population.

But federal law barred Americans from renouncing their citizenship while living in the United States during wartime. So Attorney General Francis Biddle proposed that Congress amend the law to enable such renunciations.[59] Congress debated Biddle's proposal in the spring of 1944. No one questioned the proposed law's purpose or its constitutionality, and all praised its intent. Representative Adolph J. Sabath, a Democrat from Illinois, spoke for many when he declared, "Let them renounce their citizenship. The sooner we get rid of them, as I have stated, the better it will be for us." Sabath, a naturalized citizen, concluded, "If they do not recognize the greatest and most liberal country in the world and fail to appreciate it, we have no use for them." Senator Richard Russell, a Democrat from Georgia, supported the bill because he wanted to swap the incarcerated Japanese Americans for US prisoners of war in Japan, stating he was "hopeful that a number of Japanese will take advantage of the procedure outlined in the bill so that we may offer them to the Imperial Government of Japan in exchange for American citizens who are now being held in territory occupied by the Japanese."[60]

The bill passed both houses of Congress by overwhelming majorities. On July 1, 1944, President Roosevelt signed the amendment into law, and the Department of Justice began to establish renunciation procedures at the ten camps.

On the afternoon of November 24, 1945, in a light drizzle, Kurihara joined more than one thousand men, women, and children of Japanese descent as they lined up along the Seattle docks, waiting to board the USS *General G. M. Randall*. The ship was scheduled to depart for Japan early the next morning.

Before boarding, the passengers were strip-searched by US immigration officials, who inspected baggage and clothing to ensure that they were not carrying US currency or other contraband. At least one newspaper described the group as "jubilant" to have "renounced American citizenship" and to be returning "home." But for many, including Kurihara, this would be the first time they had ever set foot in Japan.

At first, only a few hundred Japanese Americans chose to renounce their citizenship under the new federal law. But by the end of December 1944, twelve hundred had filed renunciation applications. That number crept up to forty-six hundred by the end of January, and another fifteen hundred applied in the following months, though some did not complete the process. During a four-month period from December 1944 through March 1945, over 5,589 incarcerated Japanese Americans renounced their citizenship in the land of their birth, amounting to one out of every fourteen Americans of Japanese descent. Forced to come up with a name for this new, unprecedented group of expatriated American citizens, the government labeled them "native American aliens."[61]

Some had been coerced into giving up their citizenship by a group of militant segregationists who terrorized their fellow prisoners. An elderly inmate who publicly criticized the group was attacked with clubs and a hammer. In one camp, a man known to be friendly with the white administrators was beaten so severely that he suffered brain damage and temporarily lost his eyesight. The administrators could not, or would not, protect from physical harm those who wished to keep their citizenship.[62]

For others, renouncing citizenship was a way to avoid being forced out of the camps and back into a society that would prefer them dead or deported. Prisoners returning to their home communities in early 1945 reported threats, harassment, vandalism, and violence. Property owned by those of Japanese ancestry was burned to the ground, and one returning evacuee reported cowering behind locked doors as carloads of men drove by his home, firing bullets into the windows. "What do they want us to do?" asked one Japanese American prisoner. "Go back to California and get filled full of lead?" Another said, "Yeah, you're free all right if you go out [of the camp]. You've got civil rights. Civil rights to have your head cut off!"[63]

Some later explained that they renounced their citizenship to ensure that they would remain together as a family, fearing that otherwise the noncitizen parents would be deported away from the native-born citizen children. Haruko Inouye, who was twenty years old when she renounced, described the choice as a "matter of family unity," and eighteen-year-old Akiko Fukuhara's parents insisted she give up her citizenship so they could all stay together. Inouye and Fukuhara were 2 of the 1,004 prisoners who were under twenty-one when they filed their renunciation applications, many of whom did so out of fear of being permanently separated from their Issei parents.[64]

And for many, including Kurihara, renunciation was an expression of "grief, disappointment, anger, and sometimes rage, against what [the imprisoned] considered disloyalty on a mammoth scale—America's disloyalty to them."[65]

Kurihara had always considered himself to be "100 percent American." His identity as an American citizen had pushed him to move from Hawai'i to the mainland United States, change his name, adopt the Catholic religion, enlist to fight on behalf of the United States in World War I, and seek to join the war effort at the start of World War II. His biographer, Eileen Tamura, concluded that "in his very bones, Kurihara was as American as one could be." But on the day that the government ordered Japanese Americans into camps, he explained that he had "definitely sworn severence [*sic*] of my allegiance to the United States, and became 100 percent pro-Japanese."[66]

In truth, Kurihara's decision to renounce his American citizenship took longer to crystallize. But by January 1945, he had made up his mind. He signed the forms and appeared for the requisite interview before a Department of Justice official to declare that he no longer wished to be called an American. When asked his reasons for renouncing, he responded, "I have come to realize there is no such thing as democracy in the United States with the exception for the white people."[67]

Many renunciants had not realized that giving up their US citizenship would lead to their immediate deportation to Japan. But when word got out that nearly six thousand Japanese Americans had renounced their citizenship, the press and politicians were quick to argue that they should all immediately be removed from the country. "We should not have to fool around with any of these Japs who have acknowledged they are disloyal, or with their families," Congressman Clair Engle, a Democrat from California, told reporters, for as "long as they remain in this country, they are a source of danger." Newspaper editorials declared those "who renounced their citizenship here should be returned to their own country. There is no place for them in America."[68]

In July 1945, President Harry Truman issued Presidential Proclamation 2655, declaring that "all dangerous enemy aliens" were "subject to removal from the United States." The Department of Justice concluded that proclamation applied to the renunciants and began to deport them.

When California civil rights attorney Wayne Collins heard about the renunciations, he was apoplectic. Collins, a wiry man with bright eyes and a "hot temper," had fought for the rights of Japanese Americans throughout the war, bringing (and losing) a case challenging their incarceration before the US Supreme Court. He was often criticized for employing emotional rhetoric in his legal briefs, and he angered courts and government attorneys by comparing the US government's race-based imprisonment of US citizens to Nazi Germany's racial policies.

In the fall of 1945, Collins filed a complaint on behalf of those who had lost their citizenship, arguing renunciation by those imprisoned in government camps was inherently coercive and that permitting renunciation under those conditions would "destroy not only the grant of [birthright citizenship in] the Fourteenth Amendment but impair the foundation of the Constitution itself." After obtaining a temporary injunction, he reportedly raced with the judge's order in hand to the waterfront three miles away to stop a ship from sailing with unwilling renunciants on board.[69]

But for Joseph Kurihara and thousands of others, it was too late—they were already gone.

Kurihara and the other passengers on the USS *Randall* were among the first to arrive in Japan, landing in Tokyo Bay in early December 1945. What they found there shocked them. Most of Japan's major cities had been bombed to smithereens. As many as nine million Japanese were homeless, and food was scarce. The renunciants were horrified to see the bodies of dead children "lying on the ground, naked, and their bellies were swelled as a result of malnutrition." In the year following the war's end, the average civilian in Japan ate one-third the calories allotted to the US soldiers who were stationed there. One renunciant described "walk[ing] through the streets, and the stores had nothing in them . . . there was hardly anything to eat. I wanted to return to America again, but of course, it was too late."[70]

Like all deported renunciants, Kurihara had to forfeit all his savings and property in the United States, bringing only the 370 pounds of luggage and $60 in cash he was permitted to carry with him to Japan. So he had to find work and find it quickly. But that would not be easy. Kurihara was fifty years old, did not speak Japanese fluently, and was unfamiliar with Japanese customs and traditions. A Japanese manufacturer spoke for many when he said, "I do not hire [the renunciants]," explaining, "They may look Japanese to you. They don't to me."[71]

Kurihara was finally forced to accept a job with the US military occupying Japan. Because most renunciants were bilingual and had some cultural fluency, they proved invaluable, and the military employed more than a thousand of them in the years immediately after the war. But Kurihara was never going to be happy employed by the government that had imprisoned him.

As his biographer observed, Kurihara recognized the "absurdity" of having "rejected . . . the country that rejected him," only to be forced to work for the same government that had imprisoned him as a danger to national security. A year later he quit, found a new job, and moved to a quiet neighborhood in Tokyo where he boarded with a family who described him as "polite, uncomplaining, and cheerful." His Japanese improved to the point where he made friends and was accepted by his new homeland.[72]

Many of the native-born Japanese American renunciants found the adjustment even more difficult than did Kurihara. On the whole, the Niseis' language skills were "atrocious," according to observers, and they had difficulty adapting to Japanese cultural norms. They found it uncomfortable to sit on the *tatami* mats, so they often ate their meals Western style, on chairs pulled up to tables with legs. Many disliked the food, preferring toast with butter and coffee to the usual Japanese breakfast of tea, rice, bean soup, and pickles. Japanese family and neighbors criticized the Nisei, and particularly the Nisei women, as "too abrupt, not gentle and refined," and too willing to "go . . . about [their] own business, thinking that others should not interfere." An anthropologist who studied renunciants' adjustment to life in Japan in 1953 found that even eight years later, the Nisei were unable to assimilate, and consequently "are still preoccupied with the idea of regaining their American citizenship. . . . Their hopes and dreams are to return to America with their immediate families."[73]

Fourteen years later, on a lovely spring day in May of 1959, a crowd of dignitaries gathered in the majestic office of Attorney General William P. Rogers, at the US Department of Justice in downtown Washington, DC. They had convened in a "solemn ceremony" to commemorate the Justice Department's completion of a program "righting the wrong done to Americans of Japanese ancestry" by returning to them their citizenship.[74]

"Our country did make a mistake," Rogers admitted, when it imprisoned Japanese Americans and then encouraged them to renounce their citizenship. Of the 5,589 Japanese Americans who had renounced their citizenship, 5,409 had petitioned to have their citizenship restored, and the government had granted 4,978 of those requests. That number included 1,327 who had left the United States for Japan at the end of the war and could now come back. As Rogers acknowledged, the fact that 97 percent of the renunciants asked for their citizenship back was proof, if any was needed, that they were coerced into giving up their citizenship by the conditions of their imprisonment.

He failed to mention, however, that the government had fought Wayne Collins's lawsuit seeking to restore the renunciants' citizenship for more than a decade. It was only in 1956 that the United States abruptly reversed course and agreed to quickly return those renunciants' citizenship, worn down by the endless courtroom battles and perhaps by shifting public opinion as well. For one renunciant who won back his citizenship and returned to the United States thanks to Collins's lawsuit, the moment was bittersweet. When asked how he felt, he responded, "I have lost ten years in Japan."[75]

Assistant Attorney General George C. Doub had overseen the restoration of citizenship. When it was his turn to speak, he declared that the United States must learn from its errors. "Americans must discipline themselves to resist hysteria and emotional stress in times of alarms and danger," he instructed, "in order that American ideals of justice" prevail even in times of crisis. He concluded that he could only hope that the Nisei would "have the charity to forgive their government."[76]

When Kurihara left for Japan in 1945, he had assumed that the revocation of his citizenship was permanent and that he would never return to the United States. He wrote to a friend shortly after arriving that "my life is dedicated to Japan."[77]

Then, almost fourteen years later, his brother sent him a newspaper article describing the May 20, 1959, ceremony and the attorney general's acknowledgment that it had been a "mistake" to incarcerate innocents on the basis of their race. Kurihara was elated, writing later that he "immediately forgave with joy" after learning that the government had recognized the wrong it had done him.[78]

But permission to apply for restoration of citizenship was not enough for Kurihara. Several years later, he wrote to Attorney General Robert Kennedy to ask why the government had not "contacted" him about giving him his citizenship back or taken "any steps to compensate" him and other loyal Japanese American veterans who had been so badly treated by their government. Beyond the government's blanket apology and the opportunity to petition for restoration of his citizenship, Kurihara wanted an individualized remedy. Ever principled, Kurihara rejected the idea that *he* should come begging to the United States to take him back. As the wronged party, Kurihara believed that the United States should reach out to all those imprisoned, proactively offering to return their citizenship and compensating them financially for all they had lost.[79]

Kurihara had made this same argument as far back as July 1942, during a speech at Camp Manzanar. Even as many of his fellow prisoners had convinced themselves that mass incarceration was essential to national security, Kurihara was adamant that they were victims of a terrible injustice. "Let America redeem herself," he declared in a speech while imprisoned at Camp Manzanar, "by fully compensating us for the sufferings we were made to endure—mentally, physically, and economically."[80]

Many years later, that compensation finally came. After a long and hard-fought campaign, Congress voted on August 10, 1988, to grant victims of its race-based incarceration policy $20,000 each. On October 9, 1990, government officials gave the first reparation checks to nine elderly survivors of the camps, together with a formal letter of apology signed by President George H. W. Bush. During that ceremony, Attorney General Dick Thornburgh dropped to his knees to present the check to those in wheelchairs—a gesture of supplication that would have appealed to Kurihara.[81]

But Kurihara did not live to see it. He had died in his Tokyo home of a stroke on November 26, 1965, when he was seventy years old, his brother and sister at his side. Among his personal possessions was the six-year-old newspaper clipping in which government officials acknowledged that it had all been a terrible mistake.[82]

Like Joseph Kurihara, Fritz Kuhn spent much of World War II under lock and key. Unlike Kurihara, the government had to prevail in two separate trials to justify Kuhn's incarceration. In 1939, he was convicted in New York state court of embezzling funds from the German American Bund, and he spent the next three and a half years in the Clinton Correctional Facility.[83] After he was denaturalized in 1943, he was sent to a federal internment camp for enemy aliens, then deported to Germany shortly after the war ended.

Kuhn's legal troubles were not over once he reached Germany. In 1947, he was arrested as part of a denazification program and sent to Dachau, a former Nazi concentration camp that had been repurposed by the Allies as a prison for German war criminals.[84]

In March 1949, from a jail cell in Dachau, Kuhn wrote to the US government asking to have his citizenship reinstated so that he could return to the United States. Apparently, Kuhn now valued his nine years of US citizenship over his German *blut*, and he had heard that at least some denaturalized Bundists had won the right to get their citizenship back.[85]

The US government's aggressive denaturalization program to strip citizenship from anyone affiliated with Communist or fascist organizations had attracted the attention of the US Supreme Court. In 1945, the court reversed the denaturalization of a Bund member who had stated publicly that "he would be glad to live under the regime of Hitler." In an opinion written

by Justice Felix Frankfurter—the sole Jewish justice, and often the target of
the Bundists' anti-Semitic screeds—the court expressed its discomfort with
the government's denaturalization campaign against the German American
Bund, declaring "we must be . . . watchful that citizenship, once bestowed,
should not be in jeopardy . . . through a too easy finding that citizenship
was disloyally acquired." The court explained that American citizenship came
with the "freedom to speak foolishly" without fear of expulsion. As a result of
the decision, the government was barred from relying on membership in suspect organizations as a primary basis for denaturalization, forcing it to abandon dozens of denaturalization cases.[86]

Kuhn hoped that this decision might apply to him as well. But it was not
to be. The government took the position that the Supreme Court's opinion did
not apply retroactively—a highly questionable conclusion that nonetheless
would have required a full-fledged legal battle to overcome. In any case, evidence of Kuhn's disloyalty at the time of his naturalization extended well beyond his membership in the Bund, so the Supreme Court's precedent did not
squarely apply to his case. In a decision reviewed by top US officials, including President Harry Truman, the government cited these and other reasons
to deny former *Bundesführer* Fritz Kuhn's petition to regain his American
citizenship. Kuhn died on December 14, 1951, alone and penniless, a citizen
of Germany.[87]

Emma Goldman

Harry Bridges

CHAPTER 7

SUSPECT CITIZEN

When dawn broke over San Francisco Bay on July 5, 1934, the city's dock-workers had been on strike for nearly two months. A dozen freighters sat idle in the harbor, their cargo rotting in their holds. Others had moved on, hoping to unload at ports farther south, but as they would soon learn, the strike had paralyzed the docks from Seattle to San Diego. Two months earlier, the newly formed International Longshoremen's Association, representing the twelve thousand men who loaded and unloaded millions of tons of cargo up and down the Pacific Coast, had voted to go on strike. Within days, they were joined by tens of thousands of other marine workers, including the boilermakers and machinists, the Marine Cooks and Stewards Association, and the International Seamen's Union. Work along San Francisco's dock, formerly among the busiest in the world, had slowed to a crawl.[1]

Not that it was quiet. Every morning, thousands of striking workers gathered along the Embarcadero—the paved ribbon running the length of San Francisco's waterfront—to march three or four abreast, those in front hoisting American flags and their union's banner, beating time on drums as they strode up and down the waterfront. They were there not only to protest low wages and brutal working conditions, but also to prevent anyone else from taking their place. A cry of "SCABS!" would ring out as the strikers swarmed truckloads of would-be replacement workers, preventing them from unloading the ships. Inevitably, the police would descend, wielding "long hardwood clubs . . . onto skulls with sickening force, again and again and again till a face was hardly recognizable." Strikers scattered as the police arrived, then regrouped, ready to block the train lines and swarm the newly arriving scabs, and the cycle would start all over again.[2]

Before the strike, the Embarcadero had been the nerve center of San Francisco, the access point for eighty-two docks accommodating up to 250 vessels at a time in its seventeen miles of berthing space. Trucks clattered across its cobblestones, their gaping maws to be emptied of one load and quickly filled with stacks of cut lumber, burlap bags of coffee, rolls of hemp, and whatever else the shipowners could hawk to America's population of 126 million and counting. In the mornings, white-collar workers descended from the hills of Marin and Oakland, swarming off the ferries to their jobs in office buildings up, down, and around Market Street, the city's commercial center. Scurrying among them all were the longshoremen, the city's worker ants, dressed in thick black canvas pants and hobnailed boots, lifting and carrying the cargo that fueled a nation.[3]

Now, all that activity had ground to a halt—replaced by clashes between the police and the strikers that grew more violent with each passing day.

Alfred Renton Bridges, chairman of the Joint Marine Strike Committee representing the twenty-seven thousand striking employees, arrived at union headquarters near dawn on the morning of July 5, just as he had done nearly every day since the strike began on May 9. Bridges—known simply as "Harry" to his fellow longshoremen—was a tall, lean man with sharp features who still spoke with the inflections of his native Australia despite having lived for over a decade in the United States. He had left school at thirteen, defying his father's wish that he join him in his suburban, middle-class life as a real estate agent, and found work on freighters traveling from Victoria to Tasmania and back again. Despite barely surviving two shipwrecks—once reportedly by clinging to his mandolin, an instrument he played beautifully throughout his life—Bridges fell in love with life on the open water.[4]

Then, in April 1920, when he was nineteen years old, Bridges arrived in San Francisco and decided to stay, paying the $10 head tax that earned him the legal right to remain indefinitely in the United States. He drifted around the country, and eventually married and had a daughter, making life at sea less attractive. So Bridges traded in travel and adventure for the backbreaking labor of moving cargo from ship to shore and then back again, arriving at dawn every morning in the longshoreman's uniform of flat white cap and hickory shirt, a cargo hook tucked in the back pocket of his black canvas pants.[5]

"The hook must never hang," was the longshoreman's creed—meaning the cargo must be ready to go the moment the cargo hook is lowered into the hold. And when Bridges was working, it didn't. By all accounts, he was tireless, surprisingly strong despite his light frame, and never one to slow the pace or complain. The work permanently maimed him, the constant strain on muscles and tendons leaving one hand "crippled like a claw" for the rest of his life. In 1929, Bridges worked for days on a broken foot smashed between two cases. An employee "didn't go and make a claim for injury," he said, because doing so would "cost the company money"—and likely get the employee blacklisted. "Everybody knew in advance that if you went to the company union and made a beef, you lost your job," Bridges explained.[6]

But Bridges was convinced that if they united as one, the Pacific Coast's dockworkers could negotiate better conditions and higher wages for all. His unswerving faith in the power of collective action inspired his coworkers to select him to lead the San Francisco Joint Marine Strike Committee and convinced the Pacific Coast's twelve thousand longshoremen to walk off their jobs at the nadir of the worst depression the country had ever known.

When the union first went out on strike, the shipowners had been confident they could crush it quickly, just as they had crushed a similar strike in 1919. By 1934, the United States was in the depths of the Great Depression, entering a fifth year of stagnating wages, deflated currency, and rampant unemployment—a world in which soup lines, abandoned homes, and grinding poverty had become the norm, not the exception. Even the employed were suffering. Like many of his coworkers, Bridges had been forced to move with his family into ever smaller and more decrepit apartments, and even then the $15-a-month rent amounted to more than a third of his take-home pay. So the employers were sure they could find plenty of desperate men to take the strikers' places, especially among the "colored" population, normally excluded from such work altogether—a racial divide that employers were happy to exploit when it suited them. And the shipowners also had San Francisco's mayor, Angelo Rossi, and his police force squarely on their side. The strikers didn't stand a chance.[7]

As the employers quickly realized, however, things were different this time. Under Bridges's leadership, the dockworkers were united up and down the coast, preventing the shipowners from "play[ing] one port against the other" as they had in the past. Bridges insisted that African Americans be admitted into the union on the same terms as everyone else, undermining the employers' efforts to use black longshoremen as strikebreakers. (For many years, Bridges worked on cross-racial labor issues with Revels Cayton, an African American West Coast labor leader who was named for his grandfather, Senator Hiram Rhodes Revels.) Bridges surprised employers by turning down a bribe offered to him alone of fifty thousand dollars—the equivalent of about a million dollars today—without blinking an eye. And from the start, Bridges had infuriated the old-guard union leadership by mandating that the rank and file be given a chance to vote on any settlement with the employers, which prevented the salaried union officials from caving to employers without checking in with the working men they represented.[8]

So, on July 5, 1934, the employers and strikers were in a standoff. Neither one was close to winning, and yet neither was willing to back down.

By 8 a.m. that morning, the police and strikers were back in their places, only this time whatever restraint the two sides exercised in the past was gone. Police drove the strikers into the alleys off the Embarcadero, wielding batons and hurling vials of tear gas. The chaos spread quickly along the waterfront and beyond, as tear gas settled in a white haze over the financial district. Commuters arriving by ferry fled as "bullets ricocheted off the concrete walls of several Embarcadero piers" and "men dropped, bloody, unconscious" to the ground. A woman disembarking from a street car screamed and then collapsed as she was struck in the temple by a stray bullet—one of hundreds of people who were wounded by the hail of gunfire. "Don't think of this as a riot," reported one journalist, it was "a hundred riots, big and little, first here, now there."[9]

In what became known as the "Battle of Rincon Hill," Bridges led a group of men up a steep, grassy rise just off the Embarcadero, where "screaming strikers picked up rocks, bolts, spikes, and pieces of concrete, anything handy—and sent them hurtling into the bluecoated throng." Using sawed-off shotguns and revolvers, the police fired back, first over the heads and then into the bodies of the mass of men in front of them. Explosions from tear gas set the dry grass on the hillside alight, and a light breeze quickly turned the blaze into a conflagration. The fire department rushed in, using its high-pressure hoses both to drive back the strikers and extinguish the flames.[10]

When "Bloody Thursday" finally drew to a close, men "lay bloody, unconscious, or in convulsions—in the gutters, on the sidewalks, in the streets," and two strikers had been shot dead by the police. Newspapers reported that 109 people, some innocent bystanders, had been injured in the fighting, though that number did not count all those unwilling to risk jail by seeking medical help. "Blood ran red in the streets of San Francisco yesterday," declared the *San Francisco Chronicle*. By that evening, California governor Frank Merriam had called out nearly two thousand National Guardsmen to police the waterfront, equipped with tear gas, bayonets, machine guns, and tanks.[11]

The following week, Bridges did what Governor Merriam and Mayor Rossi most feared: he joined with other labor leaders in calling for a general strike of San Francisco's 125,000 union men in the Bay Area—about 20 percent of the city's total population. On Monday, June 16, 1934, the city of San Francisco shut down. Restaurants and businesses locked their doors and propped hastily scrawled signs reading "Closed Till the Boys Win," and "We're with You Fellows. Stick It Out" in their windows. Picket lines across highways leading into the city stopped all incoming trucks save those carrying food for the city's residents. Gasoline stations closed as gas ran out. Tram drivers refused to show up for work. For the next three days, San Franciscans stayed home.[12]

"And we won," Bridges told the *New York Times* in an interview fifty years later—the "first general strike that was ever won." Within a month, Harry Bridges and his union had obtained nearly all the concessions they demanded, including control over the hiring process, an end to the employer-controlled union, a reduction in hours, and a raise in pay. "Everybody was pulling together in 1934," Bridges explained years later. "We had a beautiful united front."[13]

It was the longshoremen's greatest victory, a lesson in the power of collective action. Bridges became a national labor leader, his name known from coast to coast. In 1937, *Time* magazine put him on its cover as the labor organizer who had "hurtl[ed]" to "national fame" during the San Francisco general strike. Bridges had permanently altered the relationship between labor and capital in the Pacific Coast maritime industry, and possibly throughout the nation as a whole. And the rank and file gave him all the credit.[14]

Unfortunately for Bridges, so did the employers, local officials, and members of Congress who watched, appalled, as San Francisco underwent what some newspapers called a "Bolshevik Revolution."

In 1934, Communism had taken a terrifying hold on the American imagination, and not without reason. As the worldwide depression entered its fifth year, Communist Russia gained influence and adherents around the world. In 1917, the Russian working class had rebelled, taking over the government, executing Czar Nicholas and his family and eventually declaring itself a new country: the Union of Soviet Socialist Republics. Fifteen years later, the Great Depression was bringing down governments and unraveling the fabric of society throughout the world. Rampant inflation and a crumbling economy had helped propel Hitler and the Nazis into power in Germany. Fascists would soon be battling Communists for control of Spain, and Italy was already under the control of fascist dictator Benito Mussolini. In the United States, hungry men and women picked through garbage dumps for food, and five hundred children marched through downtown Chicago, demanding that the school system provide them with lunch.[15]

In these desperate times, the American Communist Party grew from a few thousand radicals at the start of the 1930s into a powerful and dynamic organization of fifty-five thousand and counting by the decade's end. Throughout the world, it appeared that the experiment with democracy and capitalism had failed, and that a new world order would soon take over.[16]

Many believed—or claimed to believe—that the labor unrest in San Francisco and along the Pacific Coast was the opening salvo in an attempted Communist takeover of the United States, and that Harry Bridges was its leader. In a telegram sent to President Roosevelt on June 18, 1934, the head of the anti-union

Industrial Association stated that "Communists have captured control of the Longshoremen's Union" and warned of "destruction of property and serious loss of life" if they were not stopped. A Commerce Department official wrote to a friend in the White House that a "damned lot of alien communist agitators . . . have been able to set up a so-called union," and named Bridges as the primary culprit.[17]

Newspapers piled on, reporting as fact wild conjecture based on the slimmest of reeds. The *Chicago Tribune* concluded that "quantities of communist literature . . . printed in Russian" seized from the Bay Area was proof that "the soviet government in Russia" is "seeking to advance revolution in the United States with a view of bringing about a 'proletarian dictatorship.'" The "strike amounted to civil war," announced the *San Francisco Examiner*, describing it as a "Communist uprising" and an "attempt by force and violence to depose all constituted authority and to destroy established American institutions." The *Los Angeles Times* insisted that the general strike in San Francisco was "an insurrection, a Communist-inspired and led revolt against organized government" that must be suppressed "with any force that may be necessary."[18]

Government officials up and down the West Coast further fanned the flames. Governor Merriam declared that "strike activities were in the hands of the communists," and San Francisco mayor Rossi went on the radio to accuse the organizers of the strike of seeking the "overthrow of this government, and of the Government of the United States."[19]

This Red Scare hysteria, combined with business and government leaders' determination to end the labor unrest, led to one conclusion: Harry Bridges must go.

On May 22, 1934, when the strike was less than two weeks old, Commissioner General of Immigration Daniel MacCormack sent the California Immigration and Naturalization Service (INS) district director an urgent telegram to start the ball rolling. "It has been reported to us that aliens illegally in the country are active in fomenting longshoremans [*sic*] strike at SanFrancisco [*sic*]," he wrote. MacCormack instructed the INS official to "take steps to determine . . . whether illegal aliens are involved," and in particular to "confidentially ascertain the status of one Bridges," though he warned him to be "exceedingly careful to avoid what may be considered intervention by the immigration service in labor disputes."[20]

Bridges's immigration status was no secret. That he was born and raised in Australia was obvious the moment he opened his mouth. Although he had lived in the United States legally for fourteen years, was married, and had a US citizen child, Bridges was not an American.

Not that he hadn't tried to change that. For ten years, Bridges had sought citizenship, but due to delay, bureaucratic errors, and the high cost of the application fee, he had never naturalized. That failure left him vulnerable. As an alien, even one who was a long-term, permanent resident of the United States with a US citizen family, Bridges was at risk of being deported and permanently barred from the United States.[21]

Almost exactly eleven years later, on June 18, 1945, the Supreme Court of the United States convened in the nation's steamy capital for the last session of the term before justices scattered for the summer break, escaping to summer homes in New England and out west. Everyone knew that they would give the final word on whether Harry Bridges could remain in the United States.[22]

In April of that year, Bridges's lawyers had faced off against the government in that same courtroom, the oral argument stretching over two days. The government argued Bridges was a member of the Communist Party of America, a group they claimed was intent on the violent overthrow of the US government. If they could prove both those suppositions as fact, then by federal statute Harry Bridges would be permanently exiled from the United States.

Bridges denied being a member of the Communist Party, and further argued that the government was punishing him for his speech, violating his constitutional rights under the First Amendment to the US Constitution. But the government asserted that the First Amendment could not interfere with its sovereign power "to rid itself of those deemed inimical to the national welfare." Now, it was for the justices to decide.[23]

The Supreme Court case was the culmination of the government's decade-long effort to deport Harry Bridges—an effort that began within days of the successful San Francisco dockworkers' strike. In 1939, Bridges endured a nine-and-a-half-week deportation hearing, which involved dozens of witnesses and generated 7,724 pages of trial transcript, all attempting to prove that Bridges was a member of the Communist Party—charges that Bridges took the stand to deny under penalty of perjury. At the end of all that effort, the government did not just lose; it was humiliated. The government had appointed the dean of Harvard Law School, James M. Landis—a man of impeccable credibility—to serve as judge. In a scathing opinion, Landis found not only that there was no evidence that Bridges was a member of the Communist Party but also that the government's witnesses had perjured themselves. Landis described the testimony of one witness as riddled with "evasion, qualification, and contradiction," another's as "worthless," and a third as a serial perjurer who was "unworthy of credence." Bridges could remain in the United States.[24]

But the government would not give up so easily. In 1940, members of the House of Representatives were nearly unanimous in their support for an unprecedented, and likely unconstitutional, bill explicitly targeting "the alien, Harry Renton Bridges" for deportation. The Senate's version of the law permitted the government to deport any noncitizen who had *ever* been a member of the Communist Party, with Bridges clearly in mind. One congressman announced with "joy" that the new legislation "changes the law so that the Department of Justice should have little trouble in deporting Harry Bridges."[25]

In its never-ending investigation of Bridges, the government left no stone unturned. The Federal Bureau of Investigation tapped Bridges's phone, read his mail, trailed him around San Francisco, combed through his trash, and searched his various hotel rooms—all without a warrant. The surveillance was at times laughingly obvious. Bridges could hardly help but notice suited G-men staring at him over the tops of newspapers as he entered restaurants and coffee shops or lurking in doorways as he left his home for meetings. But Bridges was not one to be easily intimidated. A 1941 *New Yorker* article gleefully recounted how he had "some fun with the F.B.I." during a visit to New York City, setting up an imaginary meeting with an unnamed "big shot" to lure his assigned tail on a wild goose chase through the city.[26]

By the end of 1941, however, even Bridges was no longer finding any humor in his situation. That year, he endured a second ten-week deportation hearing under the newly enacted federal statute that had been drafted to ensure his deportation. This time he lost. He then won his appeal before a unanimous Board of Immigration Appeals, only to have that decision reversed by Attorney General Francis Biddle, acting unilaterally. When Biddle informed President Franklin Roosevelt of his decision, Roosevelt whistled, stubbed out his cigarette, and declared, "I'm sorry to hear that." He had become fond of that "mandolin player," as he referred to Bridges, despite the trouble he · caused. Nonetheless, Roosevelt chose not to overrule Biddle.[27]

So Bridges's only hope was his appeal to the US Supreme Court. On June 18, 1945, eleven years after the general strike that forever changed the face of US labor, Bridges would hear the final word.

The courtroom was packed, as it always is for the last day of the term when the court typically announces decisions in its most important cases. At exactly 10:30 a.m., the gavel slammed onto the sound block and the marshal chanted, "Oyez! Oyez! Oyez!" The crowd rose to its feet as the justices shuffled in and took their place at the bench. As was his custom, Attorney General Biddle was likely to have been in the front row, ready to hear the justices pronounce on his decision to overrule the Board of Immigration Appeals and order Bridges's deportation.[28]

Justice William O. Douglas cleared his throat and began reading from the truncated version of his opinion for the majority. But Biddle did not need to hear a word to know what was coming. Douglas was one of the most liberal members of the court, ever suspicious of government abuse of power. If he was the author of the majority opinion, then the government had lost.

Deportation "visits a great hardship on the individual, and deprives him of the right to stay and live and work in this land of freedom," Douglas began. The majority of the court concluded that Bridges had done nothing to deserve that penalty. The government's evidence showed only that Bridges "cooperat[ed] with Communist groups for the attainment of wholly lawful objectives," and did not support the conclusion that he sought the violent overthrow of the US government. "Freedom of speech and of press is accorded aliens residing in this country," Douglas reminded the government. Like all residents of the United States, citizen or not, Bridges was "entitled to that protection."[29]

Douglas did not speculate on the government's motives in seeking to deport Bridges twice within two years. But in his concurring opinion, Justice Frank Murphy, another liberal justice, did not hold back. "Seldom if ever in the history of this nation," Murphy declared, "has there been such a concentrated and relentless crusade to deport an individual because he dared to exercise the freedom that belongs to him as a human being and that is guaranteed to him by the Constitution."[30]

Back in San Francisco, Bridges woke to the good news. He celebrated by filing his naturalization papers, officially becoming an American citizen on September 17, 1945, before a judge in San Francisco Superior Court. After stating under oath that he was not a member of the Communist Party, he raised his right arm and with "tears in his eyes" took the oath of allegiance in front of an audience that included his twenty-one-year-old daughter. "American citizenship is a priceless possession," he told the press when he first announced he would apply for US citizenship. To that statement he now added his intention "to cherish these privileges always." He was safe now, forever protected by his citizenship from being deported for his actions or his words.[31]

Or so he must have thought.

More than a quarter century before, in the "darkest hours" of a freezing December evening in 1919, the famed anarchist and former American citizen

Emma Goldman was escorted out of her prison cell on Ellis Island to a barge in New York Harbor. Together with 248 fellow "undesirables," and nearly as many armed soldiers, she was "marched single file between two lines of guards" to the SS *Buford*, a battered army transport that dated back to the Spanish–American War. The *Buford*, dubbed the "Soviet Ark" by the press, was forcibly deporting Goldman and hundreds of others to Russia, many of whom had been rounded up in massive raids of suspected Communists orchestrated by Attorney General A. Mitchell Palmer. As the boat pulled out of the harbor, Goldman could see the New York skyline through the porthole, her "beloved city," as well as the Statue of Liberty's outstretched arm. She did not expect to lay eyes on them again.[32]

Among those present to witness her departure was a twenty-four-year-old obscure government official named J. Edgar Hoover. He arrived at the South Brooklyn pier at four in the morning to revel in the culmination of a long campaign to rid the country of a woman he called the "Red Queen of Anarchy." "Other 'Soviet Arks' will sail for Europe, just as often as it is necessary to rid the country of dangerous radicals," Hoover told the press, a quote that earned him the first of many newspaper headlines.[33]

Goldman had first laid eyes on the Statue of Liberty in 1885, when she watched it "emerg[e] from the mist" as she stood on the deck of an arriving steamship full of immigrants like herself. Born in the Russian Empire in 1869, she had emigrated with her family as a teenager, fleeing anti-Semitic pogroms and grinding poverty. She found work in a corset factory in Rochester, New York, and by seventeen was married to Jacob Kersner, a fellow immigrant who shared her love of books and offered her an escape from life under the thumb of an autocratic father. Kersner had arrived several years before, and he had naturalized before the two were married. Under the law at the time, Goldman's marriage to an American citizen automatically bestowed citizenship on her as well.[34]

The marriage was short-lived. The quiet life of wife and mother was not for Goldman. She divorced him within the year, then left for New York City.[35]

In the years that followed, Emma Goldman rose from obscurity to inspire, uplift, and enrage her fellow Americans. She became the world's most famous anarchist—a political philosophy that rejected all forms of government. "I believe in man governing himself," she declared. "*Each* man."[36]

Anarchism burst into the American consciousness at the turn of the century, a radical reaction to a world of brutal and oppressive monarchies, exploitative capitalist democracies, and the rising tide of fascism. Like Harry

Bridges, Goldman was inspired to fight for the working class, of which she was a member. As a teenager, she had labored for twelve-hour shifts in clothing factories for wages too low to support even the most basic of life's necessities. Later, as a midwife delivering babies in New York's Lower East Side, she witnessed the desperate lives of new immigrants packed into tenement slums. Anarchism seemed to her the only reasonable response to the ruling class's abuse of governmental and private power.[37]

But anarchism terrified the American establishment, and Goldman terrified them most of all. The Bolshevik Revolution in Russia, the spread of the "Red Scourge" through Europe, and the rise of terrorism at home led many to fear anarchists would violently overthrow the US government. Some anarchists did not hesitate to use random acts of violence in an effort to topple governments, and Goldman herself provided behind-the-scenes assistance in the failed assassination of anti-union industrialist Henry Clay Frick. To many, Emma Goldman was a real threat—"a red spectre, a wild-eyed inciter of violence, shrieking madly against government, and getting weak-minded folks to kill Kings."[38]

A century later, it is hard to muster much alarm from pictures of this shortish, plumpish, rather rumpled woman glaring at the camera over the tops of round spectacles. In frozen black and white, she has the look of someone's dour grandmother, not a fire-breathing radical regularly run out of town by the local police force.

But photographs don't do her justice. In person, she was not magnetic as much as she exhibited the properties of a magnet—either attracting or repelling every human being who came into her orbit. Her speeches drew crowds in the tens of thousands—men and women who arrived skeptical and left enraged at the world they lived in. She inspired violent and desperate acts despite never personally engaging in violence. President William McKinley's assassin had been among her adoring audience. Although she had not encouraged him, or even known of his plan, she outraged the mourning nation when she praised his principles and refused to condemn his actions.[39]

Everywhere she went, mayors and police chiefs shut down her lecture halls and rescinded her speaking permits. But every effort to silence her resulted in more publicity and even larger audiences at the next venue. She seemed unstoppable—that is, until government officials came up with an ingenious solution to rid themselves of "Red Emma."

On March 8, 1908, Secretary of Commerce and Labor Oscar Straus wrote to US district attorney Edwin Sims asking him to "ascertain whether Emma Goldman is or is not an American citizen"—a query that would be echoed twenty-six years later for Harry Bridges. If Goldman "claims naturalization,"

Straus wished to know "whether that claim is well founded." The goal, his letter made clear, was to determine "what facts are necessary in order to issue an
order of arrest, and to bring about deportation."[40]

The United States was built on lenient immigration and naturalization laws
and policies, at least for whites. But at the dawn of the twentieth century, as
immigrants flooded the United States from southern and eastern Europe in
unprecedented numbers, Congress concluded that it had made naturalization
far too easy. So it passed the 1906 Naturalization Act, tightening up requirements for becoming a naturalized citizen and for the first time enabling the
government to denaturalize those who had acquired US citizenship. Over the
next fifty years, Congress would expand the government's power to revoke
citizenship from those who had proven to be disloyal, unworthy, or otherwise
"un-American." As Emma Goldman would soon discover, the new laws made
citizenship conditional.[41]

The thousands of American women married to noncitizens after Congress enacted the Expatriation Act of 1907—including Ethel Mackenzie and
Ruth Bryan Owen—constituted one group who lost their citizenship under these new laws. They were not alone. Under the Nationality Act of 1940,
the Subversive Activities Control Act of 1950 (also known as the McCarran
Act), and the McCarran-Walter Act of 1952, native-born Americans who had
dodged the draft, joined a foreign army, or voted in a foreign election could
also be stripped of their citizenship for their activities. As legal historian
Patrick Weil has explained, however, it was naturalized citizens like Emma
Goldman and Harry Bridges who were the "main target of crusaders against
un-Americanism."[42]

The new laws treated naturalized citizens as holding that status as a privilege, not a right. Naturalized citizens lost their citizenship for all the same acts
that jeopardized the citizenship of the native born, and also if they returned
to their home country for at least two years or lived in another country for
five. Denaturalization was also permitted "on the ground of fraud or on the
ground that such certificate of citizenship was illegally procured"—standards
that could lead to denaturalization for minor errors in naturalization applications filed long in the past. Not surprisingly, naturalized citizens who had
become a thorn in the government's side were the most likely to face such
scrutiny, as Emma Goldman would learn.[43]

After a thorough investigation, government officials reported that Goldman's
claim to citizenship came through her marriage to Jacob Kersner. They also

found that Kersner had been naturalized before the age of eighteen and after fewer than five years' residence in the United States, making his naturalization in violation of the laws in place at the time. On September 24, 1908, the government initiated an action to denaturalize Kersner on the ground that he had committed naturalization fraud nearly a quarter century before.

No matter that Kersner's citizenship had been certified by a court, that the errors in the timing of the citizenship application were apparently inadvertent, or that he had been a US citizen for the past twenty-four years. Kersner would be collateral damage in the government's quest to denaturalize and deport his former wife.

Publicly, government officials denied that denaturalizing Kersner had anything to do with Goldman. Privately, they said otherwise. One government official crowed that denaturalization would have the "very salutary moral effect" of "depriv[ing] Emma Goldman of that feeling of security which she now manifests, believing herself to be a citizen of the United States." Another admitted that the ultimate design of the proceeding was not to enforce the naturalization laws, but rather to "deprive [Goldman] of an asylum she now enjoys as the wife of an American citizen." In a letter to the attorney general in April 1909 reporting that Kersner had been successfully denaturalized, the US attorney who had overseen the proceedings acknowledged what they both knew: the suit "was entered for the purpose of depriving Emma Goldman of her rights of citizenship."[44]

In January 1909, Goldman wrote to a friend that at first she took the whole matter "as a joke," but "now it turns out serious; altogether too serious," and she was "worried to death over it." In April of that same year, Kersner's citizenship was canceled, which automatically terminated Goldman's citizenship as well. Still, it took the government another ten years to remove her, in part because denaturalization did not automatically justify deportation of a noncitizen who obeyed US laws. But then, in 1917, Goldman was arrested for criticizing America's involvement in World War I, violating the Espionage Act—a law that today would surely be struck down as an unconstitutional infringement on free speech. She served two years in jail, after which she was transported to Ellis Island and then marched aboard the "Soviet Ark" and forcibly deported with several hundred other "radicals" to Bolshevik Russia.[45]

Goldman would spend the rest of her life pining to return to the country that, for all her criticism, she considered her home. She felt herself to be "an American in the truest sense, spiritually rather than by the grace of a mere scrap of paper." She loved what she called "the other America"— the America of "rebels and radicals, the dreamers and dissenters and poets." She knew better than most what the worst of American officialdom was capable of doing, and yet she had not expected deportation for "mere opinion's sake."[46]

Many years after her deportation, Goldman published an essay entitled *A Woman Without a Country*, in which she wrote of the pain of exile. "I know from personal experience what it means to be torn out of the environment of a lifetime, dug out by the very root from the soil you have had your being in, compelled to leave the world to which all your energies have been devoted, and to part from the nearest and dearest to you." She noted bitterly that "citizenship has become bankrupt: it has lost its essential meaning, its one-time guarantee."

And yet, defiant to the last, she insisted that she continued to be a spiritual citizen of the United States despite her denaturalization. Her America was one of "men and women with ideals, with aspirations for a better day; the America of social rebellion and spiritual promise, of the glorious 'undesirables' against whom all the exile, expatriation, and deportation laws are aimed." She concluded, "It is to that America that I am proud to belong."[47]

If Harry Bridges was familiar with Emma Goldman's story, he would have known that his newly obtained US citizenship did not protect him. Indeed, it had only gotten easier to denaturalize and deport troublemakers in the intervening years, and the government was aggressively using every legal avenue available to challenge the citizenship status of its political enemies.[48]

In March of 1942, shortly after losing his initial effort to get Harry Bridges deported, Attorney General Biddle launched the first systematic federal denaturalization program in the nation's history—the same program under which Fritz Julius Kuhn and other members of the German American Bund had been denaturalized during World War II. To become a citizen, a would-be American had to take an oath of allegiance to the United States and the US Constitution. Biddle's Justice Department took the position that an affiliation with Communists, fascists, or other radical groups, even years after naturalization, suggested that the naturalized citizen had lied when taking the oath, which was itself grounds for revoking citizenship.[49]

The government's focus on suspected Communists only increased with the end of World War II. The second Red Scare gathered speed in the wake of the Communists' victory in China, the descent of the Iron Curtain over Eastern Europe, and the Korean War. The House Un-American Activities Committee aggressively investigated any person or group challenging "the form of government as guaranteed by our Constitution." The committee pressured witnesses to "name names" and made vague and sweeping accusations that resulted in the blacklisting of suspected Communists, particularly those in the entertainment industry. Senator Joseph McCarthy adopted the same tactics for his Senate investigations.[50]

McCarthy and his supporters decided that it was not enough for the government to declare people's conduct "un-American"; it would *make* those people un-American by taking away their citizenship. Throughout the second half of the 1940s and into the 1950s, denaturalizations moved forward at a breakneck pace against journalists, as well as political and labor leaders. Aiding that effort, Congress passed the Subversive Activities Control Act of 1950, which barred members of fascist or Communist organizations from becoming citizens and further provided that affiliation with such an organization within five years of becoming a citizen would constitute naturalization fraud.

Using the new law, US attorneys targeted labor leaders and political activists with Communist affiliations—men and women whose actions and beliefs rendered them un-American in the eyes of their government. In 1953, the government sought to denaturalize Paul Novick, the "pugnacious" founder and editor in chief of the left-leaning Yiddish daily the *Morning Freiheit*, claiming he had lied at his naturalization hearing twenty-six years before when he failed to admit his membership in the Workers (Communist) Party.[51] James J. Matles, the left-wing leader of the United Electrical, Radio and Machine Workers Union, and Stanley Nowak, a former state senator from Michigan who had helped to organize autoworkers in Detroit, were both initially stripped of their citizenship but had that status restored in separate rulings by the US Supreme Court. Others were not so lucky. Sam Sweet, Nicholai Chomiak, and George Charnowola, all from Detroit, were denaturalized on the grounds that they had concealed their membership in the Communist Party. Many more who lost their citizenship could not afford the legal fight, simply accepting the loss of citizenship and, frequently, their deportation following shortly thereafter.[52]

Denaturalization is most often associated with totalitarian regimes such as Nazi Germany or the Soviet Union. But by the end of the twentieth century, the US government had denaturalized at least twenty-two thousand people—more than any other democracy before or since.[53] The effect of the denaturalization campaign was to silence those who might otherwise have taken leadership positions in politics, journalism, and the labor movement. By publicly targeting men and women like Goldman, Novick, and Bridges, the government hoped to intimidate into silence tens of thousands of foreign-born citizens who were similarly vulnerable.

Shortly before noon on Tuesday, April 4, 1950, in San Francisco's federal courthouse, the jury shuffled into the juror box, "each face grim." After months of trial followed by four days of deliberation, the eight men and four women were about to deliver the verdict in the government's third attempt to remove

Harry Bridges from the United States, this time by criminally prosecuting him for naturalization fraud. One audience member exclaimed, "Oh Jesus, look at them," before he was loudly hushed. A woman in the audience began to cry.[54]

All rose as the judge entered, arranged himself behind the bench, then asked, "Ladies and Gentlemen of the jury, have you reached a verdict?"

The foreman, a candy salesman from Oakland, responded, "Yes, your honor, we have."

The courtroom held its breath.

This trial had lasted five months, encompassing eighty-one days of testimony and resulting in a two-million-word transcript. Bridges had been questioned on the stand for nine and a half days, spending his breaks chain-smoking and playing chess with his lawyers. The *New York Times* declared him "the most investigated man in the United States."[55]

This time the government had charged Bridges with perjuring himself during his naturalization proceedings when he stated under oath that he was not a member of the Communist Party, and also with conspiring to defraud the government by concealing his membership. If convicted, he would not only be stripped of his citizenship and deported from the United States, he would first serve up to seven years in jail.

The foreman passed the verdict to the judge, who read it silently before handing to his clerk to read aloud.

"Guilty."

With that, the "courtroom became a bedlam of noise and confusion." A federal marshal seized Bridges and began to handcuff him, but then Bridges's lawyer convinced the judge he should be allowed to remain free on bail while the case was appealed. Bridges's wife rushed to embrace him. Bridges was the only person in the room who did not visible react. Unflappable as ever, witnesses described him as "relaxed" despite the tumult around him.[56]

Many rushed to praise the verdict. Richard Nixon, then a member of Congress, released a statement urging the Department of Justice to "immediately . . . cancel [Bridges's] citizenship and deport him," declaring that the "tragedy of the case is that Bridges was not deported from this country 12 years ago." An editorial in Wisconsin's *La Crosse Tribune* concluded, "It is surely to the benefit of the United States that Harry Bridges no longer has the privilege of citizenship," though that paper feared his role would be taken over by "another of his same stripe, who cannot be deported." Under the headline "Good Riddance," the *Star Press* of Muncie, Indiana, stated flatly that the "American people will be glad to get rid of him."[57]

But Bridges would not be forced from his country without a fight. Three years of appeals followed, until yet again, remarkably, Bridges's case reached the US Supreme Court. The stakes for Bridges were even higher than before. If he lost, he would not only lose his citizenship and go to jail, he would be stateless and might be incarcerated indefinitely if Australia decided not to take him back—a distinct possibility.[58]

When the case was argued before the court on the afternoon of May 4, 1953, Bridges, free on $25,000 bail, was in the audience, "listen[ing] intently" as the justices battled with legal counsel over his fate. He could not have been reassured by what he heard, for the justices appeared deeply divided. Once again, Bridges would have to wait until the last day of the Supreme Court's term to learn whether he could retain his freedom and his citizenship.[59]

Finally, on June 15, 1954, the Supreme Court announced its decision. By a narrow majority, it reversed the jury's verdict and declared that Bridges could remain a US citizen. The court did not reach the question whether Bridges was a member of the Communist Party, holding only that the government had failed to indict him within the three year-statute of limitations for denaturalization fraud. But for Bridges, the only thing that mattered was that he had retained his citizenship and his freedom.[60]

"Supreme Court Frees Bridges," the New York Times declared in a front-page headline. The weeks of trial, the conviction, the multiyear jail sentence, and the likely deportation to follow had all been erased from the law books. Bridges was "jubilant," declaring that he hoped the decision would help others hounded by the government solely "because of their beliefs or opinions."[61]

But it was too soon to celebrate. The government can denaturalize its citizens in two different ways: it can choose to charge the naturalized citizen with the crime of naturalization fraud, which comes with a fine and jail time as well as loss of citizenship; or it can choose to pursue denaturalization under the civil code, which carries no jail time but also is unconstrained by a statute of limitations or by the prohibition against double jeopardy. A civil denaturalization can be filed at any time, even many decades after the target became a citizen. So there was nothing to stop the government from seeking to denaturalize Bridges yet again.

And it did.

In June 1955, in the same San Francisco courthouse where Bridges had endured his criminal trial, he now defended himself against the government's *fourth* attempt to remove him from the United States. This trial lasted for six weeks, and was before a federal judge, not a jury. Once again, the government argued that Bridges had lied at his naturalization proceedings when he declared he was not a Communist. Once again, the government called on a string of witnesses claiming Bridges was a member of the Communist Party. Once again, Bridges testified that he was not.

Once again, and for the last time, Bridges won. The judge found the testimony of the witnesses "tinged and colored with discrepancies" and biased by "animosities." He refused to denaturalize Bridges despite the "extra-judicial clamor" for his removal from the United States. Bridges had won his last battle to keep his citizenship.[62]

Bridges had one more skirmish to fight to protect his rights to equal citizenship, this time his right to marry. In 1958, while visiting Nevada, the now-divorced Bridges tried to obtain a license to marry Noriko Sawada, a Japanese American. Like Joseph Kurihara and 120,000 other American citizens of Japanese descent, Sawada spent most of World War II imprisoned in a camp—an experience that inspired her to become a civil rights activist, which is how she eventually met Bridges. But after concluding that Sawada was of the "yellow race," the clerk denied them permission to marry under Nevada's 1846 anti-miscegenation law. That state was one of approximately two dozen at the time with such laws still on the books. (Three years later, Barack Obama would be born to a white mother who had married his black father in Hawai'i, which permitted mixed-race marriages.)

Bridges argued that her race was irrelevant and pointed out that Sawada had been born in the United States and was an American citizen, just as he now was. But the clerk, unconsciously echoing Fritz Kuhn, told him, "It's not a matter of where you were born. It's the blood. It's against the law here." They could easily have married in another state, but neither Bridges nor Sawada could tolerate the injustice. So instead Bridges called his lawyers and notified the press. Embarrassed by the nationwide coverage that followed, which included an article in *Time* magazine, the Nevada state legislature quickly repealed its anti-miscegenation law. Sawada and Bridges married and remained together until his death thirty-one years later.[63]

Bridges remained in the United States for the rest of life, slowly evolving from suspect alien to citizen hero. In 1966, folk singer Pete Seeger released "The Ballad of Harry Bridges," which begins, "Let me tell you of a sailor . . . an honest union leader that the bosses tried to frame," and included as part of its refrain, "We're not a-goin' to let them send Harry o'er the sea."

In 1978, a year after he retired, Bridges was honored at the National Portrait Gallery in Washington, DC, before an audience that included the US secretary of labor. "When the old bastard's retiring, people say, 'He's not so bad after all," Bridges observed with a laugh. When he died in March 1990, at age eighty-eight, the San Francisco ports shut down for the afternoon in his honor, and San Francisco's mayor ordered the city's flags to be flown at half-staff, declaring that "all of San Francisco mourns this loss." Eleven years later, San Francisco mayor Willie Brown and California governor Gray Davis declared July 28, 2001—what would have been Bridges's one hundredth birthday—"Harry Bridges Day." The plaza in front of the Ferry Building on San Francisco's Embarcadero now bears his name, honoring him at the same site where he and the longshoremen he led were shot at and beaten by San Francisco's police force during the 1934 strike. As the *New York Times* observed, "yesterday's radical" had become "today's prophet."[64]

And yet Harry Bridges's story was not quite over.

In 1991, a year after Bridges's death, the former Soviet Union opened up its archives. According to those records, it appeared that Bridges had been a member of the Communist Party all along, and a high-ranking one at that. Letters among members of the Communist Party of the United States of America repeatedly referred to him as "Comrade Bridges," and in 1936 he was elected to the Central Committee under the alias "Rossi"—an inside joke, for Rossi was the last name of San Francisco's mayor at the time, whom Bridges despised.[65]

What does this change? Certainly, it complicates Bridges's story. That Bridges joined and then remained in the Communist Party demonstrates a surprising degree of recklessness. Why would Bridges risk everything by formally becoming a member—a status that rendered him deportable and barred his naturalization? He had lied repeatedly under oath, insisting during multiple court hearings and during his naturalization ceremony that he was not a member of the Communist Party. In declaring his innocence of the charges against him, Bridges said, "I wasn't exactly a fool; I wasn't a member."[66] Yet it turns out he *was* that foolish, though the government could never prove it during his lifetime.

In most ways, though, as historian and leading Bridges's scholar Robert Cherny argues, this new information changes nothing.[67] Bridges always readily admitted working closely with Communist Party members and sharing many of the party's goals, even as he insisted he had never formally joined that organization.[68] No one believes that Bridges was controlled by the Soviet Union or the Communist Party, or let either set his union's agenda. Nor do his Communist Party credentials change the fact that the government pursued him for his speech and actions on behalf of the workers he represented— conduct that is not only legal but also constitutionally protected—and did so using evidence that government lawyers knew to be false and witnesses they knew to have perjured themselves.[69]

The nation stumbled during the first and second Red Scares by blacklisting, prosecuting, denaturalizing, deporting, and generally hounding law-abiding individuals, letting fear justify a blatant disregard for civil liberties. But historians of this era agree that the victims of this persecution were, in fact, either members of the Communist Party or closely affiliated with it. The government erred not because it chose the wrong people as targets of its harassment, but rather because it was wrong to target people for nothing more than their ideology, speech, and affiliations.[70]

Emilia Castañeda de Valenciana

Ignacio Piña

CHAPTER 8

EXPELLED CITIZEN

Ignacio Piña's mother was making homemade flour tortillas when the men with guns came to the door. She had just slid a hot rolled tortilla onto his plate, dripping with melted butter, when he looked up to see them in the doorway. The man in front, a few feet inside the house, was holding a gun pointed at Ignacio's mother. Another man stayed outside, gun drawn as well. The one in front said, "Come on, let's go! Come on!" He indicated with a wave of the gun's muzzle that he meant all of them had to leave—Ignacio, his mother, and his sisters and brothers.

"Where?" his mother asked.

"No questions!" The man in front said, and then repeated, "Come on, out!"[1]

You don't argue with a gun. Even at six years old, Ignacio knew that. So he followed his mother and siblings out the door. On that September day in 1931, they left their house in Pocatello, Idaho, with the clothes they were wearing and nothing else. Not their winter coats or their boots. Not the new jeans Ignacio's mother had bought him for his first day of school—the day he had been looking forward to for months. Not even the official documents that his parents kept locked away in their trunk, including the birth certificates proving that each of their six children had been born in the United States.[2]

The men drove them to the field where Ignacio's father and older sister were preparing the sugar beets for harvest. The men forced them into the car, too, and then filled up a second car with other Mexicans working the same fields. They took them all to the local jail, putting Ignacio, his siblings, and his mother in one cell and his father in another with the other men. One day stretched to two, then to a week, with nothing to do but stare at the walls of their prison. Ignacio "could not understand why we were in jail if we were not criminals."[3]

Finally, ten days later, the officials had rounded up enough people to fill a train, five boxcars full, that would take them first to El Paso, Texas, before

crossing into Mexico. Ignacio was full of questions: "Where is this train going?" and, most important, "What's going to happen [to] us?" But his parents
had no answers, so he stopped asking. He could see that many of the families
were just like his. Mexican immigrants who had lived in the United States legally for decades, working in the fields or in the trades, together with their
native-born American children. Years later, Ignacio remembered "looking
around at the people . . . they looked so sad. Because many were suffering the
same things we were facing. They were kicked out too."[4]

For Emilia Castañeda de Valenciana, the news that America would no longer be home came not from strangers with guns but from her father. She was
nine years old in the fall of 1935 and had just started in the fourth grade at
the Malabar School in Los Angeles. Her father, Natividad Castañeda, sat her
and her brother Francisco down and told them that they would all be going
to Mexico. Natividad had been born in Mexico, but he had not been back for
more than twenty years. For Emilia and her brother, both born and raised in
the United States, Mexico was a "foreign country thousands of miles away."[5]

Natividad, square shouldered and handsome, was a stonemason who had
immigrated legally to the United States around 1910, quickly finding well-
paying work in construction in and around Los Angeles. Soon he married another Mexican immigrant, Emilia and Francisco's mother, Gregoria. After the
children were born, they saved enough to buy a duplex on Folsom Street, in
the Boyle Heights neighborhood of Los Angeles. Emilia remembers that they
had leather furniture, brass beds, and an RCA Victrola in the living room. A
picket fence surrounded a yard filled with fruit trees, chicken coops, and rab-
bits. They were by no means rich, but Natividad and Gregoria had made a
good life for their family.[6]

Then, in October 1929, the US stock market collapsed, and the economy
crashed with it. Seemingly overnight, the United States went from having too
many jobs to too many workers. By 1933, more than twelve million people
were unemployed, amounting to nearly 25 percent of the labor force. Finding work was tough for everyone, but the situation was far worse for Mexican
immigrants.[7]

Natividad was one of the millions suddenly out of work. At first, the family lived off Gregoria's wages as a domestic worker for a wealthy family in
West Los Angeles. They were scraping by until Gregoria got sick. *La gripa*, she
thought, and tried all the traditional remedies, but nothing could make her
well. Finally Gregoria went to the hospital. She was diagnosed with tuberculosis and sent to an institution, where she was isolated to avoid contaminat-
ing others. With no income, the family lost their house and went on welfare,

moving from one apartment to another and picking up free groceries from state-funded warehouses.[8]

Even so, Sunday, May 20, 1934, was supposed to be a happy day for the Castañeda family. Emilia had turned eight years old the month before, and this sunny Sunday morning was the day of her first Communion—a bright spot in what had otherwise been a hard year. Emilia wore a veil and a white dress provided by one of the Catholic charities, and her father had covered the black stripes on her saddle shoes with white shoe polish. At Mass that morning she knelt at the Communion rail for the first time, accepting the small disc of bread onto her tongue from the parish priest, proof that she had reached the age of reason. It was only later that day that she learned her mother had died.[9]

Natividad, impoverished and now alone, decided his family of three had no choice but to leave the United States.

On the day of their departure, they arrived at the station before dawn to find it crowded with families of Mexican descent taking the same train. "We were crying . . . many people were crying," Emilia remembers, because "we were going to an unknown place."[10]

Ignacio's and Emilia's parents were part of a wave of Mexican migration to the United States that swelled in the late 1800s and crested after the Mexican Revolution in 1910. Mexican workers were heavily recruited by US employers to build the railroads, mine ore and copper, and plant and harvest crops in the newly irrigated American Southwest. The demand only increased in the wake of federal legislation restricting entry of immigrants groups—first the Chinese, then Japanese, and then, in 1924, immigrants from southern and eastern Europe as well.[11]

At the start of the twentieth century, jobs were scarce in Mexico, and workers there were paid a fraction of what they could earn in the United States.[12] In 1910, the Mexican Revolution brought chaos and danger, as well as economic disruption to an already struggling country. So Mexicans eagerly took up the invitation, flocking across the border to help build a rapidly expanding United States.[13]

Scholars estimate that about 1 million Mexicans emigrated to the United States during the first three decades of the twentieth century. By 1930, the census listed 1,422,533 persons of Mexican heritage living in the United States—a number equal to 10 percent of the entire Mexican population.[14] Many settled down, married, and had children who, like Ignacio and Emilia, were US citizens at birth. The children attended American schools and spoke fluent English. They knew Mexico only from their parents' stories of a country they had never seen.[15]

And then came the Great Depression.

"American jobs for real Americans." That was the motto of Herbert Hoover's administration after the economy cratered, and it was echoed by states and localities across the country. "The slogan has gone out over the city [of Los Angeles] and is being adhered to—'Employ no Mexican while a white man is unemployed,'" wrote George Clements, manager of the Los Angeles Chamber of Commerce's Agriculture Department. Government officials scrambled to ensure that jobs, especially good jobs, were off-limits to immigrants. Hoover's secretary of labor, William Doak, pressured companies such as Ford, U.S. Steel, and Southern Pacific Railroad to lay off their Mexican immigrant employees, and encouraged states and localities to pass ordinances prohibiting the hiring of anyone of Mexican descent, even legal permanent residents and US citizens, though they had to be careful to frame such laws in race-neutral terms. States did not need much urging. They rushed to bar non-citizens from working as lawyers, accountants, teachers, and on public works projects, using citizenship as a proxy for race. Some even required citizenship to obtain a fishing license or register a mining claim.[16]

It did not matter that many of those affected were legal immigrants who had lived in the United States for many decades, as was true for Emilia's and Ignacio's fathers. It did not even matter that some were naturalized or native-born citizens, and therefore should not have fallen within the law's purview. Excluding workers of Mexican descent from employment "is a question of pigment, not a question of citizenship or right," the general manager of the LA Chamber of Commerce wrote to Clements in 1931. Or, as Emilia Castañeda put it, "there was work only for the chosen ones. Not Mexicans."[17]

Barring Mexican immigrants from employment only exacerbated the problem, however, leaving states and localities to provide food and housing to newly destitute families. So government officials concluded that everyone would be better off if they could force or persuade residents of Mexican descent to leave, regardless of their immigration status or citizenship.

On a sunny Sunday afternoon in Los Angeles in February 1931, about four hundred people were milling about in La Placita Park, located in the center of the city and a gathering place for Los Angeles's Mexican community. Men would spend hours there, debating Mexican or American politics, or as historian Doug Monroy put it, simply doing "a helluvalot of complaining" to a sympathetic crowd. Women and children came and went, stopping in at the park after shopping at one of the nearby markets or attending mass at La Placita church. Mariachi bands would riff for anyone who would pay them a few pennies, and popular street performers quickly generated a crowd.

According to Monroy, "In the days before television and radio, if you wanted stimulation and excitement, you went to La Placita."[18]

But on that particular Sunday afternoon, a group of unfamiliar men joined the usual crowd. Most were dressed in plainclothes, but a few wore the olive-drab uniforms of the Immigration and Naturalization Service. These immigration officials had come from as far as San Francisco and Nogales, Arizona, and they had spent the past ten days preparing for this moment. At exactly 3 p.m., several officers stationed themselves at La Placita's gates, and the rest fanned out around the park.[19]

As the crowd caught sight of the men, some cried "*Razzia!*" (Raid!) and tried to scatter, but officers wielding batons and guns prevented anyone from leaving. The officials lined up the park's four hundred occupants, requiring each one to produce papers proving citizenship or legal status before they were allowed to leave. Those who lacked documentation were detained for follow-up questions or placed in flatbed trucks that encircled the park, and then driven to the train station, where commissioned trains took them over the border and deep into Mexico. The immediate goal was to ensure that those removed would never return. But the larger purpose of the very public La Placita raid was to send a message: it was time for Mexicans to go home.[20]

The La Placita raid was one of the first federal government efforts to round up and deport all noncitizens illegally in the United States, estimated at about four hundred thousand people in the 1930s. Although the intended targets were undocumented, the process swept up legal immigrants and citizens as well.[21]

A subsequent government investigation found that immigration officials "forcibly detain[ed] groups of people many of whom are aliens lawfully in this country, or even United States citizens, without any warrant of arrest or search." Suspects were jailed and interrogated for hours, typically with no lawyer present. As one federal judge put it, "one man" acts "as inquisitor, interpreter, prosecutor, and judge," leading to a result "stripped of the conditions which make for justice." The investigation concluded that the "apprehension and examination of supposed aliens are often characterized by methods unconstitutional, tyrannic, and oppressive." Moreover, it was "not only aliens who are involved in deportation proceedings; the rights of United States citizens are often infringed" because they, too, are "subjected to these illegal searches and seizures."[22]

Nonetheless, some state and local officials thought this federal effort was not enough. In 1931, C. P. Visel, director of Los Angeles County's unemployment relief, sent a telegram to his federal counterpart in Washington complaining that the "United States Department of Immigration [was] incapacitated to handle" the removal of the tens of thousands of Mexican immigrants in his district. He offered to help "pick them all up through police and sheriff channels." Visel concluded, "Please advise as to method of getting rid [*sic*]. We need their jobs for needy citizens."[23]

Unwilling to wait for a response from Washington, the next day Visel wrote to the LA Chamber of Commerce that "between 20,000 and 25,000 deportable aliens" lived in LA, and it "would be a great relief to the unemployment situation if some method could be devised to scare these people out of our city."[24] Under Visel's leadership, Los Angeles County launched a deportation campaign, though it was eventually relabeled a "repatriation" program after county attorneys warned that only federal officials had the legal authority to remove people from the United States. The term was inaccurate. As the daughter of one native-born US citizen forced out of the United States put it, "You cannot be repatriated to a place you've never been."[25]

Renaming the program did not render it legal. In testimony before the California State Senate in 2003, law professor Kevin R. Johnson explained that the "'repatriation' took place without any legal protections in place or any kind of due process," making all of the removals—whether of undocumented immigrants, legal residents, or US citizens—"unconstitutional . . . [and] illegal, because no modicum of process was followed." Nonetheless, Los Angeles County's repatriation campaign resulted in the removal of tens of thousands of residents of Mexican heritage from the county and served as a model for cities and counties across the American Southwest.[26]

States and localities used a variety of methods to remove "unwanted Mexicans." Sometimes, as was the case for Ignacio Piña and his family, sheriffs and local law enforcement forcibly deported families of Mexican heritage. At other times, private citizens acting independently of the authorities scared or intimidated workers of Mexican descent into leaving the country. Young Anglo men would arrive at Mexican labor camps throughout the Southwest, announcing that if the Mexican workers did not leave by the next day, "we will burn you out." On June 4, 1931, a member of LA's Chamber of Commerce wrote that "efforts have been made by some individuals to scare Mexicans who have property here into selling it at a fraction of its value, on the ground that they were about to be deported." He continued, "Many Mexicans are absolutely terrorized and are ready to do anything to get out." As the letter suggests, state and local officials were well aware of these threats yet did nothing to stop them.[27]

Government officials also scoured hospitals and sanatoriums for sick and destitute patients who could be sent to Mexico against their will. On May 16, 1938, the superintendent of charities for Los Angeles County documented the removal of a number of patients of Mexican heritage from a county hospital, including an eighty-six-year-old woman; a patient described as "tubercular"; a patient suffering paralysis; and seven children ranging from ages three to fifteen—all almost certainly US citizens. It is hard to imagine that any of these people left willingly.[28]

More often, though, removal occurred through coercion rather than outright force, as was the case for Emilia Castañeda's family. Barred from most jobs, even longtime residents like Emilia's father concluded they had no choice but to leave. To encourage departure, welfare offices offered to pay for families of Mexican heritage to travel to Mexico and at the same time would threaten to cut off their benefits if they chose to stay. Some state officials threatened to take children away from parents on welfare if they did not leave the United States immediately. The Mexican government assisted the efforts to entice individuals of Mexican descent to come to Mexico, holding out promises of land, jobs, and other benefits that often failed to materialize for those who took them up on the offer.[29]

Even when the initial decision to leave was voluntary, the "repatriates" were not allowed to change their minds. In one case, the occupants of a repatriation train requested permission to get off but were told they now had no choice but to leave the country. Several young men then jumped out a train window while passing through Laredo, Texas, but were caught the next day and sent to Mexico. Government officials often went to the trouble of personally escorting families across the border to "prevent . . . their return" to the United States. Although such assisted removals were costly, government officials concluded they were cheaper than continuing to feed and house those on welfare or in county facilities. Los Angeles County further defrayed its costs by reimbursing itself from the sale of homes and household goods that the departing families were forced to leave behind.[30]

No one knows exactly how many residents of Mexican descent were forced, coerced, or pressured by their economic circumstances to leave the United States during the Great Depression. Some historians argue the number is north of 1 million people, while others believe it is closer to 350,000. At even the lower estimates, close to one-quarter of the total population of Hispanic descent in the United States left the country during the 1930s. And all agree that a significant number of US citizens were among them, estimating that number at about 60 percent of all those who left, most the children of Mexican immigrants legally residing in the United States.[31]

The problem of "mixed" families—families with both immigrants and US citizens—remains a vexing one today, and no one thinks the answer is to separate the noncitizen parents from their US citizen children. Yet the removal of so many young and vulnerable US citizens to a country ill equipped to educate and support them should have given the government pause. It did not. As a June 16, 1931, memo between members of LA's Chamber of Commerce made clear, officials were well aware that many of those removed were US citizens, and yet they viewed them as something other than "real" Americans. "All of them are certainly not foreign born, probably the bulk of them being native born," the officials agreed, "but nonetheless Mexican."[32]

Life had been hard in the United States for Ignacio Piña and his family, but Mexico proved fatal. With no other choice, the Piñas lived in the slums of Mexico City. In an interview years later, Ignacio described how "our clothes were rotting away, and it was all we had." The family was always hungry, so he and his older brother "stole bananas, oranges, guayabas . . . whatever we could from the stands at the park so we could eat."[33] Soon after arriving, his entire family contracted typhoid fever from drinking contaminated water. The people of Mexico were also reeling from the impact of the worldwide economic depression, so they did not embrace the Piñas or the hundreds of thousands of families like them. "We were misfits there," Ignacio stated flatly. "We weren't welcome."[34]

In 1935, Ignacio's father died of black lung disease, likely caused by his work in the coal mines in Utah. "My mother was left destitute, with six of us, in a country we knew nothing about," Ignacio remembered. He dropped out of school in the sixth grade so he could start working to support his family, mostly shining shoes for a few *centavos* a pair.[35]

Life was not much better for Emilia Castañeda and her family. When they arrived at the train station in Gómez Palacio, Mexico, a *cargador* (porter) carried their trunk across town on his back, bracing it with a cloth tied to his forehead. Instead of shoes, the man wore *huaraches*—strips of tire tied to his feet to create makeshift sandals. Emilia remembered thinking that the *cargador* must be very poor not to be able to afford shoes. But by the following year her brother had outgrown his only pair of shoes and wore *huaraches* too.[36]

At first they moved in with an aunt, her son, and his six children. Because the only living space was a one-room house, the children were forced to sleep outside, getting "soaked to the bones" when it rained. Bathrooms were a hole in the ground. Later, after they moved into a larger home, they all slept inside on a dirt floor, and Emilia's father hung up food on wires to prevent the rats from eating it at night. They never saw a doctor or a dentist, and Emilia and her brother never owned a toothbrush.[37]

In Mexico, Emilia was "completely occupied by survival." She spent her days starting the fire for cooking, hauling water from blocks away, washing clothes by hand, and caring for her brother. Shortly after they arrived Emilia's brother got sick, possibly with typhoid. Her father was often away for work, so she was responsible for helping Francisco eat, bathe, and get in and out of bed. Later, Emilia was ill as well, with what the neighbors called *atiriciada*— depression or maybe homesickness. She couldn't eat, and she would sit on the ground and "cry and cry."[38]

Emilia struggled in school because she did not speak much Spanish when she arrived. Other children "picked on us because we didn't belong there [and they] didn't want us in their country," she explained. She was mystified when one of her cousins referred to her, tauntingly, as a *repatriada*. It was clearly an insult, but Emilia was confused. How could she be a repatriate to a country she had never been to? "I knew I wasn't a *repatriada*," she said later, "because I was an American."[39]

Officials in charge of the mass repatriation program knew that most of those removed, including the US citizens, would not be able to return to the United States. Indeed, that was the goal.

LA Chamber of Commerce member George Clements traveled to the border to witness the removals. He observed that most of those removed "had been told that they could come back whenever they wanted to," but concluded that "it is not the truth." The deportees had each been given a "departure card" stating that they had been receiving welfare, a fact that would bar their return under laws prohibiting entry into the United States of noncitizens likely to become a public charge. Clements also noted that their children, "even though born in America," are also "without very much hope of ever coming back into the United States" because "the burden of proof" of citizenship was "placed entirely on the individual."[40]

As Clements predicted, many tried but failed to establish their right to return to the United States. *Repatriado* Pablo Guerrero had been deported from the United States with his wife and children on December 8, 1932. Eighteen months later he wrote to Los Angeles County, explaining that "all of my children were born in the U. S. of A." They wanted to return to the United States, and he asked for help in obtaining passports proving his children's citizenship. But his letter went unanswered, and the record is silent as to whether he or his children ever managed to come back to the United States.[41]

Concepción Covarrubias was born in Los Angeles in 1924 to parents who had lived in the United States for more than a decade. Her mother died when she was ten years old, and afterward social workers came to the house and told her father, "If you're still here at midnight, we'll take the kids away." So the family, including Concepción and her native-born US citizen brother José, left for Mexico. Neither Concepción nor her brother brought with them any proof that they were US citizens, and neither one realized they had a right to return to the United States. It was Concepción's son who discovered that his mother was a US citizen, and he crossed the border illegally three times to search for her birth certificate before he finally found it among Los Angeles County records in the mid-1980s. Concepción finally returned to the United States in 2004, after living more than seventy years in Mexico.[42]

Many other US citizens removed during the 1930s never came back. "I just accepted it," one woman explained, "What was I supposed to do?" When another US citizen still living in Mexico was asked, "Do you consider yourself American? Or Mexican?" he responded, "Well, not one or the other. . . . It's a lost identity. I don't even know what I am."[43]

Emilia Castañeda spent her eighteenth birthday on a train going north, first across the US–Mexico border and then up the coast of California. After nine years in Mexico, she was finally returning to the United States. It was April of 1944, so the cars were packed with US soldiers preparing to join the war in the Pacific. She spent most of the journey sitting on her suitcase in an aisle. A petite woman, with glossy black hair and wide cheekbones, she remembered that the servicemen were "surprised that I could speak a little bit of English" until she explained that she was an American citizen, just like them. When a friend in Mexico had asked her why she wanted to go back, she responded, "I belong there."[44]

Emilia had remained in touch with her godmother in the United States, and she reached out to her for help returning to the United States. After locating the birth certificate proving that Emilia had been born in California, Emilia's godmother sent her money to pay for the journey and offered her a place to stay when she arrived. Emilia knew she was lucky. Most of the deported had no way to return to the United States "because they had nobody to contact to be able to get their birth certificate to prove that they were American citizens."[45]

After Emilia arrived in California, she got a job in a candy factory, slowly paying her godmother back for the cost of the journey and for her room and board. Eventually she married and had children, all of whom attended college. She worked most of her life and volunteered at her church and her children's school, and she and her husband saved up and bought their own home. She registered to vote as soon as she was eligible. In 2003, when Emilia was seventy-seven years old, she testified before a committee of the California State Senate that was investigating the mass repatriation of residents of Mexican descent from California. She spoke softly, at first struggling to position the microphone so that she could be heard. At the end, she told the legislators that despite her ordeal, she had become "a successful, contributing American."[46]

Acting in part on the basis of Emilia's testimony, the California legislature passed a law formally apologizing to those expelled. The law described how hundreds of thousands of "American citizens and legal residents of Mexican ancestry were forced to go to Mexico," which it declared to be "fundamental violations of . . . basic civil liberties and constitutional rights." As required by the law, a plaque commemorating these events was installed at La Plaza de Cultura y Artes on North Main Street in Los Angeles, just a few hundred feet from the site of the La Placita raid. Emilia attended the plaque's installation ceremony with her daughter, Christine Valenciana, and Christine's husband, Francisco Balderrama. (Valenciana and Balderrama are professors in the California State University system who have studied and written about the mass repatriation; Balderrama is the coauthor of *Decade of Betrayal*, one of the leading historical accounts of these events.) In 2015, when she was eighty-nine years old, Emilia spoke about her experience with a class of fourth graders at Bell Gardens Elementary School. With the help of their teacher, the students then successfully lobbied the California legislature to pass a bill requiring that the State Board of Education consider including the history of mass repatriation in the curriculum in California's public schools.[47]

For Ignacio Piña, returning to the United States felt close to impossible. He had lost much of his English and spent his days struggling just to get enough to eat. But his older sisters retained the language, which helped them get jobs in tourist hotels in Mexico City. Those jobs paid higher wages and came with occasional perks. In 1939, when Ignacio was fourteen years old, his sister came home with free tickets to the Movie Palace, a big theater in Mexico City that showed all the new releases. "Let's celebrate," she told him, and took him to see the most recent blockbuster, *The Wizard of Oz*. Ignacio surprised them both when he started to cry halfway through the reel. When she asked him what was wrong, he said, "I want to go home too."[48]

A few years later, the United States entered the Second World War. Ignacio went to the American Embassy to ask how he could fight for his country. Officials there were incredulous. "You're Mexican," they told him. He told them they were wrong, that he was born in the United States of America, but he could not obtain the documents to prove it.[49]

For Ignacio, it was his English-speaking older sister who found the way home. She saved up the money they needed, then tracked down the family's birth certificates in the United States. One by one, the family came back. Ignacio returned to the United States in 1947, when he was twenty-two years old, after sixteen years of what he calls "pure hell" in the slums of Mexico City.[50]

And then the cycle of mass removal and migration began all over again. In December 1941, the United States entered the Second World War. The US economy recovered, then roared into high gear. With so many American men off at war, the owners of the fertile fields of the American Southwest once again were in desperate need of short-term workers to sow, tend, and harvest the grapes, walnuts, apples, oranges, and cotton that were their staple crops.

So the United States and Mexico together launched what would come to be called the Bracero Program, named for the colloquial Spanish term for laborer, which brought Mexican nationals into the United States as contract laborers. The program started small, amounting to no more than seventy thousand workers a year, but by 1950 over two hundred thousand workers annually were arriving with Bracero contracts, and that number doubled by 1954. In total, the government issued over five million labor contracts before the program ended in 1964. Although the jobs paid more than those in Mexico, the work could be brutal. As one grower put it, "We used to own our slaves. Now we just rent them."[51]

The Bracero Program was intended to bring in guest workers, typically men, who would stay in the country for no more than a few months while they harvested crops before returning to their families and homes in Mexico. But the arrival of short-term contract laborers had the unintended effect of increasing permanent immigration to the United States. Friends and family of Bracero workers emigrated without contracts—some legally, some not. US employers also encouraged unauthorized immigration outside the program, preferring to hire workers under the table to avoid the expense and red tape that accompanied the legal laborers.[52] Whatever their legal status on arrival, the new arrivals were increasingly likely to settle down, have families, and stay permanently, even when the temporary work they were hired to do was finished for the season. As the Swiss novelist Max Frisch commented in response to similar developments in Europe: "We asked for workers. We got people instead."[53]

At dawn on a Thursday morning in June 1954, hundreds of federal, state, and local officers fanned out over East Los Angeles, forming a human "dragnet" to round up undocumented immigrants. The East Los Angeles Sheriff's Station was the launching point for teams of officers who "questioned and arrested scores of aliens on street corners, in factories, in foundries, in brickyards . . . [and] in private homes."[54]

Officials made no secret of the fact that their intended targets were Mexican immigrants—or "wetbacks," in the pejorative terminology of the day, for they were assumed to have arrived in the United States soaking wet from forging the Rio Grande. The government focused on "areas of dense population of Mexican descent," where officials "question[ed] suspected wetbacks on the streets, in stores, and, particularly, in bars and cafes." The California Highway Patrol set up road blocks, stopping "suspected wetbacks" driving through East LA neighborhoods. The effort mirrored the La Placita raid nearly a quarter of century before, but this time the government's target was the population of an entire city, not a single public park. Like the La Placita raid, the 1954 roundup was designed to attract attention and generate publicity.[55]

It succeeded. Newspapers covered the roundup on their front pages, and included photos of men, women, and children being escorted to dozens of buses parked around the city to serve as "mobile jails." Employees at well-known Los Angeles establishments such as the Beverly Hilton, Biltmore Hotel, Los Angeles Athletic Club, and the Brown Derby were targets, and journalists were there to cover the mayhem that followed. One man fleeing from immigration officials was chased across rooftops before he was finally caught near a ventilator shaft. Another raced through a crowded restaurant, pursued by uniformed, gun-wielding officers as the well-heeled diners looked on.[56]

The aftermath of these raids was also highly visible. Buses took the detainees to Elysian Park Recreation Center—a popular public park in Central Los Angeles, now the site of Dodger Stadium—where thousands of detainees were held in full view of the public. The *Los Angeles Times* observed that the detainees "ranged from fuzzy-cheeked boys in their teens to horny-handed field workers in their 50s and 60s." That same paper included a photo of the "youngest internee," a ten-month-old baby named Sandra Martinez who was almost certainly an American citizen.[57]

The Los Angeles raid was the opening salvo in a massive campaign that would result in the departure or forced removal of over one million residents of Mexican heritage from the United States from 1954 through 1956.

The raids had been at least a year in the making. In 1953, Immigration and Naturalization Service (INS) commissioner Argyle Mackey warned of "the human tide of 'wetbacks,'" who were accused of taking jobs from American citizens, committing crimes, and overwhelming public services. Willard Kelly, the assistant commissioner of the Border Control, called the arriving Mexican immigrants "the greatest peacetime invasion ever complacently suffered by any country."[58]

Something had to be done, and Lieutenant General Joseph Swing was the man to do it. Swing had served in the US Army, leading troops into battle in the First and Second World Wars before being tapped by Eisenhower to take over the leadership of the INS. In the spring of 1954, he announced that the immigration service was launching a massive, quasi-military roundup of undocumented immigrants. The goal, Swing explained, was to stem the "alarming, ever-increasing flood tide" of undocumented immigrants from Mexico that he, too, described as an "actual invasion of the United States."[59]

Swing established hundreds of twelve-man teams, each equipped with radios, automobiles, jeeps, trucks, buses, and planes, to conduct raids of communities known to have a high percentage of Mexican immigrants. These "special mobile forces" targeted not just the borders but also major cities such as Los Angeles, San Francisco, and Chicago. Although the operation was high-tech for its era, Swing also increased the use of dogs, both to aid the roundup and to further intimidate immigrants from Mexico into leaving. Officially, the roundup was known as the "Special Mobile Force Operation," but just about everyone called it "Operation Wetback."[60]

At its height, Operation Wetback was responsible for three thousand arrests a day. Swing reported that it removed a total of 801,069 Mexican migrants from 1953 through 1955—though these numbers are contested. In any case, Operation Wetback did not aim merely to deport Mexican immigrants by force, but also to frighten the population into "self-deporting." And it largely succeeded. Although accurate numbers are hard to come by, historians estimate that in total approximately 1.5 million US residents of Mexican descent left the country during the first half of the 1950s, many voluntarily to avoid government deportation. Testifying before Congress in January of 1955, Lieutenant General Swing declared victory. The "wetback problem no longer exists" he told Congress, concluding the "border has been secured."[61]

As was true for the mass repatriations of the 1930s, Operation Wetback affected US citizens as well as undocumented immigrants. During the raids in 1954 and after, legal immigrants and US citizens of Mexican heritage were stopped, questioned, arrested, and sometimes even deported if they could not quickly prove their status to the immigration officials charged with removing as many people as possible. The burden was on those of Mexican descent to prove their citizenship.

The small town of Loomis, California, in Placer County is located near the state capital of Sacramento, about six hundred miles north of the Mexican border. Today, Loomis's population hovers around six thousand, and the town's motto is "A small town is like a large family." In the 1950s, Loomis was best known for the fruit that grew abundantly in its Mediterranean climate—pears and peaches throughout the spring, oranges in summer, and apples in the fall. Workers spent the summer and fall planting, tending, and harvesting the fruit, then packed it in wooden boxes to be shipped on beds of ice throughout the Southwest.

On a warm June day in 1954 at the height of Operation Wetback, two immigration officers driving a company car stopped at the Earl Fruit Company, a small wooden building fronting Walnut Street in downtown Loomis. The men were dressed in the new "snappy forest-green uniforms" provided to INS officers, complete with black shoes and hard-brimmed Stetsons. Sam Browne belts were slung across their chests, and each had a pistol holstered at their hip. The officers walked inside and asked to see the manager. They wanted to know if there were any "wetbacks" employed there.

The manager said there were not. But the officers weren't satisfied. After they prodded, the manager admitted that the company employed a young man of Mexican descent named Joe Vigil. The officers insisted they speak with him. When Vigil appeared before them, one of the immigration officers "forcefully" grabbed Vigil's shoulder while keeping his other hand resting on his gun. He demanded in Spanish that Vigil show him some identification. When Vigil produced his draft card and social security card, the officer exploded in anger.

"That's no damn good, any damn wetback can get those cards," the officer barked. "I want to see your birth certificate."

Victor Mar, a foreman for the company, was watching. He had known Vigil for years—they were neighbors as well as coworkers. Disturbed, he stepped in to assure the officers that Vigil was a US citizen. But they ignored him, insisting that Vigil take them to his home where he claimed he had additional documents that could prove his citizenship. Worried, Mar came with them, and the men all arrived at Vigil's small, single-family home on a quiet residential street. Once they arrived, Vigil quickly found his birth certificate and certificate of baptism, both showing he had been born in the United States. Only then did the officers reluctantly let Vigil go back to work. The incident only came to light because Victor Mar wrote to his senators and US representative complaining that Vigil had been subject to the type of abuse "that no American citizen should have to stand for."[62]

Vigil was not the only US citizen caught up in Operation Wetback. Immigration officers engaged in raids and sweeps of workplaces, parks, and neighborhoods occupied by hundreds of people of Mexican descent. The assumption was that any person who appeared to have Mexican heritage was a noncitizen until he could prove otherwise. The Border Patrol delegated the task of apprehending undocumented immigrants to state and local officials, who had no training to assist them in separating out undocumented immigrants from legal immigrants and US citizens. Government officials even signed an agreement with an Indian tribe on a reservation north of Yuma, Arizona, agreeing to pay between $2.50 and $3.00 a head for any "wetback" on the reservation who was turned over to authorities, again with no screening to ensure that those detained were, in fact, undocumented immigrants. Only much later did officials acknowledge that at times they failed to determine the status of those they arrested, admitting it was likely that US citizens as well as legal immigrants to the United States had been inadvertently deported.[63]

In 1954, at the height of Operation Wetback, Emilia Castañeda helped bring her brother Francisco back to the United States. As her godmother had done for her, she tracked down his birth certificate and helped him obtain the paperwork he needed to prove his citizenship and cross the border. When he first arrived in the United States, he lived with Emilia and her family.

Early one morning shortly after he arrived, "U.S. immigration came pounding at the door," waking up the entire family. When Emilia's husband asked them what they wanted, they declared that the family "had an alien living with [them]," and they demanded to come in. Emilia's husband refused, and because the officers had no warrant they had to leave. Testifying about that moment before the California State Senate decades later, Emilia explained, "In Mexico, we were called *repatriados*. In the United States, we were called aliens." But Emilia and her brother fell into neither category. They were both native-born US citizens.[64]

Kamala Harris

CHAPTER 9

TWENTY-FIRST-CENTURY CITIZEN

O n October 10, 2008, the election that would decide whether Barack Obama or John McCain would be the next president of the United States was less than a month away. McCain was capping off a hectic week of campaigning with a Friday night rally at Lakeville South High School, a wealthy suburb of Minneapolis. The crowd of mostly white, elderly voters was restless, full of a nervous, angry energy. Everyone in the room knew that their preferred candidate was behind in the polls, and daily losing ground to Obama, the young, first-term African American senator who had only recently burst onto the political scene.[1]

Tensions were high when McCain passed the microphone to audience member Gayle Quinnell, a seventy-five-year-old McCain volunteer from Shakopee, Minnesota, wearing a bright-red "McCain-Palin" T-shirt. Quinnell got to her feet as she spoke. "I can't trust Obama," she told McCain plaintively as he stood just a few feet away, and then added what she assumed to be fact: "He's an Arab."[2]

McCain started shaking his head as she spoke, and he quickly took back the microphone. "No ma'am," he told her firmly. "He's a decent family man. A citizen." Quinnell looked puzzled as McCain publicly contradicted her, and she remained unconvinced. When reporters spoke to her after the event, she explained that Obama's father was a Muslim, and so "he's still got Muslim in him."[3]

Quinnell's assertion that Obama was an Arab and a Muslim was a harbinger of the "birther movement" that dogged Obama during the eight years he served as the first African American president of the United States. Birthers contend that Obama could not legally take office because he had been born outside the United States, and therefore was not "a natural born Citizen" as is constitutionally required to be president of the United States. Questions about Obama's birthplace and citizenship were often accompanied by rumors that he was a Muslim who had been educated at an Indonesian madrassa, and that he was an Arab—a grab bag of mistaken racial and religious attributions that had nothing to do with citizenship or eligibility for the presidency but instead seemed to boil down to this: Barack Obama was not a "real American."[4]

No evidence supported these claims. Early in his campaign, Obama released his "certificate of live birth," which stated that he was born on August 4, 1961, in the Kapiolani Maternity and Gynecological Hospital in Honolulu, Hawai'i (one of the fifty states that make up the United States of America). Countless relatives, classmates, neighbors, and teachers could attest that Obama was born in Hawai'i and had spent much of his childhood there. So, at first, the mainstream press made a joke of the matter, describing the birther claims as "nutty" and "goof[y]."[5]

Yet the rumors lived on. An initial lawsuit claiming Obama was not a citizen eligible to be president was quickly dismissed, but others soon followed. Although most political leaders disavowed the claims, a few supported them. US representative Nathan Deal, a Republican from Georgia who would later become that state's governor, publicly expressed doubts about Obama's citizenship and asked to see his birth certificate. Louisiana senator David Vitter, also a Republican, declared: "I support conservative legal organizations and others who would bring [a case challenging Obama's citizenship] to court."[6]

More than two years into Obama's presidency, just as the rumors appeared to be dying out, a reality television star named Donald Trump took up the cause. "Why doesn't he show his birth certificate?" Trump asked during a guest appearance on a morning television show in the spring of 2011. "Maybe it says he is a Muslim," Trump speculated on Fox News in March of that year—information that not only would have no place on a birth certificate but also has nothing to do with citizenship. Shortly after, Trump declared on NBC's *Today* show, "I'm starting to think that he was not born here." A *New York Times* poll showed that a quarter of all Americans, and 45 percent of Republicans, believed that Obama was born outside the United States. "All of a sudden, the media could only talk about Donald Trump and the president's birth certificate," one Obama advisor commented. "It was coming up in Obama's press interviews. It was becoming clear we had a problem."[7]

Obama had already weathered his fair share of political and personal attacks, but the claim that he was not born an American citizen—so ridiculous, so demonstrably untrue, and yet so persistent—seemed to gnaw at him. During an overnight stay in his Chicago home in 2011, Obama took the time from his busy schedule to search through boxes of his possessions to look for further proof of the location of his birth. He subsequently directed his personal lawyers to apply for a waiver under Hawaiian law to obtain his official long-form birth certificate and then chose to appear at a press conference announcing its release.[8]

On April 27, 2011, in what the *New York Times* described as "dramatic television," Obama strode into the White House briefing room and took the podium. The major television networks broke from their scheduled programming to broadcast the scene live. Obama began by saying he "[has] watched with bemusement" and then had "been puzzled" as the rumors swirling around his citizenship status "just kept on going." By releasing his long-form birth certificate, he hoped to convince the "vast majority of the American people, as well as the press" that he was a citizen at birth eligible to be president. Alluding to Trump without naming him, he implored Americans not to be "distracted" by "side shows and carnival barkers." America will not be able to solve its serious problems, Obama admonished, if we "just make stuff up and pretend that facts are not facts," adding that the nation does "not have time for this kind of silliness."[9]

And yet, apparently, it did. In January 2016, near the end of Obama's eight years as president, 52 percent of Americans, including 71 percent of registered Republicans, stated that they were not convinced that Barack Obama had been born in the United States.[10]

As Obama's struggle to prove his citizenship shows, citizenship stripping lives on in the twenty-first century, albeit at times altered by changing technologies, new legal processes, and modified norms. Obama's effort to defend his citizenship is reminiscent of the battle to seat Hiram Revels as the first black member of Congress in 1870 and Ruth Bryan Owen as the first woman representative from the American South in the US House of Representatives in 1928. Although attacks on Obama's citizenship originated in the "nether regions of the internet" rather than in the halls of Congress, the impetus to challenge his legitimacy was the same.[11]

The birther movement mostly took place in the private sphere, but citizenship stripping in the twenty-first century is also enshrined in federal laws, regulations, and policies that enable government officials to revoke citizenship—either by taking away that status or by making it very difficult to prove it to officials' satisfaction. As in the past, these laws and policies bring with them significant consequences for their targets, undermining their right to vote along with many of the other rights of full membership in the society, including the most important right of all: to enter and remain in the United States of America. Whatever form it takes, citizenship stripping in the twenty-first century, as in the preceding years, has symbolic as well as legal consequences. For it implicitly declares to all those affected, "*you* are not American."

By half past nine in the morning on August 24, 2009, the line of traffic to cross the "Old Bridge" from Matamoros, Mexico, to Brownsville, Texas, snaked down the highway, the heat shimmering around the stalled traffic. Three generations of the Castro family occupied one of the cars, the air conditioning running at full blast as they waited their turn to present their documents to US Customs and Border Patrol officials and cross into the United States. It was a familiar trip for Trinidad Castro and her two daughters, twenty-nine-year-old Laura and twenty-five-year-old Yuliana. But this time they brought the family's newest member, Yuliana's four-week-old daughter Camila Abigail, strapped in a car seat in the back.[12]

Crossing the US–Mexico southern border is a weekly, sometimes daily, activity for many of those living in the "Borderlands," as the swath of land on either side of the Rio Grande River is known. More often than not, family, job, school, friends, and home are scattered on either side of that line, a magnetic force pulling the Borderlands' residents back and forth across it on a regular basis.

Before the Treaty of Guadalupe Hidalgo ended the Mexican-American War in 1848, there was no international border along the Rio Grande River. "We didn't cross the border, the border crossed us," immigrants' rights activists liked to say. Even after the territory north of the Rio Grande officially became the United States, the line marking the frontier between the two nations was more theoretical than real. For decades, there was no wall, no uniformed men, not even a marker to stop those on one side of that line from crossing to the other.[13]

By the time the Castros were crossing, in August 2009, all that had changed. A twenty-foot slatted steel fence lined with a tangle of barbed wire ran along hundreds of miles of the Texas–Mexico border. No one, whatever their nationality, was permitted to enter the United States outside of the official ports of entry, such as the one at the Old Bridge near Brownsville, Texas, that the Castro family waited to cross that morning.

Crossing that line had recently gotten harder. Up until 2009, to enter the United States from Mexico, an American citizen need do nothing more than show a birth certificate or a US driver's license. Even a baptismal certificate from an American church would do. But that year a new law went into effect requiring that US citizens show their passports or an "Enhanced Driver's

License" containing biographic and biometric data to prove their citizenship when crossing the border.[14]

The Castro family were as prepared as they could be. Laura, Yuliana, and Yuliana's daughter Camila, had all been born in Texas, making them US citizens at birth. Laura had already applied for and received her US passport, which she had ready to show border officials. Yuliana had applied but had yet to receive hers, so she had brought her Texas birth certificate, a picture ID, and proof that her passport application was pending, in compliance with government policy for those awaiting passports. She also brought her daughter's birth certificate. Although Yuliana and Laura's mother was not a US citizen, she had a visa permitting entry into the United States. These documents had always been sufficient to permit the family to enter the country in the past.[15]

But not this time. The US Customs and Border Patrol official who examined their paperwork noted that Yuliana's birth certificate had been signed by Trinidad Saldivar, a midwife who had assisted at the births of thousands of babies on either side of the border. Although the Castro family had no way to know it, Saldivar's name had been added to the US government's list of "suspect birth attendants"—a list of about 250 doctors, midwives, nurses, and other health practitioners who the government believed had lied about the birth location of at least some of the babies they had assisted in bringing into the world. Starting in 2008, the US government took the position that anyone born near the southern border and outside an institutional setting—and in particular, anyone whose birth certificate was signed by a person on the government's "suspect birth attendant" list—would have to produce additional documentation to prove their citizenship.[16]

The government's policy stemmed from admissions of fraud by some midwives, a few of whom had been convicted of signing US birth certificates for babies born in Mexico. But these same midwives had also signed birth certificates of thousands of babies who were legitimately born in the United States. And many on the government's suspect birth attendants list, apparently including Trinidad Saldivar, had neither confessed nor been convicted of signing fraudulent birth certificates. Exactly who is on that list, or why their names appear, is unknown to anyone outside of the US government. In any case, the government now questions the birth certificates of *anyone* born outside an institutional setting and near the border, regardless of whether the birth attendant involved was suspected of fraud. "Normally, a birth certificate is sufficient to prove citizenship," a US State Department spokesperson explained, "but because of a history of fraudulently filed [birth certificates] on the Southwest border, we don't have much faith in the (midwife-granted) document."[17]

Births outside of hospitals and with the aid of lay midwives, known as *parteras*, was and is common in Brownsville and the surrounding area. The approximately 1.3 million people who live in the four rural counties that make up the Rio Grande Valley in Texas are mostly poor and without health insurance, and there are few hospitals serving the area. In an environment where few could afford a hospital birth, or even be confident they could reach a hospital in time to give birth there, a trusted *partera* was a sensible alternative.

The exact number of Americans denied passports or barred from entering the United States on these grounds is unknown, but it surely rises into the tens of thousands. A single attorney working on the issue near the border estimates that over the past ten years he has handled two hundred lawsuits and advised about a thousand more people seeking to prove their citizenship after the State Department rejected their birth certificates.[18]

For the Castro family, the red flag raised by *partera* Saldivar's signature on Yuliana's birth certificate triggered a cascade of events that affected the family for months to come. The Castros were pulled from the line of traffic and diverted to secondary inspection. The three women were then questioned for ten hours while baby Camila screamed as only a newborn can. At the end of their ordeal, border officials seized all their documentation and refused them entry into the United States. As far as the US Border and Customs officials were concerned, none of the Castros were American citizens entitled to enter the United States.[19]

Those, like the Castros, who are denied entry into the United States or renewals of their passports have few options. The individual bears the burden of proving their own citizenship. The problem is how to do that when the primary proof of birth location, and thus citizenship, is the same official birth certificate that the federal government has deemed unreliable. Those trying to prove their citizenship to the government's satisfaction have scrambled to gather medical records, school transcripts, and even pages from the family Bible noting the date and place of their birth—all evidence that a State Department website suggests can support their claim to citizenship. But what is the citizen to do when such documents are expensive to purchase or impossible to find? And why is a handwritten date and place of birth in a family's Bible or a certificate of attendance from a primary school considered more reliable evidence of US citizenship than the state-issued birth certificate that the government has already rejected? Government officials will not answer such questions.[20]

Many months later, and with the help of family and friends in the United States, the Castros ultimately succeeded in proving their citizenship and were allowed to enter the United States. Unknown is the number who could not do so.[21]

In previous eras, government laws and policies explicitly revoked citizenship. In the twenty-first century, citizenship is most often jeopardized by laws and policies that make proving citizen status next to impossible for those who lack access to the reams of paperwork that have become part and parcel of modern life. Keeping track of birth certificates, parents' birth and residence records, social security numbers, and school documents—all of which can be vital to demonstrating US citizenship—is difficult for those without a stable address or the money and resources to obtain copies of these records from official sources. Locating legal documentation of one's very existence is as much evidence of social status and wealth as of citizenship. It seems that in the twenty-first century, US citizenship is only secure for those who can afford to prove it.

The modern-day inspection of documents is a throwback to the visual inspection of "appearances and bodies" that governed citizenship determination in the era before passports and other identity documents became the norm. In the nineteenth century, steamship passengers' race, ethnicity, hair style, clothing, and accent were all weighed when determining whether they were citizens entitled to admission or aliens to be barred. As one historian explained, the "body was held to provide something close to absolute evidence of an individual's true identity," and officials charged with policing the nation's borders "assum[ed] that a citizen would be easily recognizable as such" from appearance alone.[22]

At the turn of the twentieth century, native-born citizens of Chinese descent such as Wong Kim Ark underwent a version of that same scrutiny. Several years after the Supreme Court ruled in his favor, establishing that he, along with everyone else born in the United States, was a birthright citizen under the Fourteenth Amendment, Wong was arrested in the borderlands of Texas and detained until, once again, he could prove his US citizenship to officials' satisfaction. His children went through a rigorous screening process as well, and his eldest son was imprisoned on Angel Island and then forced to leave the United States after failing to convince immigration officials that Wong was his father. The Wong family's very appearance, it seems, rendered them presumptively un-American.

Starting at the end of the twentieth century, official documents such as passports and birth certificates replaced border officials' visual inspection. No longer could immigration officials reject all those they deemed to appear "foreign." Today, however, the skeptical inspection of the would-be American's physical appearance has been replaced by a sometimes equally skeptical inspection of that person's documents—often influenced as much by the individual's race and ethnicity as it was in the nineteenth century. For surely it is no coincidence that government policies presumptively finding birth certificates insufficient evidence of birth in the United States are primarily applied to those living near the nation's border—a population that is nearly 90 percent Hispanic. (It is hard to imagine the federal government questioning the citizenship of millions of residents of upstate New York because some midwives signed fraudulent birth certificates for babies born in Canada.) Nor can it be mere happenstance that the vast majority of Americans who are mistakenly detained and at times even deported from the United States are not white.[23]

In the summer of 2019, Francisco Erwin Galicia, a rising high school senior, was on his way to a soccer tryout with friends when his car was stopped at a Border Patrol checkpoint in the town of Falfurrias, Texas. Immigration officials have the legal right to stop and search anyone within one hundred miles of the US border, even if they have no reason to suspect an immigration violation or other crime. About two-thirds of the US population live within that zone. So, even though Galicia was ninety miles from the southern border, he was nonetheless required to prove his citizenship.

Galicia, who was born in Dallas, Texas, showed officials his Texas birth certificate, Texas ID card, and his social security card—documents that, like many of the Borderlands' residents, he carried with him at all times for just this reason. But officials insisted the documents were fake and arrested him. Because of further confusion over documentation—in part because Galicia's mother had once mistakenly applied for a US tourist ID card on his behalf so that he could cross the border to visit relatives in Mexico—Galicia was held in immigration detention for a month before being released.[24]

Mark Lyttle was also nowhere near the border when he first came to the attention of the Immigration and Customs Enforcement (ICE). He was living in North Carolina when he was convicted of a misdemeanor and sentenced to one hundred days in prison. A clerk at the Goldsboro, North Carolina, correctional facility mistakenly recorded his place of birth as "Mexico" and his citizenship status as "alien." Bizarrely, an ICE officer conducting a subsequent interview concluded that "Mark Lyttle" was an alias and that his real name was "Jose Thomas." Although Lyttle apparently informed ICE that his mother's name was Mary and she was a US citizen, an ICE official later scratched out his answers and claimed his mother was "Maria" and was a non-citizen. At times, Lyttle gave confusing and conflicting information about his background, compounding these errors. ICE officers were aware that Lyttle suffered from mental illness and had obvious cognitive deficiencies, which should have given them pause. But Lyttle, like all presumed noncitizens, had no right to government-provided counsel to defend him, even after he insisted that he was a US citizen.

At the end of his criminal sentence, Lyttle was ordered deported. He was flown in shackles to Hidalgo, Texas, where he was forced to walk across the international bridge from Texas to Reynosa, Mexico, wearing his prison-issued green jumpsuit with only three dollars in his pocket. Lyttle spent months living on the streets and eating out of trash cans before he finally made contact with his family in the United States, who convinced officials to allow him to return.[25]

Mark Lyttle was a US citizen, born and raised in North Carolina. He did not speak Spanish, had never been to Mexico, and his English was, in the words of one observer, "indelibly local." ICE had access to fingerprints and other biometric records taken from Lyttle's previous arrests that confirmed he was a US citizen. Yet at every turn, government officials disregarded the copious evidence of his US citizenship. Why? One reporter noted that "Lyttle is brown-skinned," and speculated that his skin tone alone appears to have undermined the significant evidence of his citizenship in the eyes of immigration officials assigned his case.[26]

Errors will occasionally occur even in well-functioning administrative systems. But Galicia's and Lyttle's experiences are not one-offs or random mistakes. Political scientist Jacqueline Stevens, who has closely studied the issue, estimates that at any time about 1 percent of the population held in detention by Immigration and Customs Enforcement are US citizens—the vast majority nonwhite. That amounts to approximately three thousand Americans mistakenly detained by immigration officials every year, an unknown number of whom are deported, never to return.[27]

Proving citizenship can also pose an obstacle to exercising one of the most fundamental rights of citizenship in the twenty-first century: the right to vote. Today, all citizens over the age of eighteen have a constitutional right to vote, save a controversial exception for convicted felons in some states. In contrast, noncitizens are barred from voting in almost every election—federal, state, or local—and are subject to harsh criminal penalties for doing so. Once again, however, the key to accessing citizenship rights is not only being a citizen, but also proving it.[28]

Jo French was born at home in Arkansas in 1941, and later moved to Kansas. When she tried to register to vote in advance of the 2014 Kansas elections, she was blocked by a new law, known as the "Secure and Fair Elections Act" (SAFE Act), which required would-be voters to prove their citizenship before registering to vote.

Enacted in 2013, the SAFE Act was the brainchild of then Kansas secretary of state Kris Kobach, who claimed the law would prevent noncitizens from intentionally or accidentally gaining access to the ballot. Voters could no longer rely on their Kansas driver's license and personal attestations of citizenship, and instead had to produce a birth certificate, passport, or some other documentary proof of that status—documents that many Americans do not possess. In the words of the president of the Kansas League of Women Voters, the new law "creat[ed] barriers to the vote" for all citizens, forcing them to navigate a "complex network of hoops and jumps" before they could register to vote in their state. By 2016, over thirty-one thousand people were barred from registering because they lacked evidence of their US citizenship.[29]

French was one of them. Although she was determined to vote, the path was not easy. To prove her citizenship, French produced her family's Bible recording her birth date, her baptismal records, and a high school transcript. She then had to drive forty miles to a hearing before the State Election Board, which lasted over thirty minutes. She was seventy-five years old and had health issues that made driving long distances difficult, so she enlisted a friend to take her to the hearing and back. Ultimately, she succeeded, though from start to finish the process of registering to vote took more than five months. And French was one of the lucky ones. Others in her situation were unable to locate and pay for the required documents or take the time off work required to prove their citizenship.[30]

The SAFE Act was premised on Kobach's oft-repeated claim that "voter fraud is a national problem." But at a 2016 trial challenging the law, Kobach could provide little evidence to support it. After six days of testimony, a federal district court judge struck down the SAFE Act as violating both the US Constitution and federal law, finding that the burden it placed on voters was unacceptably high, especially considering that the problem it was designed to fix was nonexistent. The judge found that between 1999 and 2013, only thirty-nine noncitizens were mistakenly registered to vote in Kansas, and most of those registrations were the result of "administrative error, confusion or mistake," and not intentional fraud.[31]

Remarkably, despite her ordeal, French supported the law. Kobach called her as a witness at the trial. Yet her testimony weakened Kobach's case further when she admitted that the length and the difficulty of the process troubled her, as did the government's initial refusal to credit her claim to citizenship. "I was hurt that no one believed me that I was an American citizen," she said, adding later, "I just couldn't imagine having to go through this procedure to prove I live here and I can vote." And she told one reporter she thought it "was strange that I had to go through this procedure to be able to vote. . . . I don't look funny. I don't talk funny, I've been here all my life." French seemed to subconsciously equate citizenship with accent and appearance—both legally irrelevant to citizenship, and yet still powerful markers of that status for many.[32]

Citizenship stripping in the twenty-first century at times has resurrected battles thought long won and over.

In 1909, the government denaturalized the infamous anarchist Emma Goldman because it wanted, in the words of a government official, to "deprive [her] of that feeling of security" that comes from "believing herself to be a citizen of the United States." Goldman's denaturalization was the first of many politically based denaturalizations to follow—a precursor to the massive denaturalization campaign intended to undermine the "feeling of security" of millions of other naturalized Americans.

Some of the targets were less sympathetic than others. Fritz Kuhn, leader of the German American Bund, lost his citizenship and was deported to Germany after spewing hatred toward Jews and declaring that his German *blut* trumped his US citizenship. But once the government got a taste for the power to choose its citizenry, it widened its net, targeting politically troublesome Communist sympathizers, among them successful labor leaders such as Harry Bridges and gadfly journalists like Paul Novick. The government argued that the men's recent activities and affiliation with the Communist Party suggested they lacked the requisite "attachment" to the US Constitution at the time of their naturalization—a claim that chilled all naturalized citizens from engaging in speech and conduct that would bring them to the attention of their government.

In 1967, the US Supreme Court finally put an end to the government's aggressive denaturalization campaign in *Afroyim v. Rusk*, declaring that the Fourteenth Amendment guarantees every American citizen, whether by birth or naturalization, "a constitutional right to remain a citizen." The court explained that the "very nature of our free government makes it completely incongruous to have a rule of law under which a group of citizens temporarily in office can deprive another group of citizens of their citizenship."

For the next fifty years, the government denaturalized no more than a handful of people each year, typically those who had committed significant human rights violations and then had lied about it to obtain citizenship. As a leading scholar of the history of denaturalization in the United States explained, "Citizenship had moved from an era when it was provisional, qualified, and unsecure to one in which it was nearly unconditionally guaranteed."[33]

That is, until today.

On April 2, 2019, Parvez Khan arrived at the federal courthouse in Jackson-
ville, Florida, with Betty Louise, his wife of twenty years. Khan, a sixty-two-
year-old bus driver from Branford, Florida, wore a gray jacket over dark
pants—not quite a suit, but perhaps as close as his wardrobe allowed. Despite
a middle-aged bulge and the start of a bald patch, he gave the impression of
youthful optimism, smiling often and greeting his attorneys cheerfully. The
group had arrived early, so Khan and his wife sat side by side on a bench outside the courtroom.

Parvez Khan is the first person to go to trial under "Operation Janus," the
name of the Trump administration's mass denaturalization campaign. Janus,
the Roman god charged with overseeing life's transitions, is typically depicted
with two heads, one facing forward and the other backward, to symbolize
how the past inevitably affects the future. He is an appropriate namesake for a
government campaign that will review the records of hundreds of thousands
of naturalized American citizens, many of whom, like Khan, have been US
citizens for over a decade. Although prosecution for all but the most serious
crimes is constrained by a statute of limitations, there is no such limit on revoking citizenship through denaturalization. For all of these Americans, even
minor problems or errors long in their past may now upend their lives and
radically alter their futures.

Operation Janus began under the Obama administration after the government realized that it had failed to upload fingerprints from immigration
records in the early 1990s to its centralized database. The mistake allowed
some individuals to naturalize even though they had been ordered deported
under a different name. But the Obama administration proceeded with cau-
tion, instructing officials only to denaturalize those who appeared to pose a
danger to the United States. After the Trump administration took over, however, the program grew exponentially. In 2018, the US Citizenship and Immigration Services announced that it was opening a new office in Los Angeles,
to be staffed by dozens of attorneys and analysts, devoted to investigating the
files of over seven hundred thousand naturalized American citizens. Later
that same year, the Department of Homeland Security requested $207.6 mil-
lion to fund these investigations, and announced it expected to refer 1,600
cases to the Department of Justice for denaturalization proceedings over the
next few years. In February 2020, the Department of Justice created a new section dedicated entirely to prosecuting such cases.[34]

These numbers were a sharp break from the norms that had developed
over the past fifty years against denaturalization—norms that grew out of the
Supreme Court's decision in *Afroyim v. Rusk* striking down as unconstitutional the government's aggressive use of denaturalization to target labor lead-

ers and other activists. In light of *Afroyim*, does the Constitution allow the government to denaturalize thousands of citizens?

According to the government, it does. Although *Afroyim v. Rusk* barred the federal government from denaturalizing citizens on the basis of their speech, conduct, and political affiliations, the court noted that naturalized citizens could still lose their citizenship for fraud or error in the naturalization process. That exception makes sense. After all, if a war criminal lies about his past to gain admission to the United States, the government must have the power to take back fraudulently conferred citizenship.

But the government now reads the fraud or error exception broadly, allowing it to take away citizenship for almost *any* error in the naturalization process, even a minor and inadvertent one, and even if the error comes to light decades after the naturalized citizen received citizenship. The process of seeking a green card and then citizenship is long and convoluted, and the difficulties are compounded by cultural and linguistic confusion. In 2017, a government attorney argued before the US Supreme Court that a naturalized citizen could lose his citizenship for failing to note on his naturalization application that he had once driven over the speed limit, or parked illegally, even if he never received a ticket or fine for doing so. With that as the standard, it is hard to imagine going through the multi-year process of obtaining a green card and then citizenship *without* making some mistakes along the way.[35]

Baljinder Singh may have lost his citizenship for just such a minor error. He arrived in the United States as a teenager from India. But the government recorded his first name as "Davinder" and not "Baljinder," perhaps due to an interpreter's error. Singh then failed to update his address after being released from immigration custody to an adult guardian, so he failed to get notice or show up at an immigration hearing under the mis-recorded name. As a result, unbeknownst to him, he was ordered deported in absentia. In the meantime, Singh followed all the steps required to become a citizen: He immediately applied for asylum, eventually married a US citizen, obtained his green card and then his citizenship. Singh has lived in the United States for over half his life and had been a citizen for more than ten years. The government never claimed he posed a national security risk or had a criminal record. Yet because of the initial error regarding his paperwork, in January 2018 he became the first American stripped of his citizenship under Operation Janus.[36]

Shortly after 9 a.m., the government calls Parvez Khan as its first witness. He is sworn in, then leans forward in the witness chair, hands clasped in front of him, seemingly eager to answer the government attorney's questions. His testimony quickly reveals what everyone in the room already knows. Khan arrived in Los Angeles, California, in December 1991 on a flight from Pakistan, and sought admission to the United States using a false passport and visa that he had purchased because he was unable to obtain a visa to enter the United States under his own name. He was detained for a month, then released and went to stay with his brother, Suhail Khan, a legal immigrant living in Florida.

Khan testified that he assumed when the authorities released him from detention that the problems with his initial illegal entry were resolved. Khan spoke little English at the time, and the government did not provide him with an Urdu interpreter, so he did not understand much of the process that led to his detention and subsequent release. Khan also never received the follow-up notices the government mailed to his lawyer, and never learned that he had been ordered deported by an immigration judge. He then married Betty Louise, a US citizen, and eventually obtained a green card and then naturalized, assuming he was legally entitled to become an American citizen. Like the other targets of Operation Janus, the government had not flagged the issue when he filed his naturalization papers because it had failed to upload his fingerprints into a central database that it uses to check naturalization applicants against those ordered deported.

Khan is no saint, and his illegal entry into the United States under a falsified visa was a serious immigration violation. But if it had it been raised earlier, Khan could have applied for a waiver that may have permitted him to remain in the United States and naturalize despite the initial illegal entry. Khan has lived in the United States for nearly three decades, more than ten as a citizen, and he has a US citizen wife and son. He has no criminal convictions, and the government makes no claim that he poses a national security risk. So it is hard to understand why three government lawyers have gathered in a federal courthouse at a cost of tens of thousands of dollars to take away his citizenship and, presumably, to deport him from the United States.

The government's aggressive mass denaturalization campaign undermines the security of *all* of the United States' naturalized citizens, not just the named targets in denaturalization cases. As journalist Masha Gessen explained, Operation Janus "itself is undoing the naturalization of more than twenty million naturalized citizens in the American population by taking away their assumption of permanence." Gessen, who grew up in the Soviet Union and is a naturalized US citizen, was drawing from her own experience when she explained how fear of imprisonment or deportation can chill speech and conduct. She concluded, "All of them—all of us—are second-class citizens now."37

Khan's brother discovered that new reality firsthand when he testified for his brother at the denaturalization trial. When it was the government's turn to cross-examine Suhail, the attorney did not ask about Parvez Khan. Instead, he began by questioning *Suhail's* citizenship status, asking when and how Suhail had obtained his green card and his citizenship, and strongly implying that he had committed marriage fraud.

Parvez Khan's attorney interrupted, rising from his seat as he spoke. "Your honor, I'm going to have to register a strong objection to this whole line of questioning . . . [about] his immigration record," he told the judge. "I think it's totally intimidating to try to scare the witness from saying anything." But the government attorney pleaded for "leeway," explaining his questions went to the witness's credibility, and the judge allowed it.

By testifying on behalf of his brother, Suhail Khan had brought himself to the attention of the US government. Now his citizenship is at risk as well.[38]

The history of citizenship stripping in the United States is the story of a nation struggling with its own identity. Is it the society that the Declaration of Independence proclaimed it would be, treating all as created equal and giving the people the power to choose their government, rather than letting the government choose its people? Does it welcome immigrants and integrate them and their children, as the Statue of Liberty's upraised arm suggests? Did it shed its reliance on race and caste with the adoption of the Fourteenth Amendment's guarantee of citizenship and equality for all born or naturalized in the United States, as the framers of that amendment intended?

Or, in the words of Joseph Kurihara, is it a nation in which "democracy [is only] . . . for the white people?" Does it continue to view some born in the United States as mere "technical citizens," as was the case for Wong Kim Ark and his children, who were deprived of the right to enter and remain in the United States at the whim of immigration officials? Does it see its naturalized citizens as conditional members of the society, at perpetual risk of being targeted for denaturalization and removal for their speech or conduct, as Harry Bridges and Emma Goldman had been?

The history of citizenship stripping reveals that the United States is both nations at once. On the one hand, the country has embraced immigrants and their families, welcoming more foreigners to its shores than any other nation and adopting laws allowing easy access to citizenship—at first, only for whites, but since 1952, citizenship has been available by law on equal terms for all races. The United States considers equality, free speech, and tolerance of difference to be among its founding values, and these ideals are prominently enshrined in its constitutional commitments. On the other hand, the United States has often second-guessed those same choices, as illustrated by the stories in this book. After extending citizenship broadly, the nation at times tried to snatch it back from individuals and groups who appeared something other than "real Americans" on account of race, ethnicity, religion, political orientation, or choice of marriage partner. Citizenship stripping exemplifies the bundle of contradictions that is the United States of America.[39]

The decision to revoke or deny citizenship sends a more powerful and pointed message even than the laws and policies governing immigration and the acquisition of US citizenship. The significance of the choice to cast a citizen out is at least as great as the decision to allow a noncitizen in. The loss of all the rights and privileges of citizenship, as well as what Emma Goldman described as "the assurance of having some spot you can call your own," was often devastating to those who had assumed that they were secure in their citizenship and their home. And for the nation as a whole, the act of "casting out" carries important symbolic value, defining not just those who are excluded but also all who are allowed to remain.

Citizenship stripping in the United States has often paralleled the nation's history of racism and xenophobia, sometimes serving as a proxy for overt discrimination on those same grounds. Although the law has long prohibited de jure discrimination on the basis of race, ethnicity, or national origin, it is legally permissible to deny many rights and privileges to noncitizens.

When the United States wanted to rid itself of persons of Chinese descent in the late nineteenth century, it barred Chinese immigrants from entering. But its only means of preventing native-born Americans like Wong Kim Ark from returning to the United States was to try to convince the Supreme Court that they were not Americans either. In 1907, Congress disapproved of women who chose to marry foreigners, and so it expelled from the citizenry those women who did so. At the height of the Great Depression, state and local officials coerced or forced families of Hispanic descent to leave the country because they viewed them as a drain on social services. But they could only accomplish that goal by coercing the removal of families containing US citizens, assuming correctly that it would be difficult to impossible for many of those citizens to return. During World War II, the United States wanted to expel Japanese Americans, or better yet trade them for white Americans held as prisoners of war in Japan, but that required first taking away their citizenship so that they legally became the "other" the nation had always considered them to be. And during the Red Scare, the government used affiliation with the Communist Party as a basis for denaturalizing journalists and labor leaders as a means to silence disfavored speech and protest.

Revoking citizenship has its roots in the oldest American contradiction of all: a nation founded on freedom, liberty, and equality that at the same time permitted slavery. Free blacks occupied a dangerous space in the antebellum United States, their very presence undermining racialized justifications for slavery. That some black people could exercise all the rights of US citizenship—freedom of movement, property ownership, the right to vote and serve in government—was impossible to reconcile with the racist justifications for treating other blacks as property. Chief Justice Taney's opinion in *Dred Scott v. Sandford* denied the citizenship of free blacks in an attempt to reconcile the "utter and flagrant inconsisten[cy]," as he put it, of a nation that declared all men are equal even as it treated four million of them as property. Seeking to eliminate that dissonance, Taney concluded that free blacks were noncitizens with "no rights which the white man was bound to respect." He assumed that the elimination of citizenship of all blacks would further justify the enslavement of most. In the end, that decision helped precipitate the Civil War, the end of slavery, and the addition of birthright citizenship to the US Constitution—putting in words, if not always in action, the conception of a nation in which everyone born or naturalized had equal citizenship status.

And yet, in the twenty-first century, even birthright citizenship remains insecure, at least for some.

Two and a half years into his presidency, in the middle of a slow news week, President Trump announced that his administration was "seriously" looking at the possibility of ending birthright citizenship for the children of immigrants. "You walk over the border, have a baby—congratulations, the baby is now a U.S. citizen. . . . It's frankly ridiculous," Trump told a gaggle of reporters gathered outside the White House on August 21, 2019. His comments echoed those made in October 2018, when he declared that he believed he could end the "crazy, lunatic" policy of birthright citizenship unilaterally, through an executive order, and were similar to claims made during his campaign for president. Trump had already tried to rescind President Obama's efforts to grant some measure of security to the "Dreamers"—the eight hundred thousand people who had been brought to the United States by their parents as children, and who were sociologically but not legally Americans. Now, President Trump suggested he had the unilateral power to impose the illegal status of the parents on their children.[40] In August 2020, Trump took that argument a step further by questioning the citizenship of Senator Kamala Harris, the Democratic vice presidential nominee. Senator Harris had been born in the United States to *legal* immigrants. Apparently, Trump now embraced the baseless legal theory that birth on US soil did not convey citizenship unless the parents were not only legally in the country but were also permanent residents of the United States.[41]

Trump's arguments were reminiscent of those made over one hundred years ago by Solicitor General Holmes Conrad, who argued before the US Supreme Court in *United States v. Wong Kim Ark* that the Fourteenth Amendment's birthright citizenship guarantee did not apply to children born to Chinese immigrants living in the United States. That amendment declares that "all persons born or naturalized in the United States, and subject to the jurisdiction thereof, are citizens of the United States." In 1897, Conrad argued that the children of Chinese immigrants were not "subject to the jurisdiction" of the United States because children and parents of Chinese ancestry owed their allegiance to the emperor of China.[42]

The Supreme Court flatly rejected that idea, holding that the qualifying language of "subject to the jurisdiction thereof" was intended to exclude only members of Indian tribes living on reservations, children of diplomatic representatives, and children of a foreign military occupation—long-standing exceptions to the common law rule of birthright citizenship. In all those cases, the parents (and thus their children) were *not* within the full jurisdiction of the United States because they were not subject to the full range of civil and legal sanctions that could be imposed on all other residents. This put them in marked contrast to the children of aliens—whether legal immigrants, such as Wong's parents, or immigrants who had entered or remained in the United States without permission, as is true for millions of people in the United States today—all of whom are subject to all federal and state laws. For that reason, the Supreme Court held in *Wong Kim Ark* that the "fourteenth amendment affirms the ancient and fundamental rule of citizenship by birth within the territory"—whatever the race, religion, or immigration status of that child's parents.[43]

Nonetheless, in 2019, President Trump and a few of his supporters latched onto the same argument that failed for Solicitor General Conrad, arguing that the children of undocumented immigrants were not "subject to the jurisdiction" of the United States automatically covered by the Fourteenth Amendment's citizenship guarantee. Also like Conrad, President Trump and the other proponents of this argument did not acknowledge the enormous ramifications of such a change in law and policy.

Eliminating birthright citizenship for the children of undocumented immigrants would create a perpetual, hereditary caste of "un-Americans"—men, women, and children who would live and work in the United States without legal status and always in fear of deportation. As of this writing, in 2020, approximately eleven million undocumented immigrants reside in the United States. If every child with one undocumented parent—and by extension, all future generations of those families—are not US citizens, then overnight the number of undocumented would increase by over four million. By 2050, it would balloon to twenty-four million. All of the problems that accompany undocumented immigrants—from depressed wages to unsafe working conditions to fear of reporting domestic violence, theft, and corruption—would be magnified with the birth of each "illegal child." And proving citizenship would be harder than ever, requiring proof not only of location of birth, but also of the immigration status of one's parents. The burden would likely be borne by those of Hispanic descent, who would be presumptively viewed as noncitizens until they could show that their parents, perhaps even their grandparents or great-grandparents, were legally present in the United States. That single change in the law would recreate a nation divided by "caste" and governed by "oligarchy of the skin"—the very wrongs that, as Senator Charles Sumner explained over 150 years ago, the Fourteenth Amendment was designed to end.[44]

Perhaps those who seek to strip birthright citizenship from the children of undocumented immigrants do not consider the consequences because the rhetoric matters more than the reality. They know it's unlikely that the US Supreme Court will reverse its century-old decision in *Wong Kim Ark*, ignoring both the letter and the spirit of the Fourteenth Amendment to do so. They seek not to change the law, but send a message—the same message conveyed to Dred and Harriet Scott and Hiram Revels, to Wong Kim Ark and his children, to Ethel Mackenzie and Ruth Bryan Owen, to Joseph Kurihara and his fellow Japanese Americans imprisoned during World War II, to Emma Goldman and Harry Bridges, and to forced "*repatriados*" such as Emilia Castañeda and Ignacio Peña, among millions of others. *You are not us*, they are telling those children; *you are not American*. And whatever the law says now, you never will be.

ACKNOWLEDGMENTS

It is customary to thank one's spouse at the *end* of a book's acknowledgments, but I am going to begin by thanking my husband because he was essential to every aspect of the process. He was the first reader of every word, listened patiently as I agonized over every narrative choice, and shouldered more than his share of household chores and childcare at key moments in the process—particularly when the book came due just as we were locked in an apartment in France during a global pandemic. And somehow he kept his sense of humor through it all, for which I'm especially grateful.

I am also grateful to the institutions that provided financial support as I researched and wrote the book. American University provided both summer research grants and research leave that enabled me to do the bulk of my research, and I was lucky to receive generous fellowships from the American Council of Learned Societies and the Collegium de Lyon to support me while I completed the writing.

Also essential in every way was my brilliant agent, Jessica Papin. I hope to benefit from her wise counsel for many years to come. Helene Atwan, my editor at Beacon Press, improved the manuscript enormously, and she and the entire Beacon Press team were a pleasure to work with from start to finish. I am very lucky that my book is in their capable hands.

I am indebted to the many accomplished scholars who generously took time from their busy schedules to shares sources, answer questions, or read portions of the book. I am particularly thankful to Candice Bredbenner, Robert Cherny, Garrett Epps, Mark Graber, Kevin Johnson, John Reeves, Rachel Rosenbloom, Lucy Salyer, Julie Soo, Peter Spiro, Eileen Tamura, Lee Terán, Lea Vander Velde, and Hanako Wakatsuki for their careful review of chapters of this book. I am grateful as well to Peter Afrasiabi, Raymond Balderrama, Bethany Berger, Patricia Biggs, Linda Bosniak, Joseph Dunn, Anne Galiski, Ruth Ann (Abels) Hager, Aziz Huq, Andrew Kent, Barbara Takei, Christine Valenciana, Charles Wollenberg, Sandra Wong, and Judy Yung, who provided helpful information through telephone conversations, interviews, and email exchanges. I received valuable feedback at an early stage of this project from scholars at the 2018 European University Institute's GobalCit Annual Conference and at the 2018 ImmProf Conference, and from my fabulous colleagues at the Collegium de Lyon. In particular, I am thankful to Professors Hervé Joly and Marie-Laure Basilien-Gainche for providing the supportive and enriching environment I needed to finish this book while living with my family in Lyon. Finally, I am very grateful to Dick Fallon, Gerry Neuman, and Alex Tsesis, who, when this book was nothing more than a page-long proposal, were extraordinarily generous with their assistance.

This book tells the story of citizenship stripping over more than 150 years of US history though the voices of those affected, so it required many hours of archival research. American University librarians William Ryan, Shannon Roddy, and Ripple Weistling provided exceptional research support, tracking down sources within minutes of receiving my emails, whatever hour of the day or night. I also benefited from the expert assistance of archivists at the National Archives and Records Administration, the University of Miami Otto G. Richter Library, the Bancroft Library at the University of California, Berkeley, the Lawrence de Graaf Center for Oral and Public History at California State University, Fullerton, the Schomburg Center for Research in Black Culture at the New York Public Library, the Supreme Court Library, and the Schlesinger Library at the Radcliffe Institute for Advanced Study.

I want to acknowledge as well the men and women whose stories were buried in those archives, and who became the subject of this book. As often as possible, I used their own words to describe what it meant to them to lose their citizenship and how they fought back. I am grateful that they raised their voices loudly enough to become part of the historical record, speaking not only for themselves but for the many thousands of others who silently suffered the same fate.

I am extremely grateful to my smart and hard-working research assistants for their hours of labor. Melina Oliverio was there from the beginning with thoughtful substantive feedback and exceptionally careful cite checking. Hannah Stambaugh, Katia Barron, and Natalia Meade were also invaluable in tracking down hard-to-find sources all over Washington, DC.

I cannot thank enough the friends and family members who read drafts of the full manuscript, each of whom provided just the right mix of praise and criticism to energize me through several rewrites. Tamar Shapiro and Alexandra Lahav are brilliant writers and astute critics, as well as dear friends of many decades, and the book is much better for their insights. My brother Josh and my mother Isabella not only shared their thoughts on early drafts, but also imbued me with a lifelong love of US history that led to the writing of this book.

I also want to thank my daughters, Becca and Ella, for their helpful suggestion that I insert references to kittens throughout the text. I am afraid I did not take that sage advice, but I am very glad they were around to ensure I never took myself or this book too seriously.

Finally, I am grateful to my husband for just about everything. Yes, I thanked him at the start, but once was not enough.

NOTES

INTRODUCTION: THE SIGNIFICANCE OF CITIZENSHIP

1. "Has Committed No Crime," *San Francisco Call*, Feb. 4, 1913, 1; "McKenzie Gordon to Wed Beautiful Ethel Coope," *San Francisco Examiner*, June 10, 1909, 6; "Suffrage Leader Can't Vote Going to Kick Up Big Row," *Sacramento Star*, Jan. 30, 1913, 1.

2. "Mackenzie Gordon Will Claim Bride Today," *San Francisco Call*, Aug. 14, 1909, 11; "Will Test Law of Citizenship," *Oakland Tribune*, Feb. 3, 1913, 5; Brief for Petitioner at 3, Mackenzie v. Hare, 239 U.S. 299 (1915); "Because Suffrage Leader Can't Vote She Will Start a Row," *Wisconsin State Journal*, Feb. 4, 1913, 7.

3. "Has Committed No Crime," *San Francisco Call*; Mackenzie v. Hare, 239 U.S. 299 (1915).

4. Petition for Habeas Corpus at 3, Haw Moy v. North, 183 F. 89 (9th Cir. 1910), Record Group 276, No. 14935, National Archives and Records Administration—San Bruno, CA; Robert Barde and Gustavo J. Bobonis, "Detention at Angel Island: First Empirical Evidence," *Social Science History* 30, no. 1 (Spring 2006): 108; Haw Moy v. North, 183 F. 89 (9th Cir. 1910).

5. Salyer, *Laws Harsh as Tigers*, 208–9; Report of the Commissioner-General of Immigration, Department of Commerce and Labor, Bureau of Immigration and Naturalization, July 1, 1907, 107–8, https://babel.hathitrust.org/cgi/pt?id=uiug.30112003908420&view=1up&seq=9.

6. Lauren Etter, "Immigration Twist Gives a Laborer a Fresh Beginning," *Wall Street Journal*, May 12, 2006, A1.

7. Indictment, United States v. Garza-Aguilera, No. B-05-1049, 2005 WL 5920605 (S.D. Tex. Dec. 13, 2005); Lee J. Terán, "Mexican Children of U.S. Citizens: 'Viges Prin' and Other Tales of Challenges to Asserting Acquired U.S. Citizenship," *Scholar* 14 (2012): 656–57.

8. Etter, "Immigration Twist Gives a Laborer a Fresh Beginning."

9. William M. Grosvenor, "The Law of Conquest; The True Basis of Reconstruction," *New Englander* 24 (1865): 111, 120; Statement of Sen. Sumner, May 19, 1862, 37th Cong. 2nd Sess., *Congressional Globe*, S 2189–90 (arguing that leaders of the rebellion could be treated both as criminals and "alien enemies" under what became known as the "dual status" doctrine); J. G. Randall, *Constitutional Problems Under Lincoln*, rev. ed. (Urbana: University of Illinois Press, 1951), 67–95; Kettner, *The Development of American Citizenship*, 334–37, 340n17; Kent, "The Constitution and the Laws of War During the Civil War," 1841, 1877, 1902, 1907; *The Prize Cases*, 67 U.S. 635, 672–74 (1863).

10. "President Johnson's Amnesty Proclamation," *New York Times*, May 30, 1865, 1; "General Robert E. Lee's Parole and Citizenship," *Prologue Magazine* 37, no. 1 (2005), https://www.archives.gov/publications/prologue/2005/spring/piece-lee; "American Rebellions—Past and Present," *Evening Bulletin* (Philadelphia), republished in "American Rebellions—Past and Present," *Appleton Post* (WI), May 11, 1865, 2; "American Rebellions," *Berkshire County Eagle* (Pittsfield, MA), May 11, 1865, 1; *Orleans Independent* (Irasburg, VT), June 30, 1865, 1; Avery Craven, ed., *"To Markie": The Letters of Robert E. Lee to Martha Custis Williams* (Cambridge, MA: Harvard University Press, 1933), 68.

11. Statement of Representative Robinson, *Congressional Record*, 94th Cong., 1st Sess. (July 22, 1975), H 23947; Statement of Representative Bowen, *Congressional Record*, 94th Cong., 1st Sess. (July 22, 1975), H 23947; Statement of Representative Montgomery, *Congressional Record*, 94th Cong., 1st Sess. (July 22, 1975), H 23943; Statement of Representative Hechler, *Congressional Record*, 94th Cong., 1st Sess. (July 22, 1975), H 23946; Elizabeth Brown Pryor, *Reading the Man: A Portrait of Robert E. Lee Through His Private Letters* (New York: Penguin Books, 2007), 261–74; President Gerald R. Ford's Remarks upon Signing a Bill Restoring Rights of Citizenship to

General Robert E. Lee, S.J. Res. 23, 89 Stat. 380, Aug. 5, 1975, https://www.fordlibrarymuseum.gov /library/speeches/750473.htm.

12. James Q. Whitman, *Hitler's American Model: The United States and the Making of Nazi Race Law* (Princeton, NJ: Princeton University Press, 2017), 58.

13. Yuji Ichioka, "The Meaning of Loyalty: The Case of Kazumaro Buddy Uno," *Amerasia Journal* 23, no. 3 (Winter 1997): 44–71; "Buddy Uno," Densho Encylopedia, http://encyclopedia .densho.org/Buddy_Uno.

14. Commonwealth v. Bleischwitz, 14 Pa. D. & C. 170 (Court of Common Pleas of Pennsylvania, Montgomery County, Jan. 1, 1930).

15. "Ark with 30 Reds Sails Early Today for Unnamed Port," *New York Times*, Dec. 21, 1919; Wexler, *Emma Goldman.*

16. Emma Goldman, "A Woman Without a Country," in Weil, *Sovereign Citizen*, 188.

17. Linda Bosniak, *The Citizen and the Alien: Dilemmas of Contemporary Membership* (Princeton, NJ: Princeton University Press, 2006), 2–3.

18. Companies that rate the value of citizenship put US citizenship at the top of the list, and the US government essentially sells US citizenship through its "EB-5 investor program," which enables those willing to invest over $500,000 to obtain a visa that puts the holder on the path to citizenship.

19. Erika Lee, *America for Americans: A History of Xenophobia in the United States* (New York: Basic Books, 2019); Kunal M. Parker, *Making Foreigners: Immigration and Citizenship Law in America, 1600–2000* (Cambridge, UK: Cambridge University Press, 2015), 2.

20. Amy Taxin, "US Launches Bid to Find Citizenship Cheaters," Associated Press, June 11, 2018, https://www.apnews.com/1da389a535684a5f9d0da74081c242f3; "The Department of Justice Creates Section Dedicated to Denaturalization Cases," Department of Justice, Office of Public Affairs, Feb. 26, 2020, https://www.justice.gov/opa/pr/department-justice-creates-section-dedicated -denaturalization-cases; Masha Gessen, "In America, Naturalized Citizens No Longer Have an Assumption of Permanence," *New Yorker*, June 18, 2018, https://www.newyorker.com/news/our -columnists/in-america-naturalized-citizens-no-longer-have-an-assumption-of-permanence; Laura Bingham and Natasha Arnpriester, *Unmaking Americans: Insecure Citizenship in the United States* (Open Society Justice Initiative, 2019), 127; Rachel E. Rosenbloom, "From the Outside Looking In: U.S. Passports in the Borderlands," in *Citizenship in Question: Evidentiary Birthright and Statelessness*, ed. Benjamin N. Lawrance and Jacqueline Stevens (Durham, NC: Duke University Press, 2017), 133; Transcript of Oral Argument at 27–30, Maslenjak v. United States, 137 S. Ct. 1918 (2017) (No. 16–309); William Finnegan, "The Deportation Machine," *New Yorker*, Apr. 22, 2013; Stevens, "U.S. Government Unlawfully Detaining and Deporting U.S. Citizens as Aliens," 622, 630.

21. Katie Rogers, "Trump Encourages Racist Conspiracy Theory About Kamala Harris," *New York Times*, August 13, 2020.

22. Kyle Dropp and Brendan Nyhan, "It Lives. Birtherism Is Diminished but Far from Dead," *New York Times*, Sept. 23, 2016.

23. Lee, *America for Americans*; Kerber, "The Meaning of Citizenship," 837.

CHAPTER 1: CITIZEN SLAVE

1. VanderVelde, *Mrs. Dred Scott*, 129, 135.

2. "Visit to Dred Scott," *Frank Leslie's Illustrated Newspaper*, June 27, 1857; Hager, *Dred & Harriet Scott*, 9, 15.

3. VanderVelde, *Mrs. Dred Scott*, 135; Alfred Brunson, *A Western Pioneer*, vol. 2 (Cincinnati: Hitchcock & Walden, 1879), 125.

4. Dred Scott v. Sandford, 60 U.S. at 393, 398 (1857).

5. VanderVelde, *Mrs. Dred Scott*, 133–38; Dred Scott, 60 U.S. at 398.

6. Fehrenbacher, *The Dred Scott Case*, 580–83.

7. Petition for Leave to Sue for Freedom, filed on behalf of Harriet Scott, Apr. 6, 1848, Revised Dred Scott Case Collection; Summons in False Imprisonment, Dred Scott v. Emerson, Revised Dred Scott Case Collection; Action in False Imprisonment, Harriet Scott v. Emerson, Revised Dred Scott Case Collection. Documents in the Revised Dred Scott Case Selection are available through the Washington University Digital Gateway, http://digital.wustl.edu/d/dre/. In truth, the Scotts did not expect to collect a penny, either for their damages from the assault and imprisonment or for their years of uncompensated service as slaves after their residence in free territory. Nor is it clear that Dred and Harriet were in fact beaten or imprisoned on the date in question. The allegations were "pro forma"—the standard boilerplate that could be found in the dozens of freedom suits filed by

slaves in the 1830s and 1840s, all claiming that their sojourns to free states and territories with their masters had freed them. As everyone involved in the case knew, the claims would force the court to address the threshold issue of whether Harriet and Dred Scotts' residence in free territory had transformed them from slaves into free persons. VanderVelde, *Mrs. Dred Scott*, 233–35.

8. Dred's and Harriet Scott's cases were consolidated by the time the case reached the US Supreme Court. Lea VanderVelde, "The *Dred Scott* Case in Context," *Journal of Supreme Court History* 40, no. 3 (2015): 272.

9. "Visit to Dred Scott"; VanderVelde, *Mrs. Dred Scott*, 228. Dred Scott's birthdate is unknown, and sources refer to it as being anytime between 1795 and 1809. Hager, *Dred & Harriet Scott*, 5. Major Lawrence Taliaferro, who had owned Harriet Robinson and who served as justice of the peace at their wedding, estimated that Dred Scott was about forty years old when they married in 1836. *Id.* at 9. Slave traders took great pains to make aging slaves appear younger, such as by using black shoe polish to disguise grey hair and instructing slaves to lie about their age. Harrison Anthony Trexler, *Slavery in Missouri 1804–1865* (Baltimore: Johns Hopkins Press, 1914), 48.

10. VanderVelde, *Mrs. Dred Scott*, 228. In a December 1895 interview with the *New York Times*, Irene Emerson (by then Irene Chaffee) claimed that the wealthy, slaveholding Chouteau family of St. Louis had promoted the litigation. The Chouteau family owned more slaves than any other in St. Louis, and they had a lost a number to the same type of "freedom lawsuit" filed by Dred and Harriet Scott. Irene's brother, John Sanford, had married into the Chouteau family, and she claimed that he funded the litigation as a favor to his wife's family. VanderVelde, "The *Dred Scott* Case in Context," 274.

11. "Visit to Dred Scott"; Jennifer L. Morgan, "*Partus sequitur ventrem*: Law, Race, and Reproduction in Colonial Slavery," *Small Axe* 22, no. 1 (Mar. 2018): 1–17. Slave women in their twenties were sold for approximately $1,300 in the 1850s, while slaves in their late forties were worth less than $500. Trexler, *Slavery in Missouri*, 40–41.

12. "The Original Dred Scott, a Resident of St. Louis—a Sketch of His History," *Holmes County Republican*, Apr. 16, 1857; "Visit to Dred Scott."

13. Galusha Anderson, *The Story of A Border City During the Civil War* (Boston: Little, Brown, 1908), 182; "This Was St. Louis Slave Market Before Civil War," *St. Louis Star*, Jan. 30, 1922, 8; Walter Johnson, *Soul by Soul: Life Inside the Antebellum Slave Market* (Cambridge, MA: Harvard University Press, 1999), 130, 163.

14. "The Original Dred Scott, a Resident of St. Louis; "Visit to Dred Scott."

15. VanderVelde, *Mrs. Dred Scott*, 230–54; "The Original Dred Scott, a Resident of St. Louis."

16. Vincent C. Hopkins, *Dred Scott's Case* (New York: Russell & Russell, 1967), 24. A clerk misspelled John Sanford's name as "Sandford" when entering the case on the Supreme Court's docket.

17. Kettner, *The Development of American Citizenship*, 174–75.

18. Kettner, *The Development of American Citizenship*, 8, 187; I-Mien Tsiang, *The Question of Expatriation in America Prior to 1907* (Baltimore: Johns Hopkins University Press, 1942), 11.

19. Mark A. Graber, *Dred Scott and the Problem of Constitutional Evil* (Cambridge, UK: Cambridge University Press, 2006), 52–53; Smith, *Civic Ideals*, 115; Kettner, *The Development of American Citizenship*, 173–210.

20. Smith, *Civic Ideals*, 130; Kettner, *The Development of American Citizenship*, 227–28.

21. Akhil Reed Amar, *America's Constitution: A Biography* (New York: Random House, 2005), 251; The Federalist Papers, No. 80 (Hamilton), The Avalon Project, Documents in Law, History and Diplomacy, Yale Law School, https://avalon.law.yale.edu/18th_century/fed80.asp.

22. Martha S. Jones, "Birthright Citizenship and Reconstruction's Unfinished Revolution," *Journal of the Civil War Era*, https://www.journalofthecivilwarera.org/forum-the-future-of-reconstruction-studies/birthright-citizenship-reconstructions-unfinished-revolution/#page; Kettner, *The Development of American Citizenship*, 312–23; Amar, *America's Constitution*, 253–54; Smith, *Civic Ideals*, 126; Jones, *Birthright Citizens*, 9–12.

23. Randall Kennedy, "*Dred Scott* and African American Citizenship," in *Diversity and Citizenship: Rediscovering American Nationhood*, ed. Gary Jeffrey Jacobsohn and Susan Dunn (Lanham, MD: Rowman & Littlefield, 1996), 106.

24. George Van Santvoord, *Sketches of the Lives, Times and Judicial Services of the Chief Justices of the Supreme Court of the United States* (Albany: Weare C. Little & Co., 1882), 524; Vincent C. Hopkins, *Dred Scott's Case* (New York: Russell & Russell, 1967), 32.

25. "Supreme Court of the United States, Tuesday, February 12, 1856," *Triweekly Washington Sentinel*, Feb. 14, 1856; "United States Supreme Court—Trial for Freedom," *Baltimore Sun*, Dec. 16, 1856, 4; "Important Suit Before the Supreme Court," *National Era*, Feb. 21, 1856, 30.

26. Order for reargument issued May 12, 1856, Dred Scott v. Sandford, Supreme Court Archives; James F. Simon, *Lincoln and Chief Justice Taney: Slavery, Secession, and the President's War Powers* (New York: Simon & Schuster, 2006), 107.

27. "The Case of Dred Scott," *New-York Tribune*, Dec. 19, 1856, 5; "United States Supreme Court—Trial for Freedom," *Baltimore Sun*, Dec. 16, 1856, 4; "The Missouri Compromise Case," *Evening Star* (Washington, DC), Dec. 17, 1856; Fehrenbacher, *The Dred Scott Case*, 288.

28. Fehrenbacher, *The Dred Scott Case*, 226–27; Brian McGinty, *Lincoln and the Court* (Cambridge, MA: Harvard University Press, 2008), 20.

29. Finkelman, *Dred Scott v. Sandford*, 29; "The Case of Dred Scott," *New-York Tribune*, Dec. 19, 1856, 5.

30. "Montgomery Blair: A Prominent Figure in Political History Passes Away," *Washington Post*, July 28, 1883, 1.

31. One newspaper explained that Dred Scott "paid his lawyers whatever he could save out of his scanty earnings by cleaning rooms and doing other odd jobs about town," which he did on top of his unpaid slave labor. "Dred Scott, Life of the Famous Fugitive and Missouri Slave Litigant," *Cincinnati Enquirer*, Jan. 16, 1886, 12.

32. "A Member of Mr. Lincoln's Cabinet on the Radicals. A Highly Important Speech from Postmaster General Blair," *Evening Courier and Republic*, Oct. 15, 1863, 1; James M. McPherson, "Abolitionist and Negro Opposition to Colonization during the Civil War," *Phylon* 26, no. 4 (1965): 397–98; Leonard L. Richards, *Who Freed the Slaves? The Fight over the Thirteenth Amendment* (Chicago: University of Chicago Press, 2015), 130–31; Montgomery Blair, "Ought the Negro to Be Disenfranchised? Ought He Have Been Enfranchised?," *North American Review* 128, no. 268 (Mar. 1879): 264.

33. William Cooper, "James Buchanan: Campaigns and Elections," UVA Miller Center, https://millercenter.org/president/buchanan/campaigns-and-elections; Fehrenbacher, *The Dred Scott Case*, 291; Kenneth M. Stampp, *America in 1857: A Nation on the Brink* (Oxford, UK: Oxford University Press, 1992), 48.

34. Irons, *A People's History of the U.S. Supreme Court*, 171.

35. Irons, *A People's History of the U.S. Supreme Court*, 170–71; Stampp, *America in 1857*, 92. The news was leaked to at least a few journalists as well. Before the decision was issued, the *Berkshire County Eagle* reported that "[w]e learn from trustworthy sources" that a majority of the Court would hold the Missouri Compromise unconstitutional, that Justices Benjamin Robbins Curtis and John McLean would dissent, and that the decision would be issued around the date of Buchanan's inauguration. "The Missouri Compromise," *Berkshire County Eagle*, Mar. 6, 1857.

36. "Dred Scott, Life of the Famous Fugitive and Missouri Slave Litigant," *Cincinnati Enquirer*, Jan. 16, 1886, 12; Walter Ehrlich, *They Have No Rights: Dred Scott's Struggle for Freedom* (Westport, CT: Greenwood Press, 1979), 3.

37. Taney's conclusion that Scott was not a citizen entitled to sue was explicitly joined only by two other justices in their concurrences. Because it is debatable whether Taney spoke for a majority of the Court on this issue, it is arguably justified in reaching the other legal questions in the case.

38. Dred Scott, 60 U.S. at 406, 407.

39. Dred Scott, 60 U.S. at 405, 411, 416, 419–20.

40. Dred Scott, 60 U.S. at 410.

41. Dred Scott, 60 U.S. at 404.

42. Fehrenbacher, *The Dred Scott Case*, 284, 319; Graber, *Dred Scott and the Problem of Constitutional Evil*, 77; Richard H. Leach, "Benjamin Robbins Curtis: Judicial Misfit," *New England Quarterly* 25, no. 4 (Dec. 1952): 509, 519.

43. Dred Scott, 60 U.S. at 576, 582 (Curtis, J., *dissenting*). In his dissent, Justice McLean also argued that because "[s]everal of the States have admitted persons of color to the right of suffrage," they had been "recognized . . . as citizens." Dred Scott, 60 U.S. at 533 (McLean, J., *dissenting*).

44. Dred Scott, 60 U.S. at 576, 581 (Curtis, J., *dissenting*); Foner, *The Second Founding*, 4; Jones, *Birthright Citizens*.

45. Dred Scott, 60 U.S. at 583 (Curtis, J., *dissenting*).

46. Dred Scott, 50 U.S. at 583 (Curtis, J., *dissenting*). Under Article III of the US Constitution, a federal court cannot hear a case that arises under state law unless it is brought by a citizen of one state against a citizen of a different state.

47. Leach, "Benjamin Robbins Curtis," 521 (quoting letter from Curtis to George Ticknor, July 3, 1857); "Resignation of Judge Curtis," *Richmond Enquirer* (VA), Sept. 8, 1857.

48. "The Original Dred Scott, a Resident of St. Louis."

49. "The Original Dred Scott, a Resident of St. Louis."

50. Fehrenbacher, *The Dred Scott Case*, 231; "Democratic Slanders," *Berkshire County Eagle*, Mar. 27, 1857; Hager, *Dred & Harriet Scott*, 36 (quoting "Dred Scott's Owner," *Union and Advertiser* [Nunda, NY], Mar. 27, 1857, 2); "Dred Scott Owned by a Black Republican Member of Congress," *Detroit Free Press*, Mar. 17, 1857, 2 (excerpting portions of the *Argus* article).

51. "Dred Scott Owned by Abolitionist," *Wayne County Herald* (Honesdale, PA), Apr. 9, 1857, 2; "Congressional Nominations," *Berkshire County Eagle*, Oct. 1, 1858, 2.

52. Kenneth Clarence Kaufman, *Dred Scott's Advocate: A Biography of Roswell M. Field* (Columbia: University of Missouri Press, 1996), 167.

53. "The Case of Dred Scott," *Liberator* (Boston), Mar. 20, 1857, 47 (quoting letter from Calvin Chaffee published in the *Springfield Republican*); Hager, *Dred & Harriet Scott*, 32–43, 124, 126 (reprinting correspondence between Representative Calvin Chaffee and Montgomery Blair); Ehrlich, *They Have No Rights*, 181. Missouri law provided that only a Missouri resident had the power to free slaves residing within the state.

54. VanderVelde, *Mrs. Dred Scott*, 321–22.

55. "Dred Scott," *Advocate* (Buffalo, NY), Oct. 8, 1857; "Where the Credit Is Due," *Washington Union* (Washington, DC), June 3, 1857, 2 (crediting the pressure from the Springfield *Argus* for bringing about the Scotts' emancipation).

56. Finkelman, *Dred Scott v. Sandford*, 147, 151 (quoting "The Supreme Court of the United States," *Evening Post* [NY], Mar. 7, 1857, and "Wickedness of the Decision in the Supreme Court against the African Race," *Independent* [NY], Mar. 19, 1857).

57. Mitchell v. Wells, 37 Miss. 235, 264 (1859).

58. Hager, *Dred & Harriet Scott*, 47; "Visit to Dred Scott," *Frank Leslie's Illustrated Newspaper* (NY), June 27, 1857. The reporters quoted Dred and Harriet Scott using an idiomatic vernacular rather than Standard English—a choice it did not always make when quoting white southerners.

59. "Visit to Dred Scott"; VanderVelde, *Mrs. Dred Scott*, 320.

60. "Visit to Dred Scott"; Andrew Delbanco, *The War Before the War: Fugitive Slaves and the Struggle for America's Soul from the Revolution to the Civil War* (London: Penguin Press, 2018).

61. Trexler, *Slavery in Missouri*, 67, 83–84; Hager, *Dred & Harriet Scott*, 53.

62. Hager, *Dred & Harriet Scott*, 49, 53; Trexler, *Slavery in Missouri*, 53, 67; VanderVelde, *Mrs. Dred Scott*, 322.

CHAPTER 2: CONFEDERATE CITIZEN

1. "The Statue of Freedom," Architect of the Capitol, https://www.aoc.gov/art/other-statues /statue-freedom.

2. "Extra. Execution of Wirz," *Evening Star* (Washington, DC), Nov. 10, 1865, 1; "Our Andersonville Prisoners," *Philadelphia Inquirer*, Dec. 28, 1864, 2 (reprinting a letter to the editor of the *New-York Tribune*); Walter Lowenfels, ed., *Walt Whitman's Civil War* (New York: Da Capo Press, 1960), 216.

3. "Execution of Wirz," *New York Times*; "Extra. Execution of Wirz," *Evening Star*.

4. "The Paroled Rebel Soldiers and the General Amnesty," *New York Times*, June 4, 1865, 4; Ron Chernow, *Grant* (New York: Penguin Press, 2017), 496.

5. Reeves, *The Lost Indictment of Robert E. Lee*, 40; Cynthia Nicoletti, *Secession on Trial: The Treason Prosecution of Jefferson Davis* (Cambridge, UK: Cambridge University Press, 2017), 22; "American Rebellions—Past and Present," *Evening Bulletin* (Philadelphia), republished in "American Rebellions—Past and Present," *Appleton Post* (WI), May 11, 1865, 2; "American Rebellions," *Berkshire County Eagle*, May 11, 1865, 1; *Orleans Independent* (Irasburg, VT), June 30, 1865, 1; "Jefferson Davis and Robert E. Lee," *Cleveland Daily Leader*, May 16, 1865.

6. "Davis at Fort Monroe," *Pittsburgh Daily Post*, May 29, 1865, 2; letter from Robert E. Lee to the Board of Trustees of Washington College, Aug. 24, 1865, published in *Recollections and Letters of Robert E. Lee*, compiled by Captain Robert Edward Lee (1904; repr., Mineola, NY: Dover Publications, 2007), 181.

7. Calvin Jarrett, "The First Negro Senator," *Black World/Negro Digest*, May 1964, 16; Elizabeth Lawson, *The Gentleman from Mississippi: Our First Negro Congressman, Hiram R. Revels* (New York: privately printed, 1960), 9–10; James Oaks, "Why Slaves Can't Read," in *Thomas Jefferson and the Education of a Citizen*, ed. James Gilreath (Washington, DC: Library of Congress, 1999), 179–80.

8. Thompson, "Hiram Rhodes Revels, 1827–1901," 298; Borome, "The Autobiography of Hiram Rhoades Revels Together with Some Letters by and About Him," 81; VanderVelde, *Mrs. Dred Scott*, 301–2.

9. Thompson, "Hiram Rhodes Revels, 1827–1901," 298; Richard S. Hobbs, *The Cayton Legacy: An African American Family* (Pullman: Washington State University Press, 2002), 4. Jean Libby, Hannah Geffert, and Jimica Akinloye Kenyatta, "Hiram Revels Related to Men in John Brown's Army," Allies for Freedom, http://www.alliesforfreedom.org/files/Hiram_Revels_Related_to_Men _in_John_Brown.pdf.

10. "The Colored Senator," *Morning Democrat* (Davenport, IA), Mar. 15, 1870, 2; "The Senator from Mississippi," *Charleston Daily News* (SC), Mar. 3, 1870, 2; "Hiram R. Revels. U.S. Senator-Elect from Mississippi," *Frank Leslie's Illustrated Newspaper*, Feb. 26, 1870, 401.

11. Thompson, *Hiram R. Revels, 1827–1901*, 55 (quoting letter from Hiram Revels to Captain William D. Matthews, published in the *New York World* Jan. 31, 1870); Borome, "Autobiography of Hiram Rhoades Revels," 90. Phoeba Revels was sometimes known as "Phoebe."

12. Samuel Denny Smith, *The Negro in Congress, 1870–1901* (Chapel Hill: University of North Carolina Press, 1940), 13; William Horatio Barnes, *History of Congress: The Forty-First Congress of the United States, 1869–71* (Washington, DC: W. H. Barnes & Co., 1872), 2.

13. Blight, *Race and Reunion*, 112–13; US Commission on Civil Rights, *Political Participation* (1968), 3–4, https://www2.law.umaryland.edu/marshall/usccr/documents/cr12p753.pdf; Dray, *Capitol Men*, 84–85; Foner, *Reconstruction*, 119–23.

14. Smith, *The Negro in Congress, 1870–1901*, 13–14.

15. Frederick William Seward, *Reminiscences of a War-time Statesman and Diplomat, 1830–1915* (New York: G. P. Putnam's Sons, 1916), 255. In 1865, the *New York Times* speculated that Jefferson Davis might be released from prison "with the understanding that he is to go to Europe and not return, or in other words, to be expatriated." "The Trial of Jefferson Davis," *New York Times*, Nov. 9, 1865; Melia Robinson, "The American Confederacy Is Still Alive in a Small Brazilian City Called Americana," *Business Insider*, Jun. 8, 2015; Alan M. Tigay, "The Deepest South," *American Heritage* 49, no. 2 (Apr. 1998): 84–92.

16. Jones, *Birthright Citizens*, 35–49; James D. Lockett, "Abraham Lincoln and Colonization: An Episode That Ends in Tragedy at L'Ile a Vache, Haiti, 1863–1864," *Journal of Black Studies* 21, no. 4 (June 1991): 435; Abraham Lincoln, "Second Annual Message," Dec. 1, 1862, American Presidency Project, https://www.presidency.ucsb.edu/node/202180.

17. Kettner, *The Development of American Citizenship*, 334–37, 340n17; Randall, *Constitutional Problems Under Lincoln*, 67–68, 70–72 (describing how the Union treated Confederates as both enemy aliens and belligerent citizens); Statement of Sen. Sumner, May 19, 1862, 37th Cong., 2nd Sess., *Congressional Globe*, S2189–90 (arguing under what became known as the "dual status" theory that leaders of the rebellion could be treated both as criminals and "alien enemies"); Statement of Representative Stevens, 38th Cong., 1st Sess., *Congressional Globe* H316 (1864); *The Prize Cases*, 67 U.S. 635, 672–74 (1863); Kent, "The Constitution and the Laws of War During the Civil War," 1841, 1877, 1902, 1907n255; William M. Grosvenor, "The Law of Conquest; The True Basis of Reconstruction," *New Englander* 24 (1865): 111, 120; In re Mrs. Alexander's Cotton, 69 U.S. 404 (1864).

18. Dred Scott v. Sandford, 60 U.S. at 393, 407 (1857); Epps, *Democracy Reborn*, 86; Du Bois, *Black Reconstruction in America*, 447–48.

19. Foner, *Reconstruction*, 222–23. In 1865 only five states allowed blacks to vote, and referenda in other states to permit black suffrage repeatedly failed. Whitelaw Reid, *After the War: A Southern Tour: May 1, 1865 to May 1, 1866* (New York: Moore, Wilstach & Baldwin, 1866), http://www.gutenberg.org/files/55381/55381-h/55381-h.htm; Carl Schurz, *Report on the Conditions of the South*, 39th Cong., 1st Sess., Senate, Dec. 19, 1865, 48 (reporting that the "masses [of people in the South] are strongly opposed to colored suffrage").

20. Epps, "The Antebellum Political Background of the Fourteenth Amendment," 182–85; Epps, *Democracy Reborn*, 67; Leonard L. Richards, *The Slave Power: The Free North and Southern Domination, 1780–1860* (Baton Rouge: Louisiana State University Press, 2000), 2–3; Foner, *The Second Founding*, 21.

21. Epps, *Democracy Reborn*, 57, 88, 197; David W. Blight, *Frederick Douglass* (New York: Simon & Schuster, 2018), 475; Reid, *After the War*; Foner, *Reconstruction*, 252.

22. Epps, *Democracy Reborn*.

23. Foner, *The Second Founding*, 16.

24. Foner, *Reconstruction*, 67; Russ, "The Negro and White Disfranchisement During Radical Reconstruction," 171, 176, 178 (quoting *Boston Evening Traveller*, Mar. 11, 1868).

25. "Gen. Rosecrans and Gen R. E. Lee," *Staunton Spectator*, Sept. 8, 1868, https://www.newspapers.com/image/72188517. The document, known as the "White Sulphur Springs Manifesto," was a letter from Robert E. Lee and twenty-five other former Confederate leaders to Gen.

William S. Rosecrans, dated Aug. 26, 1868, https://leefamilyarchive.org/family-papers/letters
/letters-1866-present/9-family-papers/1172-robert-e-lee-et-al-to-william-s-rosecrans-1868-august
-26-white-sulphur-statement; Jill Lepore, "'Mourning Lincoln' and 'Lincoln's Body,'" *New York Times*, Feb. 4, 2015.

26. Johnson, "Proclamation 134"; LeRoy P. Graf, ed., *The Papers of Andrew Johnson*, vol. 7, *1864–1865* (Knoxville: University of Tennessee Press, 1986), 613; "President Johnson's Amnesty Proclamation," *New York Times*, May 30, 1865, 1, https://www.nytimes.com/1865/05/30/archives/president-johnsons-amnesty-proclamation-restoration-to-rights-of.html. Some states restricted former confederates' access to the ballot immediately after the war, and Congress subsequently included restrictions on voting in the Reconstruction Acts of 1867. Rawley, "The General Amnesty Act of 1872," 481n7.

27. Johnson, "Proclamation 134"; Heather Cox Richardson, *West from Appomattox: The Reconstruction of America After the Civil War* (New Haven, CT: Yale University Press, 2007), 43; Dorris, *Pardon and Amnesty Under Lincoln and Johnson*, 112.

28. Edwin Haviland Miller, ed., *Selected Letters of Walt Whitman* (Iowa City: University of Iowa Press, 1990), 113, 115; Reid, *After the War*.

29. Haviland, *Selected Letters of Walt Whitman*, 114.

30. "General Robert E. Lee's Parole and Citizenship," *Prologue Magazine* 37, no. 1 (2005); Dorris, *Pardon and Amnesty*, 112.

31. William C. Davis, *Jefferson Davis: The Man and His Hour* (New York: HarperCollins Publishers, 1991); James Longstreet, *From Manassas to Appomattox: Memoirs of the Civil War in America* (Philadelphia: J. B. Lippincott Company, 1896), 634.

32. Randall, *Constitutional Problems Under Lincoln*, 67–95; Kent, "The Constitution and the Laws of War During the Civil War," 1893n187. Courts that viewed rebels as having lost their citizenship rights and transformed themselves into enemy aliens nonetheless justified the charge of "treason" on the ground that these former citizens had joined a foreign army in attacking the United States.

33. Foner, *The Second Founding*.

34. Foner, *Reconstruction*, 275–76; Foner, *The Second Founding*, 56. No one knows the exact number of people affected by these provisions, but estimates are that about ten thousand to fifteen thousand lost their right to vote and hold office.

35. Brian Klaas, "Looking Back at Andrew Johnson—the President Most Like Trump," *Washington Post*, July 9, 2018; Dray, *Capitol Men*, 34; "The President's Mistake," *New York Times*, Sept. 7, 1866; Andrew Johnson, Third Annual Message to Congress, Dec. 3, 1867, University of Virginia, Miller Center, https://millercenter.org/the-presidency/presidential-speeches/december-3-1867-third-annual-message-congress; Blight, *Frederick Douglass*, 475.

36. Dorris, *Pardon and Amnesty*, 135, 141, 357; Foner, *Reconstruction*, 191.

37. Sen. Wilson, Feb. 23, 1870, 41st Cong., 2nd Sess., *Congressional Globe* 1503, https://memory.loc.gov/cgi-bin/ampage?collId=llcg&fileName=095/llcg095.db&recNum=200.

38. Sen. Howard, Feb. 24, 1870, 41st Cong., 2nd Sess., *Congressional Globe* 1543; "Forty-First Congress, Second Session: The Mississippi Senators Elect," *New York Times*, Feb. 24, 1870, 5.

39. Sen. Saulsbury, 41st Cong., 2nd Sess., *Appendix to the Congressional Globe* 130; Sen. Davis, Feb. 23, 1870, 41st Cong., 2nd Sess., *Congressional Globe* 1509.

40. Sen. Davis, Feb. 23, 1870, 41st Cong., 2nd Sess., *Congressional Globe* 1508–9; Feb. 23, 1870, 41st Cong., 2nd Sess., *Congressional Globe* 1503–8.

41. Sen. Vickers, Feb. 25, 1870, 41st Cong., 2nd Sess., *Congressional Globe* 1558; Sen. Howard, Feb. 24, 1870, 41st Cong., 2nd Sess., *Congressional Globe* 1543 (paraphrasing Democrats' objections).

42. Sen. Sumner, Feb. 25, 1870, 41st Cong., 2nd Sess., *Congressional Globe* 1566–67; Sen. Howard, Feb. 24, 1870, 41st Cong., 2nd Sess., *Congressional Globe* 1543; Sen. Sherman, Feb. 23, 1870, 41st Cong., 2nd Sess., *Congressional Globe* 1510; Sen. Nye, Feb. 23, 1870, 41st Cong., 2nd Sess., *Congressional Globe* 1513.

43. Sen. Davis, Feb. 23, 1870, 41st Cong., 2nd Sess., *Congressional Globe* 1509; Sen. Saulsbury, Feb. 24, 1870, 41st Cong., 2nd Sess., *Appendix to the Congressional Globe*, 127.

44. Sen. Sumner, Feb. 25, 1870, 41st Cong., 2nd Sess., *Congressional Globe* 1567; "Senator Revels," *Harper's Weekly*, Feb. 19, 1870, 116, https://archive.org/details/harpersweeklyv14bonn/page/114. Professor Richard Primus provides a fascinating constitutional analysis of the debate over Revels's citizenship: "The Riddle of Hiram Revels," *Harvard Law Review* 119, no. 6 (2006): 1680–734.

45. "Congress: The Colored Member Admitted to His Seat in the Senate, an Interesting Scene When the Oath Was Administered," *New York Times*, Feb. 26, 1870.

46. Borome, "Autobiography of Hiram Rhodes Revels," 81; VanderVelde, *Mrs. Dred Scott*, 301.

47. *Political Participation: A Study of the Participation by Negroes in the Electoral and Political Process in 10 Southern States Since the Passage of the Voting Rights Act of 1965*, Report of the US Commission on Civil Rights (1968), 1, 2, & 2n4, https://www2.law.umaryland.edu/marshall/usccr /documents/cr12p753.pdf; Foner, *Reconstruction*, 275–76, 323–24; David P. Currie, "The Reconstruction Congress," *University of Chicago Law Review* 75, no. 1 (Winter 2008): 424; "Louisiana: The Constitutional Convention—the Reports on Disenfranchisement—Two Days' Discussion," *New York Times*, Feb. 1, 1868.

48. Foner, *Reconstruction*, 354.

49. Lewis and Allen, "Black Voter Registration Efforts in the South," 105, 106; Foner, *Reconstruction*, 351–61; Dray, *Capitol Men*, 79 (quoting *Marion Star*).

50. Marjorie Hunter, "Lee Wins Final Skirmish: Citizenship Restored," *Globe-Gazette* (Mason City, IA), July 23, 1975.

51. *Congressional Record*, 94th Cong., 1st Sess. (July 22, 1975), H 23943–H 23948; Statement of Representative Montgomery, *Congressional Record*, 94th Cong., 1st Sess. (July 22, 1975), H 23943; Statement of Representative Butler, *Congressional Record*, 94th Cong., 1st Sess. (July 22, 1975), H 23945.

52. Statement of Representative Hechler, *Congressional Record*, 94th Cong., 1st Sess. (July 22, 1975), H 23946. A search of the Newspapers.com database for articles from July 1975 including the words "Lee," "citizenship," "Congress," and "restore" produced 321 articles. None of those articles referred to "slaves," "treason" or "traitor" other than to quote those words as they appeared in Lee's original pardon application and in Johnson's grants of amnesty. No op-eds or other commentary were critical of the decision to give Lee his citizenship. Three articles in Vermont newspapers quoted an interview with Vermont representative James M. Jeffords, who voted against giving "amnesty to a man who led the fight in defense of slavery," while at the same time denying amnesty to Vietnam War draft evaders. "Robert E. Lee Regains Citizenship," *Burlington Free Press*, Jul. 23, 1975, 1.

53. Laurel Wamsely, "John Conyers Jr., Who Represented Michigan for 5 Decades, Dies at 90," National Public Radio, Oct. 27, 2019, https://www.npr.org/2019/10/27/773919009/john -conyers-jr-who-represented-michigan-for-5-decades-dies-at-90; Hunter, "Lee Wins Final Skirmish: Citizenship Restored."

54. President Gerald R. Ford's Remarks Upon Signing a Bill Restoring Rights of Citizenship to General Robert E. Lee, S.J. Res. 23, 89 Stat. 380, Aug. 5, 1975, https://www.fordlibrarymuseum .gov/library/speeches/750473.htm.

55. Statement of Sen. Mark Hatfield, *Congressional Record*, 95th Cong., 1st Sess. (1977), S 12475.

56. William J. Cooper Jr., ed., *Jefferson Davis: The Essential Writings* (New York: Random House, 2003), 428–29.

57. US House of Representatives, Hearings before the Committee on the Judiciary, Markup, 41, July 25, 1978; Statement of Sen. Montgomery, *Congressional Record*, 95th Cong., 2nd Sess. (1978), 31619; Robert Penn Warren, "Jefferson Davis Gets His Citizenship Back," *New Yorker*, Feb. 25, 1980.

58. Blight, *Race and Reunion*, 87.

59. Michael Perman, *Struggle for Mastery: Disfranchisement in the South, 1888–1908* (Chapel Hill: University of North Carolina Press, 2001), 70; Lewis and Allen, "Black Voter Registration Efforts in the South," 107; Smith, *The Negro in Congress*, 135–36; Foner, *The Second Founding*, 129. Under Section 2 of the Fourteenth Amendment, those states that disenfranchised their black citizens should have lost a share of their representation in Congress, but that section was never enforced. Gabriel J. Chin, "Reconstruction, Felon Disenfranchisement, and the Right to Vote: Did the Fifteenth Amendment Repeal Section 2 of the Fourteenth Amendment?," *Georgetown Law Journal* 92 (2004): 259–60.

60. Gerrett Epps, "The Constitution: A Love Story," *American Prospect*, Oct. 17, 2011, https:// prospect.org/justice/constitution-love-story/.

61. Rawley, "The General Amnesty Act of 1872."

62. Greg Bailey, "Why Does This Georgia Town Honor One of America's Worst War Criminals?," *New Republic*, Nov. 10, 2015.

CHAPTER 3: BIRTHRIGHT CITIZEN

1. "Interview with Wong Kim Ark on Aug. 31, 1895," in Wong Kim Ark File 12017/42223, Immigration and Naturalization Service, Record Group 85, Archival Research Catalog Identifier 296477, National Archives and Records Administration at San Francisco–San Bruno, CA; Population of the United States, US Census, Ninth Census, Volume I, Table I, at 3, https://www2.census .gov/library/publications/decennial/1870/population/1870a-04.pdf?#; Population of the United States, US Census, Ninth Census, Volume I, Table XXII (Table of Sex, and Selected Ages), at 609; https://www2.census.gov/library/publications/decennial/1870/population/1870a-55.pdf. See also Sucheng Chan, "The Exclusion of Chinese Women, 1870–1943," in *Chinese Immigrants and American Law*, ed. Charles McClain (New York: Garland Publishing, 1994), 2; Population of the United States, US Census, Ninth Census, Volume I, Table I, at 8, https://www2.census.gov/library /publications/decennial/1870/population/1870a-04.pdf?#; Population of the United States, Ninth Census, Volume I, Table VI, at 328, https://www2.census.gov/library/publications/decennial/1870 /population/1870a-32.pdf?#; Joan B. Trauner, "The Chinese as Medical Scapegoats in San Francisco, 1870–1905," *California History* 57, no. 1 (1978): 82–83.

2. Wendy Rouse Jorae, *The Children of Chinatown: Growing Up Chinese American In San Francisco, 1850–1920* (Chapel Hill: University of North Carolina Press, 2009), 10.

3. Laverne Mau Dicker, *The Chinese in San Francisco: A Pictorial History* (New York: Dover Publications, 1979), 16; Yong Chen, *Chinese San Francisco, 1850–1943: A Trans-Pacific Community* (Stanford, CA: Stanford University Press, 2000), 64.

4. Huping Ling, *Surviving on the Gold Mountain: A History of Chinese American Women and Their Lives* (Albany: State University of New York Press, 1998), 19; Kerry Abrams, "Polygamy, Prostitution, and the Federalization of Immigration Law," *Columbia Law Review* 105, no. 3 (2005): 670, 674–75.

5. Yung, *Unbound Feet*, 21.

6. Immigration records give inconsistent dates for Wong Kim Ark's birth. In some records he was born on October 1, 1870; in others he was born on an unspecified date in 1873. The confusion may be due in part to the differences between the Chinese and Western calendar. I chose to use October 1, 1870, as his birthdate because it was listed as a precise birthdate in some documents, and because it is consistent with the age Wong gave for himself in numerous immigration interviews over many years.

7. Petition for a Writ of Habeas Corpus at 1, In re: Wong Kim Ark, Case File 11198, Admiralty Case Files 1851–1966, Archival Research Catalog Identifier 296013, United States District Courts, Northern District of California, San Francisco, Record Group 21, National Archives and Records Administration at San Francisco (San Bruno). Beth Lew-Williams, *The Chinese Must Go: Violence, Exclusion, and the Making of the Alien in America* (Cambridge, MA: Harvard University Press, 2018).

8. Yung, *Unbound Feet*, 21–22; Naturalization Act of 1870, 16 Stat. 254 (1870).

9. Scott Zesch, "Chinese Los Angeles in 1870–1871: The Makings of a Massacre," *Southern California Quarterly* 90, no. 2 (Summer 2008): 113–14, 141, 142. A total of 178 Chinese lived in Los Angeles in 1870, but many were servants who lived with their employers.

10. "Mob Violence in San Francisco Directed Against the Chinese," *Philadelphia Inquirer*, July 25, 1877; Katie Dowd, "140 Years Ago, San Francisco Was Set Ablaze During the City's Deadliest Race Riots," *San Francisco Gate*, July 23, 2017, https://www.sfgate.com/bayarea/article/1877 -san-francisco-anti-chinese-race-riots-11302710.php; "The Force of Sympathy," *New York Times*, July 25, 1877; "Outbreak in San Francisco, Rioters Attack the Chinese," *Evening Star* (Washington, DC), July 24, 1877.

11. Jorae, *The Children of Chinatown*, 12; Lee Chew, "The Life Story of a Chinaman," *Independent* 55 (Feb. 19, 1903): 417–23, reprinted in *The Life Stories of Undistinguished Americans as Told by Themselves*, ed. Hamilton Holt (New York: Routledge, Chapman, and Hall, 1990), 179–81.

12. Descriptions of Wong Kim Ark's travel to and from China and details of his life in China and the United States come primarily from the following two case files held by the National Archives: Wong Kim Ark File 12017/42223, Immigration and Naturalization Service, Record Group 85, Archival Research Catalog Identifier 296477, National Archives and Records Administration at San Francisco–San Bruno, CA; and Wong Kim Ark Case File No. 11198, Admiralty Case Files, 1851–1966, United States District Courts, Northern District of California, San Francisco, Record Group 21, Archival Research Catalog (ARC) Identifier 296013, National Archives and Records Administration at San Francisco–San Bruno. Hereafter these files will be cited as "Wong Kim Ark Files, National Archives."

13. The 1890 census records the presence of 103,607 Chinese men and only 3,868 Chinese women in the United States as a whole, though the numbers were slightly more favorable for Chinese men in California, who numbered only 69,382 in comparison with 3,090 Chinese women. Population of the United States, Eleventh Census, Vol. I, p. 488, Table 21, https://www.census.gov/library/publications/1895/dec/volume-1.html; Madeline Yuan-yin Hsu, *Dreaming of Gold, Dreaming of Home: Transnationalism and Migration Between the United States and South China, 1882–1943* (Stanford, CA: Stanford University Press, 2000), 90–123.

14. Wong Kim Ark Files, National Archives; Max Roser, Cameron Appel, and Hannah Ritchie, *Human Height*, Our World in Data, https://ourworldindata.org/human-height, accessed Dec. 13, 2019.

15. Wong Kim Ark Files, National Archives.

16. Wong Kim Ark Files, National Archives.

17. Lee, *At America's Gates*, 6–7; Gabriel J. Chin, "Segregation's Last Stronghold: Race Discrimination and the Constitutional Law of Immigration," *UCLA Law Review* 46 (Oct. 1998): 34 (quoting Sen. George, 13 *Congressional Record* 1637–38 [1882]).

18. Garrett Epps, "The Citizenship Clause Means What It Says," *Atlantic*, Oct. 30, 2018, https://www.theatlantic.com/ideas/archive/2018/10/birthright-citizenship-constitution/574381/; Foner, *The Second Founding*, xxix; Lucy E. Salyer, "*Wong Kim Ark:* The Contest over Birthright Citizenship," in Martin and Schuck, *Immigration Stories*, 66.

19. "Aliens and Citizenship," *Los Angeles Times*, Oct. 1, 1895, 3; Salyer, "*Wong Kim Ark:* The Contest over Birthright Citizenship," 63; "No Ballots for Mongols," *San Francisco Examiner*, May 2, 1896, 16.

20. Minor v. Happersett, 88 U.S. 162, 168 (1875); "A Question of Citizenship," *San Francisco Call*, Feb. 8, 1896.

21. Andy Kiersz, Leanna Garfield, and Shayanne Gal, "Migrant Detention Centers in the United States Are Under Fire for Their Horrifying Conditions—and There's at Least One in Every State," *Business Insider*, July 5, 2019, https://www.businessinsider.com/ice-immigrant-families-dhs-detention-centers-2018-6; Petition for Writ of Habeas Corpus at 2, Wong Kim Ark Files, National Archives.

22. Wong Kim Ark Files, National Archives. Wong's lawyer could have argued that because Wong had been previously admitted to the United States in 1890, the government had already resolved the question of his right to re-enter in his favor and could not change its mind now. Whatever the merits of that argument, he chose not to make it because he preferred that the "broad principle of citizenship [be] settled for all time." It is unclear whether Wong was fully informed and consulted before that choice was made. "All Asiatics Affected," *San Francisco Call*, Nov. 13, 1895.

23. Lucy Salyer, "Captives of Law: Judicial Enforcement of the Chinese Exclusion Laws, 1891–1905," in *Chinese Immigrants and American Law*, vol. 1, ed. Charles McClain (New York: Garland Publishing, 1994), 372.

24. Chinese Exclusion Case, 130 U.S. 581, 595 (1889).

25. "All Asiatics Affected: The Question of Citizenship of American-Born Chinese Sweeping," *San Francisco Call*, Nov. 13, 1895; "A Question of Citizenship," *San Francisco Call*, Feb. 8, 1896.

26. "Chinese as Citizens," *San Francisco Call*, Jan. 4, 1896, 5; "Chinese and the Law," *San Francisco Call*, Nov. 14, 1895.

27. John E. Semonche, *Charting the Future: The Supreme Court Responds to a Changing Society, 1890–1920* (Westport, CT: Greenwood Press, 1978), 4, 9.

28. Salyer, "*Wong Kim Ark:* The Contest over Birthright Citizenship," 69; "The Question of Citizenship," *San Francisco Call*, Feb. 8, 1896.

29. "Holmes Conrad," Office of the Solicitor General, https://web.archive.org/web/20081009072131/http://www.usdoj.gov/osg/aboutosg/holmescbio.htm.

30. Fong Yue Ting v. United States, 149 U.S. 698 (1893).

31. Brief for the United States [Conrad] at 49–51, United States v. Wong Kim Ark, 169 U.S. 649 (1898).

32. Brief for the United States [Conrad] at 46–48 & n.1, United States v. Wong Kim Ark, 169 U.S. 649 (1898) (quoting George Ticknor Curtis, *Constitutional History of the United States: vol. 2, From 1877 to the Present*, ed. Joseph Culbertson Clayton [New York: Harper & Bros., 1896], 376).

33. Brief for the United States [Conrad] at 16–17, United States v. Wong Kim Ark, 169 U.S. 649 (1898).

34. George D. Collins, "Are Persons Born Within the United States Ipso Facto Citizens Thereof?," *American Law Review* 18 (1884): 831–38.

35. Salyer, "*Wong Kim Ark*: The Contest over Birthright Citizenship," 65; "Bigamus Lawyer Still Has Hopes," *Fresno Morning Republican*, Dec. 30, 1907, 6; "George D. Collins v. Thomas F. O'Neil," *American Journal of International Law* 3, no. 3 (July 1909): 747–52.

36. "Attorney Collins' Part," *San Francisco Call*, Nov. 14, 1895, 11; "No Ballots for Mongols," *San Francisco Examiner*, May 2, 1896, 16.

37. Calavita, "The Paradoxes of Race, Class, Identity, and Passing," *Law & Social Inquiry* 4 (quoting an 1877 congressional report); Volpp, "Divesting Citizenship," 415.

38. Brief for the United States [Collins] at 34, United States v. Wong Kim Ark, 169 U.S. 649 (1898).

39. Brief for the United States [Collins] at 32–34, 37, United States v. Wong Kim Ark, 169 U.S. 649 (1898); "The Question of Citizenship," *San Francisco Call*, Feb. 8, 1896.

40. Brief for Wong Kim Ark [Ashton, 1896], at 14–18, United States v. Wong Kim Ark, 169 U.S. 649 (1898) (quoting Sen. Sumner, 40th Cong., 3rd Sess., *Congressional Globe* [Feb. 5, 1869] S 903).

41. The citizenship struggles of Native Americans are complex and deserve their own book. For most groups throughout US history, acquiring citizenship is a path toward obtaining the full civil, political, and social rights of membership. But for Native Americans, the imposition of citizenship was often used to undermine tribal sovereignty and traditional ways of life, as well as to appropriate tribal land. Berger, "Birthright Citizenship on Trial," 1185–258.

42. Brief for Wong Kim Ark [Ashton, 1896], at 22–24, United States v. Wong Kim Ark, 169 U.S. 649 (1898); Berger, "Birthright Citizenship on Trial," 1197–98. 43. Brief for Wong Kim Ark [Ashton, 1896], at 6-8, United States v. Wong Kim Ark, 169 U.S. 649 (1898).

44. Salyer, "*Wong Kim Ark*: The Contest over Birthright Citizenship," 77.

45. United States v. Wong Kim Ark, 169 U.S. 682, 693.

46. United States v. Wong Kim Ark, 169 U.S. 694.

47. United States v. Wong Kim Ark, 169 U.S. 731; Willard L. King, *Melville Weston Fuller: Chief Justice of the United States 1888–1910* (Chicago: University of Chicago Press, 1967), 235.

48. James W. Gordon, "Was the First Justice Harlan Anti-Chinese?," *Western New England Law Review* 36 (2014): 288–89; Goodwin Liu, "The First Justice Harlan," *California Law Review* 96 (2008): 1383–93; Gabriel J. Chin, "The *Plessy* Myth: Justice Harlan and the Chinese Cases," *Iowa Law Review* 82 (1996): 151–82; Plessy v. Ferguson, 163 U.S. 537, 559 (1896) (Harlan, J. *dissenting*).

49. Denesh Sohoni, "Unsuitable Suitors: Anti-Miscegenation Laws, Naturalization Laws, and the Construction of Asian Identities," *Law & Society Review* 41 (2007): 587, 596, Table 2; Sucheng Chan, "Against All Odds: Chinese Female Migration and Family Formation on American Soil During the Early Twentieth Century," in *Chinese American Transnationalism: The Flow of People, Resources, and Ideas between China and America During the Exclusion Era*, ed. Sucheng Chan (Philadelphia: Temple University Press, 2006), 41–42.

50. Lee, *At America's Gates*, 66; Salyer, *Laws Harsh as Tigers*, 67.

51. Salyer, *Laws Harsh as Tigers*, 65; Report of the Commissioner-General of Immigration, Department of Commerce and Labor, Bureau of Immigration and Naturalization, July 1, 1907, 107–8, https://babel.hathitrust.org/cgi/pt?id=uiug.30112003908420&view=1up&seq=9; "The Chinese Horde. Methods Adopted for Keeping Track of the Coolies," *Daily Examiner* (San Francisco), June 30, 1888; Erika Lee, "The Story of *United States v. Wong Kim Ark*," in *Race Law Stories*, ed. Rachel F. Moran and Devon W. Carbado (New York: Foundation Press, 2008), 103; Lee, *At America's Gate*, 185, 196–97, 209–12; Salyer, *Laws Harsh as Tigers*, 59–60, 150.

52. Lee, *At America's Gate*, 208; Mary Roberts Coolidge, *Chinese Immigration* (New York: Henry Holt, 1909), 324.

53. "Angel Island Immigration Station Poetry," 1910, http://www.digitalhistory.uh.edu/disp _textbook.cfm?smtid=3&psid=42.

54. "Decision Makes a Precedent," *San Francisco Chronicle*, July 19, 1904, 5.

55. "Affidavit of Frank V. Bell, October 25, 1901," Wong Kim Ark Files, National Archives.

56. Lee, "The Story of *United States v. Wong Kim Ark*," 105.

57. United States v. Wong Kim Ark, El Paso case 802(7), WTX097A1, Equity Case Files Relating to Deportation of Chinese 1892–1915, National Archives and Records Administration, El Paso.

58. Erika Lee and Judy Yung, *Angel Island: Immigrant Gateway to America* (Oxford, UK: Oxford University Press, 2010), 8.

59. All of the above information regarding Wong Yook Fun's attempt to enter the United States came from Wong Yook Fun File, Record Group 85, Archival Research Catalog Identifier 10434, National Archives and Records Administration–San Bruno, CA.

60. Wong Yook Sue File, Record Group 85, Archival Research Catalog Identifier 23517, National Archives and Records Administration—San Bruno, CA; Wong Yook Thue File, Record Group 85, Archival Research Catalog Identifier 29438, National Archives and Records Administration–San Bruno, CA; Wong Yook Jim File, Record Group 85, Archival Research Catalog Identifier 30980, National Archives and Records Administration—San Bruno, CA. Yook Jim reported that he was born on January 5, 1915, which would make him eleven years old when he arrived in the United States, though at other times he gave his age as thirteen years old. Wong Kim Ark returned to the United States from China in the fall of 1914, and responded "no" when asked in 1926 if he had "ever seen" his son before their meeting on Angel Island, which further confirms that Yook Jim was born in 1915.

61. Lee, "The Story of *United States v. Wong Kim Ark*," 102; Ngai, "Legacies of Exclusion: Illegal Chinese Immigration During the Cold War Years," 3; Salyer, *Laws Harsh as Tigers*, 44.

62. Estelle T. Lau, *Paper Families: Identity, Immigration Administration, and Chinese Exclusion* (Durham, NC: Duke University Press, 2006), 36–38; Lee, *At America's Gates*, 202; Ngai, "Legacies of Exclusion," 6.

63. US Department of Labor, *Annual Report of the Commissioner General of Immigration to the Secretary of Labor*, 1925, 22–23, https://babel.hathitrust.org/cgi/pt?id=uc1.l0054909940;view=1up;seq=203.

64. Ngai, "Legacies of Exclusion," 4–6.

65. Lee, *At America's Gates*, 197, 198, 215; Jorae, *The Children of Chinatown*, 13; Salyer, *Laws Harsh as Tigers*, 59.

66. Ngai, "Legacies of Exclusion," 4–6; Salyer, *Laws Harsh as Tigers*, 61–62.

67. Alien Case File for Wong Hang Juen (aka Wong Yook Sue).

68. Alien Case File for Wong Hang Juen (aka Wong Yook Sue).

69. K. Scott Wong, introduction to *Paper Son: One Man's Story*, by Tung Pok Chin with Winifred C. Chin (Philadelphia: Temple University Press, 2000), xvii.

70. Him Mark Lai, *Becoming Chinese American: A History of Communities and Institutions* (Walnut Creek, CA: AltaMira Press, 2004), 32.

71. Lee, *At America's Gate*, 169; *Hearings Before the President's Commission on Immigration and Naturalization*, US Congress, House of Representatives, Sept. 30, 1952, at 271, https://babel.hathitrust.org/cgi/pt?id=umn.31951d02533451a;view=1up;seq=9.

72. Gordon H. Chang and Shelley Fisher Fishkin, "The Chinese Helped Build America," *Forbes*, May 12, 2014, https://www.forbes.com/sites/forbesasia/2014/05/12/the-chinese-helped-build-america.

73. William Wong, *Yellow Journalist: Dispatches from Asian America* (Philadelphia: Temple University Press, 2001), 55.

74. Wong Yook Jim File, National Archives and Records Administration; Wong, *Yellow Journalist*, 52–55; "The Progeny of Citizen Wong," *SFWeekly*, Nov. 4, 1998, https://www.sfweekly.com/news/the-progeny-of-citizen-wong/; telephone interview with Julie D. Soo, Mar. 5, 2019; email from Julie D. Soo to the author, Apr. 14, 2020; telephone interview with Sandra Wong, Apr. 8, 2019.

CHAPTER 4: CITIZEN SUFFRAGIST
1. "Dainty Suffragette Wins Plaudits by Fiery Speech," *Oakland Tribune*, Mar. 12, 1911, 1; "Miss Pankhurst to Speak Here," *Oakland Tribune*, Mar. 9, 1911, 8.

2. Robert P. J. Cooney Jr., "California Women Suffrage Centennial: A Brief Summary of the 1911 Campaign," https://www.sos.ca.gov/elections/celebrating-womens-suffrage/california-women-suffrage-centennial.

3. Susan Englander, "'We Want the Ballot for Very Different Reasons': Clubwomen, Union Women, and the Internal Politics of the Suffrage Movement, 1896–1911," in *California Women and Politics: From the Gold Rush to the Great Depression*, ed. Robert W. Cherny, Mary Ann Irwin, and Ann Marie Wilson (Lincoln: University of Nebraska Press, 2011), 209.

4. "McKenzie Gordon to Wed Beautiful Ethel Coope," *San Francisco Examiner*, June 10, 1909, 6. Ethel was born "Ethel Coope," was known as "Ethel Mackenzie" during the early years of her marriage, but later became "Ethel Gordon" after her husband changed his name.

5. "Opposition to Suffrage Found at Both Ends of Society," *San Francisco Chronicle*, Oct. 4, 1911, 7.

6. "Opposition to Suffrage Found at Both Ends of Society."

7. "Dainty Suffragette Wins Plaudits by Fiery Speech."

8. "Dainty Suffragette Wins Plaudits by Fiery Speech."

9. "San Francisco Earthquake, 1906," National Archives, Center for Legislative Archives, https://www.archives.gov/legislative/features/sf; Carl Nolte, "The Great Quake: 1906–2006 / Rising from the Ashes," *SFGate*, Apr. 18, 2006, https://www.sfgate.com/news/article/The-Great -Quake-1906-2006-Rising-from-the-ashes-2537103.php.

10. Jessica Ellen Sewell, *Women and the Everyday City: Public Space in San Francisco, 1890–1915* (Minneapolis: University of Minnesota Press, 2011), 127–67.

11. "Suffragist Outpost Watch Voting Booths," *San Francisco Chronicle*, Oct. 11, 1911, 2.

12. "Woman Suffrage Amendment Defeated by 5000," *San Francisco Chronicle*, Oct. 11, 1911, 1; "Suffrage Defeated by Adverse Vote in San Francisco," *Los Angeles Express*, Oct. 11, 1911; "Woman Suffrage Defeated in the State of California," *Evening Times-Star* (Alameda, CA), Oct. 11, 1911, 1; "Suffrage Appears Lost—the Recall Carries," *L.A. Times*, Oct. 11, 1911, 1.

13. "Overpowered, but Not Conquered," *San Francisco Chronicle*, Oct. 11, 1911, 2; "Suffragist Outpost Watch Voting Booths."

14. "Mackenzie Gordon Here for Rest," *Desert Sun* (Palm Springs, CA), Dec. 9, 1938, 7.

15. "Popular Tenor Is in Luck," *Chicago Tribune*, Dec. 29, 1896, 4; "Mackenzie Gordon Here for Rest"; "Singing to Millions," *Wichita Daily Eagle*, Oct. 24, 1899, 8.

16. "Amusements," *Woodland Daily Democrat* (CA), Mar. 5, 1910, 3; "Popular Tenor Is in Luck."

17. "Mackenzie Gordon Here for Rest."

18. "Mackenzie Gordon Here for Rest"; "Gordon's First Public Recital," *San Francisco Chronicle*, Apr. 17, 1907, 11; "Of Local Interest," *Arizona Republic*, June 21, 1905, 5.

19. "McKenzie Gordon to Wed Beautiful Ethel Coope," *San Francisco Examiner*, June 10, 1909, 6.

20. "Society," *San Francisco Call*, Aug. 22, 1909; "Mackenzie Gordon and Miss Coope Married," *San Francisco Call*, Aug. 15, 1909, 25; "Social Notes," *San Francisco Examiner*, Aug. 16, 1909, 7; "Mackenzie Gordon Will Claim Bride Today."

21. "Will Test Law of Citizenship," *Oakland Tribune*, Feb. 3, 1913, 5; "Suffrage Leader Can't Vote Going to Kick Up Big Row," *Sacramento Star*, Jan. 30, 1913, 1; Brief for Petitioner at 3, Mackenzie v. Hare, 239 U.S. 299 (1915).

22. "875 Women Flock to Register."

23. "875 Women Flock to Register."

24. Act of Mar. 2, 1907, 34 Stat. 1228. The Act of Feb. 10, 1855, 10 Stat. 604 automatically conferred US citizenship upon all noncitizen women who married American men. Martha Mabie Gardner, *The Qualities of a Citizen: Women, Immigration, and Citizenship, 1870–1965* (Princeton, NJ: Princeton University Press, 2005), 14; Cott, "Marriage and Women's Citizenship in the United States," 1462.

25. Statement of US Representative John L. Cable, "American Citizenship Rights of Women," in *Hearing Before a Subcommittee of the Committee on Immigration, United States Senate, Seventy-Second Congress, Second Session, on S. 992, S. 2760, S3968, and S. 4169* (Washington, DC: US Government Printing Office, 1933), 9, https://www.loc.gov/law/find/hearings/pdf/0014160126A.pdf.

26. Francis A. Walker, "Restriction of Immigration," *Atlantic*, June 1896; "The Grisly Tale of Sicilian Lynchings," *Italian Tribune*, Mar. 28, 2019; John V. Baiamonte Jr., *Spirit of Vengeance: Nativism and Louisiana Justice, 1921–1924* (Baton Rouge: Louisiana State University Press, 1986), 63.

27. "Lynch Law and the Mafia," *New York Times*, Mar. 17, 1891, 4; Richard D. White Jr., *Roosevelt the Reformer: Theodore Roosevelt as Civil Service Commissioner, 1889–1895* (Tuscaloosa: University of Alabama Press, 2003), 145; US Immigration Commission, S. Doc. 61–747, in *Abstracts of Reports of the Immigration Commission, with Conclusions and Recommendations and Views of the Minority* (Washington, DC: US Government Printing Office, 1911), 13–14, 47.

28. Cott, "Marriage and Women's Citizenship in the United States," 1461.

29. US Congress, House, Committee on Immigration and Naturalization, *Relative to Citizenship of American Women Married to Foreigners*, 65th Cong., 2nd Sess., 1917, 6, 14, 17; Bredbenner, *A Nationality of Her Own*, 61–63.

30. Bredbenner, *A Nationality of Her Own*, 63–64; "Women's Suffrage in the U.S. by State," compiled by the Center for American Women and Politics, http://tag.rutgers.edu/wp-content /uploads/2014/05/suffrage-by-state.pdf.

31. "Mackenzie Gordon's Wife Wonders Why She Can't Vote," *Arizona Republican*, Oct. 20, 1913, 1.

32. Linda J. Lumsden, *Inez: The Life and Times of Inez Milholland* (Bloomington: Indiana University Press, 2003), 103; Bredbenner, *A Nationality of Her Own*, 83; *Commonwealth v.*

Bleischwitz et ux., 14 Pa. D. & C. 170 (Court of Common Pleas of Pennsylvania, Montgomery County, Jan. 24, 1930).

33. "Larch Expulsion Backed," *New York Times*, May 3, 1931; "Says Deported Woman Broke 3 Alien Laws," *Baltimore Sun*, May 3, 1931.

34. US Congress, House, Committee on Immigration and Naturalization, *Readmission of Augusta Louisa de Haven-Alten to the Status and Privileges of a Citizen of the United States: Hearings on S.J. Res. 134*, 66th Cong., 2nd Sess., 1920, 3–4.

35. US Congress, House, Committee on Immigration and Naturalization, *Readmission of Augusta Louisa de Haven-Alten to the Status and Privileges of a Citizen of the United States: Hearings on S.J. Res. 134*, 66th Cong., 2nd Sess., 1920, 3–4; Cable, "American Citizenship Rights of Women," 22–23.

36. Statements of Representatives Madden and Representative Raker, *Congressional Record*, 66th Cong., 2nd Sess. (Apr. 1, 1920), 5107.

37. Cable, "American Citizenship Rights of Women," 18–19; H.J. Resolution 238, 56th Cong., 2nd Sess., 30 Stat. 1496 (1898); US Congress, House, Committee on Immigration and Naturalization, *Readmission of Augusta Louisa de Haven-Alten to the Status and Privileges of a Citizen of the United States: Hearings on S.J. Res. 134*, 66th Cong., 2nd Sess., 1920, 3–4.

38. "Has Committed No Crime: Mrs. Mackenzie Gordon Would Vote," *San Francisco Call*, Feb. 4, 1913, 1; "She Carries Fight for Right to Vote to the Highest Court in Land," *Tacoma Times* (WA), Sept. 13, 1913, 1; "Mackenzie Gordon's Wife Wonders Why She Can't Vote," *Arizona Republican*, Oct. 20, 1913, 1.

39. "Child May Vote, Mother Cannot," *Los Angeles Times*, Apr. 8, 1913, 3; "Has Committed No Crime"; "She Carries Fight for Right to Vote to the Highest Court in Land," *Tacoma Times* (WA), Sept. 13, 1913, 1.

40. "Because Suffrage Leader Can't Vote She Will Start a Row," *Wisconsin State Journal*, Feb. 4, 1913, 7.

41. "Child May Vote, Mother Cannot."

42. "Has Committed No Crime."

43. "Rights of Women Married to Aliens," *Ogden Standard* (UT), Nov. 12, 1915, 1; "She's Carrying Fight for Right to Vote to Highest Court in the Land," *Pittsburgh Press*, Sept. 15, 1913, 21; "A Suffrage Claim," *Ottawa Citizen*, Feb. 5, 1913, 3; "Fights Law that Prevents Her Voting," *Daily Times* (Davenport, IA), Feb. 5, 1914, 4.

44. "The Marriage That Lost a Vote," *Davenport Weekly Democrat and Leader* (IA), Sept. 11, 1913, 8.

45. Charles Henry Butler, *A Century at the Bar of the Supreme Court of the United States* (New York: G. P. Putnam's Sons, 1942), 85; "The Court and Its Traditions," US Supreme Court, https://www.supremecourt.gov/about/traditions.aspx.

46. Brief for Petitioner at 2, Mackenzie v. Hare, 239 U.S. 299 (1915).

47. William D. Bader & Frank J. Williams, *Unknown Justices of the United States Supreme Court* (Buffalo: William S. Hein, 2011), 113; Clare Cushman, ed., *The Supreme Court Justices*, 2nd ed. (Washington, DC: Congressional Quarterly, 1995), 281–85; Alpheus Thomas Mason, *William Howard Taft: Chief Justice* (New York: Simon & Schuster, 1965), 213 (quoting letter from William Howard Taft to Horace D. Taft, Apr. 17, 1922).

48. Mackenzie v. Hare, 239 U.S. 299, 311 (1915); Linda K. Kerber, *No Constitutional Right to Be Ladies: Women and the Obligations of Citizenship* (New York: Hill and Wang, 1998), 42.

49. Mackenzie v. Hare, 239 U.S. 299, 312 (1915).

50. "Santa Cruz Girl Restored to Citizenship," *Santa Cruz Evening News*, Jan. 7, 1921, 1.

51. "S.F. Women Are Hit by Court Ruling," *San Francisco Chronicle*, Dec. 7, 1915, 3; "Santa Cruz Girl Restored to Citizenship."

CHAPTER 5: CITIZEN STATESWOMAN

1. Brown, *Ruth Bryan Owen*, 3–7.

2. Vickers, *The Life of Ruth Bryan Owen*, 58; Marjory S. Douglas, "Bryan Name Goes Back into National Politics," *New York Times*, Nov. 11, 1928, 8.

3. Brown, *Ruth Bryan Owen*, 3; Rice, "The Riddle of Ruth Bryan Owen," 1, 22; Frances Drewry McMullen, "The Three Ruth's in Congress," *Woman's Journal* 13 (1928): 18.

4. "Florida and the 19th Amendment," National Park Service, https://www.nps.gov/articles/florida-and-the-19th-amendment.htm. Florida's ratification of the Nineteenth Amendment on

May 13, 1969, had symbolic importance, but no legal significance. The Nineteenth Amendment was added to the US Constitution in August 1920, after three-quarters of the states ratified it.

5. Brown, *Ruth Bryan Owen*, 6–7, 54–60; Vickers, *The Life of Ruth Bryan Owen*, 40–41.

6. Brown, *Ruth Bryan Owen*, 5, 7.

7. "Bryan's Daughter Will Run," *New York Times*, Oct. 8, 1909, 1.

8. Ruth Bryan Owen to Carrie Dunlap, Nov. 18, 1915, Carrie Dunlap Papers, Box 1, Folder 44; Vickers, *The Life of Ruth Bryan Owen*, 33; Vickers, *The Life of Ruth Bryan Owen*, 33; Brown, *Ruth Bryan Owen*, 44; Ruth Bryan Owen to Carrie Dunlap, Mar. 3, 1916, Carrie Dunlap Papers, Box 1, Folder 44.

9. Vickers, *The Life of Ruth Bryan Owen*, 34; Brown, *Ruth Bryan Owen*, 71.

10. Ruth Bryan Owen to Carrie Dunlap, Dec. 25, 1918, Carrie Dunlap Papers, Box 1, Folder 44; Brown, *Ruth Bryan Owen*, 46.

11. Brown, *Ruth Bryan Owen*, 5–6, 57–60; Vickers, *The Life of Ruth Bryan Owen*, 41.

12. "Congresswoman, Unmarried, Comes to the Aid of Cupid," *Evening Report* (Lebanon, PA), Dec. 13, 1917.

13. US Congress, House, Committee on Immigration and Naturalization, *Relative to Citizenship of American Women Married to Foreigners*, 65th Cong., 2nd Sess., 1917, 8, 14.

14. US Congress, House, Committee, *Relative to Citizenship*, 19.

15. "Women's Suffrage: Tennessee and the Passage of the 19th Amendment," Tennessee Secretary of State, https://sos.tn.gov/products/tsla/womens-suffrage-tennessee-and-passage-19th-amendment, accessed Feb. 22, 2020; US Congress, House, Committee on Immigration and Naturalization, *Changes in Naturalization Laws*, 66th Cong., 2nd Sess., 1928, 18 (Statement of Representative John Jacob Rogers).

16. Bredbenner, *A Nationality of Her Own*, 80–82, 81n1; Cable, "American Citizenship Rights of Women," 27.

17. An Act Relative to the Naturalization and Citizenship of Married Women (Cable Act), § 3, 42 Stat. 1021 (1922).

18. Cable Act, §§ 3, 5, 42 Stat. 1021, 1022; Ex parte (Ng) Fung Sing, 6 F.2d 670 (W.D. Wash. 1925); Volpp, "Divesting Citizenship," 405, 407; López, *White By Law*; Cott, "Marriage and Women's Citizenship in the United States," 1467.

19. Rice, "The Riddle of Ruth Bryan Owen," 21.

20. "Bryan's Daughter Seeks Congress Seat," *New York Times*, Apr. 9, 1926.

21. "Bryan's Daughter Loses in Florida," *New York Times*, Jun. 10, 1926; Brown, *Ruth Bryan Owen*, 88.

22. Vickers, *The Life of Ruth Bryan Owen*, 55, 58, 61; Anna Rothe, ed., *Current Biography: Who's News and Why, 1944* (New York: H. W. Wilson, 1945), 523.

23. Vickers, *The Life of Ruth Bryan Owen*, 62; Marjory S. Douglas, "Bryan Name Goes Back into National Politics," *New York Times*, Nov. 11, 1928, 8; Herbert C. Plummer, "Washington Daybook," *Orlando Evening Star*, Mar. 28, 1929; Drew DeSilver, "A Record Number of Women Will Be Serving in the New Congress," Pew Research Center, Dec. 18, 2018, https://www.pewresearch.org/fact-tank/2018/12/18/record-number-women-in-congress/.

24. *Arguments and Hearings Before Election Committee No. 1*, 15–16 (hereinafter Lawson v. Owen Hearing); US Constitution, Article I, § 5.

25. "G.O.P. Contests Congress Seat," *St. Petersburg Times*, Nov. 29, 1928.

26. "To Appeal on Mrs. Owen," *New York Times*, Nov. 30, 1928; "Mrs. Owen Pokes Fun at Election Contest," *Atlanta Constitution*, Nov. 30, 1928; "Much Alive Corpse," *Fort Myers News-Press* (FL), Jan. 18, 1930, 6.

27. "Place for Mrs. Owen," *New York Times*, Dec. 8, 1929, 30; "Bryan's Daughter Making Good Congresswoman from Florida," *Palm Beach Post* (FL), Jun. 16, 1929, 8; S. J. Woolf, "A Woman's Voice in Foreign Affairs," *New York Times Magazine*, Jan. 5, 1930, 7; "Miss Faith Binkley Writes of Florida Congresswoman," *Pensacola News Journal* (FL), Mar. 28, 1929, 5; Rothe, *Current Biography*, 523; letter from Ruth Bryan Owen to Minnie Moore Willson, Feb. 27, 1928, Minnie Moore Willson Papers.

28. Lawson v. Owen Hearing, 35, 47.

29. "Much Alive Corpse"; Lawson v. Owen Hearing, 1.

30. Lawson v. Owen Hearing, 22.

31. Lawson v. Owen Hearing, 32.

32. Lawson v. Owen Hearing, 32.

33. Lawson v. Owen Hearing, 32; "Bryan's Daughter Says Citizenship Regained in 1925," *Lincoln Star*, Jan. 18, 1930; "Mrs. Owen Makes a Plea," *Winnipeg Tribune*, Jan. 29, 1930.

34. Lawson v. Owen Hearing, 47.

35. Lawson v. Owen Hearing, 54.

36. Lawson v. Owen Hearing, 61.

37. Lawson v. Owen Hearing, 54, 55, 59, 61.

38. Lawson v. Owen Hearing, 55.

39. Lawson v. Owen Hearing, 54–55.

40. "Mrs. Ruth Owen Defends Right to House Seat," *Tampa Tribune*, Jan. 19, 1930, 1, 3; "House Hears Appeal Made by Ruth Owen," *Arizona Republic*, Jan. 19, 1930, 1; "Mrs. Owen Makes a Plea"; Lawson v. Owen Hearing, 55, 57.

41. Lawson v. Owen Hearing, 58.

42. US Congress, House, Committee on Elections, *William C. Lawson-Ruth Bryan Owen Election Case*, H.R. Rep. No. 71–968, 71st Cong., 2nd Sess., 1930, 7 (hereinafter Lawson-Owen House Report).

43. Lawson-Owen House Report, 4; Statement of Representative Beedy, *Congressional Record*, 72nd Cong., 2nd Sess. (1930), 10195.

44. Lawson-Owen House Report, 7.

45. Statement of Representative Beedy, *Congressional Record*, 72nd Cong., 2nd Sess. (1930), 10195, 10198.

46. *Amendment to the Women's Citizenship Act of 1922*, 16; "A Victory for American Women," *Tampa Tribune*, Mar. 31, 1931, 6.

47. "A Victory for American Women"; S. E. Spicer, "Shouting Highly in Order, Writer Declares After Women's Bill Passes," *Cincinnati Enquirer*, Mar. 8, 1931, 16.

48. "A Victory for American Women"; "Mrs. Ruth Bryan Owen Wins Election Fight," *Tallahassee Democrat*, June 6, 1930, 3.

CHAPTER 6: *BLUT* CITIZEN

1. Bernstein, *Swastika Nation*, 1–2.

2. *A Night at the Garden,* directed by Marshall Curry (Marshall Curry Productions, 2017), https://anightatthegarden.com; Bernstein, *Swastika Nation*, 1–3, 180, 184.

3. Bernstein, *Swastika Nation*, 2; *A Night at the Garden*; Jay Maeder, "RATZIS: Fritz Kuhn and the Bund, 1939," in *Big Town, Big Time: A New York Epic: 1898–1998*, ed. Jay Maeder (New York: New York Daily News, 1999), 85.

4. Fritz Kuhn, "What Are WE?," *Deutscher Weckruf und Beobachter*, Oct. 7, 1936, quoted in Diamond, *The Nazi Movement in the United States*, 218.

5. Greg Bradsher, "Archives Receives Original Nazi Documents That 'Legalized' Persecution of Jews," *Prologue* 42, no. 4 (Winter 2010), https://www.archives.gov/publications/prologue/2010/winter/nuremberg.html.

6. Cornelia Wilhelm, "Nazi Propaganda and the Uses of the Past: Heinz Kloss and the Making of a 'German America,'" *American Studies* 47, no. 1 (2002): 59. In 1940, there were 1.2 million German immigrants in America, slightly under 1 percent of the population. Another 7.2 million were immediate descendants of German immigrant parents, and it was believed another 12 million were of more distant German descent. Citing similar figures, in the mid-1930s the Deutsches Ausland-Institut (German Foreign Institute) in Stuttgart engaged in a multiyear project intended to demonstrate that America was "as much German as Anglo-Saxon," and to prove "America was built by German immigrants, the Hitlerian 'Viking types.'" Diamond, *Nazi Movement*, 72.

7. Bernstein, *Swastika Nation*, 12, 14, 18, 20, 31, 49, 158–60, 166–73.

8. Diamond, *Nazi Movement*, 205; "The Bund Meeting," *New York Times*, Feb. 22, 1939.

9. Kurihara, *Autobiography, Speeches, and Statements*, 25.

10. 8 U.S.C. § 1405. Under the Organic Act of 1900, which made Hawai'i a US territory, all persons who were citizens of the Republic of Hawai'i on Aug. 12, 1898, automatically became US citizens on April 30, 1900, the date of the legislation's enactment. The Hawai'i Constitution of 1894 declared that all persons born in Hawai'i were Hawaiian citizens.

11. Kurihara, *Autobiography, Speeches, and Statements*, 27–28.

12. Kurihara, *Autobiography, Speeches, and Statements*, 29–30.

13. Kurihara, *Autobiography, Speeches, and Statements*, 31–37.

14. Kurihara, *Autobiography, Speeches, and Statements*, 2–3.

15. Kurihara, *Autobiography, Speeches, and Statements*, 9.

16. Volpp, "Divesting Citizenship," 411–15; *Joint Hearings before the Subcommittees of the Committees on the Judiciary, Congress of the United States, 82nd Congress, First Session, on S. 716 H.R. 2379, and H.R. 2816 Bills to Revise the Laws Relating to Immigration, Naturalization, and Nationality* (Washington, DC: US Government Printing Office, 1951), 59–60.

17. US Census Bureau, *Thirteenth Census of the United States, Statistics for Hawaii, 1910* (Washington, DC: US Government Printing Office, 1913), 9; Kurihara, *Autobiography*, 3.

18. Eric L. Muller, *American Inquisition: The Hunt for Japanese American Disloyalty in World War II* (Chapel Hill: University of North Carolina Press, 2007), 11–12.

19. Muller, *American Inquisition*, 15–16.

20. Morton Grodzins, *Americans Betrayed: Politics and the Japanese Evacuation* (Chicago: University of Chicago Press, 1949), 399; John Eric Schmitz, "Enemies Among Us: The Relocation and Repatriation of German, Italian and Japanese Americans During the Second World War" (PhD diss., American University, 2007), 277–78; "Manila Fifth Column Active," *Los Angeles Times*, Dec. 10, 1941, 4.

21. Jan Jarboe Russell, "5 Surprises About America's Imprisoning People During World War II," *Business Insider*, Jan. 21, 2015, https://www.businessinsider.com/5-surprises-about-american -internment-during-world-war-ii-2015-1.

22. *Investigation of Un-American Propaganda Activities in the United States, Hearings Before a Special Committee on Un-American Activities, House of Representatives*, 76th Cong., 1st Sess., 3705 (Aug. 16, 1939) (Testimony of Fritz Kuhn), https://babel.hathitrust.org/cgi/pt?id=umn.31951d0349 6539g&view=1up&seq=618.

23. Bernstein, *Swastika Nation*, 206, 223–24.

24. *Investigation of Un-American Propaganda Activities in the United States*, 3712, 3777, 3778, 3784; Bernstein, *Swastika Nation*, 68.

25. Diamond, *Nazi Movement*, 155; *Investigation of Un-American Propaganda Activities in the United States Before the Special Committee on Un-American Activities, House of Representatives*, 76th Cong., 1st Sess., Appendix – Part VII, "Report on the Axis Front Movement in the United States—First Section: Nazi Activities" (Washington, DC: US Government Printing Office, 1943), 60–61; Bernstein, *Swastika Nation*, 80–82; Hearing, *Investigation of Un-American Propaganda Activities in the United States*, 3757.

26. *Investigation of Un-American Propaganda Activities in the United States*, 3772.

27. *Investigation of Un-American Propaganda Activities in the United States*, 3724, 3777–78.

28. David S. Wyman, *The Abandonment of the Jews: America and the Holocaust, 1941–1945* (Lexington, MA: Plunkett Lake Press, 1984); Hazel Gaudet Erskine, "The Polls: Religious Prejudice, Part 2: Anti-Semitism," *Public Opinion Quarterly* 29, no. 4 (Winter 1965–66): 653, 655, 656, 661, https://academic.oup.com/poq/article/29/4/649/1895659; Whitman, *Hitler's American Model*, 57–58.

29. "Goodbye to Joe Starnes," *Crisis* 51, no. 6 (June 1944): 185.

30. John L. DeWitt to Henry L. Stimson, Memorandum: Final Recommendation of the Commanding General, Western Defense Command and Fourth Army, Submitted to the Secretary of War, Feb. 13, 1924, in *Final Report: Japanese Evacuation from the West Coast 1942* (Washington, DC: US Government Printing Office, 1943), appendix to chap. 3; Representative Jackson, *Congressional Record*, 78th Cong., 1st Sess. (Apr. 15, 1943), 89, pt. 3: 3397; Alan Walker, "A Slap's a Slap: General John L. DeWitt and Four Little Words," National Archives: The Text Message, Nov. 22, 2013, https://text-message.blogs.archives.gov/2013/11/22/a-slaps-a-slap-general-john-l-dewitt-and -four-little-words.

31. Henry Stimson, Diary Entry of Feb. 10, 1942, quoted in Irons, *Justice at War*, 55; Leland Ford to William Knox and J. Edgar Hoover, Jan. 16, 1942, quoted in Grodzins, *Americans Betrayed*, 65; *Congressional Record*, 77th Cong., 2nd Sess., 88, pt. 1: 502, quoted in Grodzins, *Americans Betrayed*, 66; Grodzins, *Americans Betrayed*, 77; Sens. Holman and Wallgren and Reps. Lea et al. to President Roosevelt, Feb. 13, 1942, in Stetson Conn, "The Decision to Evacuate the Japanese from the Pacific Coast," in *Command Decisions*, ed. K. R. Greenfield (Washington, DC: US Department of the Army, Office of the Chief of Military History, 1960), 135.

32. Mark Weber, "The Japanese Camps in California," *Journal of Historical Review* 2 (Spring 1980): 45.

33. Western Defense Command and Fourth Army, *Final Report: Japanese Evacuation from the West Coast, 1942* (Washington: US Government Printing Office, 1943), 145, quoted in Grodzins, *Americans Betrayed*, 2.

34. The terminology for describing the forced removal and imprisonment of Japanese and Japanese Americans during World War II is controversial. At the time of their creation, the US government described the camps for Japanese and Japanese Americans as "concentration camps." However, the term "concentration camp" is now closely associated with the Nazi death camps in Europe, where Jews and other Nazi enemies were imprisoned, enslaved, tortured, and murdered in large numbers, and therefore I have chosen not to use that term. That said, commonly used terms such as "internment" and "Japanese internment camps" obscure the fact that the Japanese and Japanese Americans were imprisoned against their will. To avoid such euphemisms, I use terms such as "prisoner," "inmate," and "incarcerated" throughout the text. I refer to the locations in which the Japanese and Japanese American population was imprisoned as "camps." "Civil Exclusion Order: Instructions to All Persons of Japanese Ancestry," No. 69, May 12, 1942, available at National Museum of American History, https://americanhistory.si.edu/collections/search/object /nmah_1694663, accessed August 24, 2020.

35. Kurihara, *Autobiography*, 39.

36. Kurihara, *Autobiography*, 38, 41; Tamura, *In Defense of Justice*, 53; email from Hanako Wakatsuki to author, August 1, 2020.

37. W. A. Swanberg, "The Spies Who Came in from the Sea," *American Heritage* 21, no. 3 (1970), https://www.americanheritage.com/spies-who-came-sea.

38. Swanberg, "Spies."

39. Swanberg, "Spies."

40. Germany had successfully performed such operations in the past. During World War I, German saboteurs had destroyed an arsenal and munitions plant in New Jersey.

41. Swanberg, "Spies"

42. Swanberg, "Spies."

43. Kurihara, "Murder in Camp Manzanar," 9.

44. Interview with Harry Yoshio Ueno, Oct. 30, 1976, conducted by Sue Kunitomi, Arthur A. Hansen, and Betty Kulberg Mitson, as part of the "Japanese American World War II Evacuation Oral History Project, Part IV: Resisters," Arthur A. Hansen, ed., California State University, Fullerton, Oral History Program, Japanese American Project, 36, http://texts.cdlib.org/view?docId =ft1f59n61r&doc.view=entire_text (hereinafter Ueno Oral History).

45. Kurihara, *Autobiography*, appendix, Speech #1, 1, 3; Tamura, *In Defense of Justice*, 61.

46. Kurihara, "Murder in Camp Manzanar," 9; Ueno Oral History, 34.

47. Ueno Oral History, 36n57.

48. Kurihara, "Murder in Camp Manzanar"; Kurihara, *Autobiography*, 49.

49. Tamura, *In Defense of Justice*, 100; Kurihara, *Autobiography*, appendix, Speech #1, 6.

50. "Fritz Kuhn Gives Up Chance to Defend Self," *Burlington Free Press*, Jan. 6, 1943, 2; Diamond, *Nazi Movement*, 346.

51. "Naturalized Foes to Lose Citizenship; Biddle Says Government Will 'Shoot Quickly' at Bundists and Other Disloyal," *New York Times*, Mar. 26, 1942.

52. Weil, *Sovereign Citizen*, 101.

53. "Bundist Shuns Trial to End His Citizenship," *Salt Lake Telegram* (UT), Jan. 5, 1943.

54. United States v. Kuhn, 49 F. Supp. 407, 413 (S.D.N.Y. 1943).

55. United States v. Kuhn, 49 F. Supp. at 412, 414, 416.

56. Under German citizenship policies in 1934, Kuhn remained a citizen of Germany even after naturalizing and becoming an American citizen in 1937. When he lost his US citizenship, he therefore remained a German citizen rather than becoming stateless.

57. The government incarcerated 112,000 Japanese and Japanese Americans in 1942. By 1944, the number of prisoners had dropped to approximately 100,000 after the government permitted some to leave to serve in the military, to attend colleges away from the West Coast, or because they had answered a loyalty questionnaire to the government's satisfaction.

58. Representative Harless, speaking on H.R. 4103, *Congressional Record*, 78th Cong., 2nd Sess. (Feb. 16, 1944), 90, pt. 2: 1787; Louis Merrick Van Patten, "Public Opinion on Japanese Americans," *Far Eastern Survey* 14, no. 15 (1945): 207–8.

59. Collins, *Native American Aliens*, 72–73; John Christgau, *Enemies: World War II Alien Internment* (Ames: Iowa State University Press, 1985), 155.

60. Representative Sabath, speaking on H.R. 4103, *Congressional Record*, 78th Cong., 2nd Sess. (Feb. 16, 1944), 90, pt. 2: 1778; Senator Russell, speaking on H.R. 4013, *Congressional Record*, 78th Cong., 2nd Sess. (June 23, 1944), 90, pt. 5: 6617.

61. Collins, *Native American Aliens*, 93, 118, 142.

62. Thomas and Nishimoto, *The Spoilage*, 312–13, 320–21, 324–25; Collins, *Native American Aliens*, 65, 78, 80.

63. Thomas and Nishimoto, *The Spoilage*, 346–47; Collins, *Native American Aliens*, 90.

64. Charles Wollenberg, *Rebel Lawyer: Wayne Collins and the Defense of Japanese American Rights* (Berkeley, CA: Heyday, 2018), 56; Christgau, *Enemies*, 180.

65. Michi Weglyn, *Years of Infamy: The Untold Story of America's Concentration Camps* (New York: William Morrow, 1976), 157; Minoru Kiyota, *Beyond Loyalty: The Story of a Kibei* (Honolulu: University of Hawai'i Press, 1997), 107, 111–12, quoted in Tamura, *In Defense of Justice*, 122.

66. Kurihara, *Autobiography*, appendix, Speech #1, 1; Tamura, *In Defense of Justice*, 151.

67. Joseph Y. Kurihara, Renunciation of United States Nationality, Jan. 15, 1945, Case File 146-54-117, US Department of Justice, FOIA, quoted in Tamura, *In Defense of Justice*, 133.

68. "6,000 Nisei Ask End of Citizenship," *Fresno Bee*, Mar. 20, 1945; "Have No Place Here," editorial, *Bakersfield Californian*, Nov. 15, 1945, 20.

69. Complaint to Rescind Renunciation of Nationality, to Declare Nationality, for Declaratory Judgment and for Injunction, Nov. 13, 1945, box 467, *Abo v. Clark*, FARC-RG-21, quoted in Christgau, "Collins Versus the World," 11; Wollenberg, *Rebel Lawyer*, 18–19, 61, 64; Jacobus ten-Broek, Edward N. Barnhart, and Floyd W. Matson, *Prejudice, War, and the Constitution: Causes and Consequences of the Evacuation of the Japanese Americans in World War II* (Berkeley: University of California Press, 1954), 320–21, in Collins, *Native American Aliens*, 143–44.

70. Tamura, *In Defense of Justice*, 133, 134; Ishida, "The Japanese American Renunciants of Okayama Prefecture," 106.

71. Ishida, "Japanese American Renunciants," 100, 138.

72. Tamura, *In Defense of Justice*, 137, 139, 140–41.

73. Ishida, "Japanese American Renunciants," 143–44, 151, 152–53.

74. "Nisei Wrong Is 'Righted,'" *Baltimore Sun*, May 21, 1959, 5.

75. Collins, *Native American Aliens*, 142; Tamura at 141.

76. "Apology to Japanese, Forgive Us, Nisei," *Cincinnati Enquirer*, May 21, 1959; "U.S. Asks Nisei Forgive Internment During II," *Berkshire Eagle* (Pittsfield, MA), May 21, 1959, 3; "Ask Relocated Nisei to Forgive 'Mistake,'" *Daily Press* (New York), May 21, 1959.

77. Kurihara, *Autobiography*, appendix ("Verbatim Excerpts from Kurihara's Manuscripts"), 9.

78. Tamura, *In Defense of Justice*, 143.

79. Tamura, *In Defense of Justice*, 143.

80. Kurihara, *Autobiography*, Speech #2, 8.

81. Michael Isikoff, "Delayed Reparations and an Apology," *Washington Post*, Oct. 10, 1990.

82. Tamura, *In Defense of Justice*, 145.

83. Weil, *Sovereign Citizen*, 93.

84. Bernstein, *Swastika Nation*, 282, 285.

85. Bernstein, *Swastika Nation*, 284. (Citing Miller, Watons, undated letter, FBI File, Apr. 12, 1949.)

86. Baumgartner v. United States, 322 U.S. 665, 674 (1944).

87. Weil, *Sovereign Citizen*, 131; "Fritz Kuhn Death in 1951 Revealed," *New York Times*, Feb. 2, 1953.

CHAPTER 7: SUSPECT CITIZEN

1. "Agree on Plan to Arbitrate in San Francisco," *Chicago Tribune*, July 22, 1934, 2; Kevin Starr, *Endangered Dreams: The Great Depression in California* (Oxford, UK: Oxford University Press, 1996), 91.

2. Harvey Schwartz, ed., *Harry Bridges: An Oral History About Longshoring, the Origins of the ILWU and the 1934 Strike*, International Longshore and Warehouse Union Oral History Collection, https://www.ilwu.org/oral-history-of-harry-bridges (hereinafter Bridges Oral History); Bruce Nelson, *Workers on the Waterfront: Seamen, Longshoremen, and Unionism in the 1930s* (Urbana: University of Illinois Press, 1988), 129.

3. Quin, *The Big Strike*, 30.

4. Robert W. Cherny, "Prelude to the Popular Front: The Communist Party in California, 1931–35," *American Communist History* 1, no. 1 (2002): 19–20; "Labor: C.I.O. to Sea," *Time* 30, no. 3 (July 19, 1937); Cherny, "Constructing a Radical Identity," 579, 582; William Serrin, "For Harry Bridges, the Heart of Unionism Still Lies with the Rank and File," *New York Times*, Dec. 1, 1985.

5. Starr, *Endangered Dreams*, 93.

6. Frances Perkins, *The Roosevelt I Knew* (New York: Viking Press, 1946), 316; Serrin, "For Harry Bridges, the Heart of Unionism"; Bridges Oral History.

7. Quin, *The Big Strike*, 31; Fred Glass, *From Mission to Microchip: A History of the California Labor Movement* (Berkeley: University of California Press, 2016), 231; Bridges Oral History. The average weekly wage of a longshoreman in 1934 was $10.45, which is approximately the same amount that Bridges reported earning. Quin, *The Big Strike*, 32.

8. Bridges Oral History; Quin, *The Big Strike*, 41, 52; Starr, *Endangered Dreams*, 84–120; Hobbs, *The Cayton Legacy*, 149–52.

9. Louis Ashlock, "Eye Witness Reminded of War Scenes," *San Bernardino County Sun*, July 6, 1934, 1; "Troops Called; 22 Shot in Riots," *Oakland Tribune*, July 5, 1934, 1; Royce Brier, "Blood Floods Gutters as Police, Strikers War," *San Francisco Chronicle*, July 6, 1934, 1. For a short video clip of the violence, see "1934 Longshore Strike," YouTube, September 19, 2007, https://youtu.be/aOAFEi1Yc9M.

10. "Troops Called; 22 Shot in Riot," *Oakland Tribune*; Quin, *The Big Strike*, 111–15; Starr, *Endangered Dreams*, 106; Henry Schmidt, "Secondary Leadership in the ILWU, 1933–1966," an oral history conducted 1974–81 by Miriam F. Stein and Estolv Ethan Ward, Regional Oral History Office, Bancroft Library, University of California, Berkeley, 1983, 93–101.

11. Nelson, *Workers on the Waterfront*, 129; Royal W. Jimerson, "Troops Guard Front! 2 Dead, 109 Hurt in Rioting," *San Francisco Chronicle*, July 6, 1934, 1; Quin, *The Big Strike*, 115, 116; Brier, "Blood Floods Gutters," 1; Larrowe, *Harry Bridges*, 67. Henry Schmidt reports that he did not see Harry Bridges during the "Battle of Rincon Hill," contradicting other sources that say he led the charge. Henry Schmidt, "Secondary Leadership in the ILWU, 1933–1966," an oral history conducted 1974–81 by Miriam F. Stein and Estolv Ethan Ward, Regional Oral History Office, Bancroft Library, University of California, Berkeley, 1983, 104.

12. Quin, *The Big Strike*, 4, 137; Starr, *Endangered Dreams*, 114; David F. Selvin, *A Terrible Anger: The 1934 Waterfront and General Strikes in San Francisco* (Detroit: Wayne State University Press, 1996), 17.

13. Serrin, "For Harry Bridges, the Heart of Unionism"; Bridges Oral History.

14. "Labor: C.I.O. to Sea," *Time* 30, no. 3 (July 19, 1937); Selvin, *A Terrible Anger*, 17.

15. Peter Irons, *A People's History of the Supreme Court: The Men and Women Whose Cases and Decisions Have Shaped Our Constitution* (New York: Penguin Books, 1999), 295.

16. Ellen Schrecker, *The Age of McCarthyism: A Brief History with Documents*, 2nd ed. (New York: Palgrave, 2002), 7.

17. Starr, *Endangered Dreams*, 101; Larrowe, *Harry Bridges*, 105–6.

18. "Labor Leaders Start Drive on Western Reds," *Chicago Tribune*, July 22, 1934, 2; "Americanism Versus Communism," *San Francisco Examiner*, July 23, 1934, 1; "The Beleaguered City," *Los Angeles Times*, July 17, 1934, 22.

19. Jimerson, "Troops Guard Front!," *San Francisco Chronicle*, July 6, 1934, 1; Quin, *The Big Strike*, 141.

20. Telegraph from MacCormack to District Director, INS, Angel Island, California, Record Group 85, Records of Immigration and Naturalization Services, 1787–2004, Series: Records Relating to Harry Bridges, 1920–1965, File Unit 12020/25037(1) Bridges, Harry Renton City Office File, National Archives and Records Administration–San Bruno.

21. C. P. Trussell, "Deportation of Bridges Is Voted by House," *Sun* (Baltimore), June 14, 1940, 1; United States v. Bridges, 133 F. Supp. 638, 644 (N.D. Cal. 1955); Peter Afrasiabi, *Burning Bridges: America's 20 Year Crusade to Deport Labor Leader Harry Bridges*, (Brooklyn: Thirlmere Books, 2016), Kindle ed., loc. 278–84.

22. "Supreme Court Clears Docket in Final Day of Close Decisions," *New York Times*, June 19, 1945. Although nine justices sit on the court, only eight would decide Bridges's case because Justice Robert Jackson had recused himself. To win, Bridges would need at least five votes; a 4–4 tie would affirm Bridges's loss in the court below.

23. Brief for Respondent United States at 98, Bridges v. Wixon, 326 U.S. 135, 154 (1945); Alien Anarchists Exclusion Act of 1918, 40 Stat. 1012 (Oct. 16, 1918); Stanley I. Kutler, *The American Inquisition: Justice and Injustice in the Cold War* (New York: Hill and Wang, 1982), 126; Murray, *Red Scare*, 14–15.

24. Larrowe, "Did the Old Left Get Due Process—the Case of Harry Bridges," 78; *In the Matter of Harry R. Bridges: Findings and Conclusions of the Trial Examiner* (Washington, DC: Government Printing Office, 1939), 18n38, 47, 147.

25. A Bill to Authorize the Deportation of Harry Renton Bridges, 1940, H.R. 9766, 76th Cong., 3rd Sess. The vote was 330–42. Kutler, *The American Inquisition*, 134–35; Representative Sam Hobbs, speaking on H.R. 5138, *Alien Registration Act of 1940*, *Congressional Record*, 76th Cong., 3rd Sess. (June 22, 1940), 86: H 9031.
26. Larrowe, *Harry Bridges*, 125; St. Clair McKelway, *Reporting at Wit's End: Tales from the New Yorker* (New York: Bloomsbury USA, 2010), 125–33. The article was first published under the title "Some Fun with the F.B.I.," published in the *New Yorker*, Oct. 11, 1941.
27. Francis Biddle, *In Brief Authority* (New York: Doubleday, 1962), 302. The decision to seek judicial review of Bridges's deportation may have been politically advantageous for the Roosevelt administration because it provided political cover and avoided a final decision for the years it would take for the case to be resolved in the courts.
28. "Supreme Court Clears Docket."
29. Bridges v. Wixon, 326 U.S. 135, 145, 148 (1945). In fact, Bridges himself was the petitioner in a Supreme Court case just a few years before that held that noncitizens were protected by the freedom of speech guaranteed by the First Amendment to the US Constitution. Bridges v. California, 314 U.S. 252 (1941).
30. Bridges, 325 U.S. at 157 (Murphy, J., *concurring*).
31. "Harry Bridges Made Citizen," *Los Angeles Times*, Sept. 18, 1945, 12; Ann Fagan Ginger, *Carol Weiss King: Human Rights Lawyer, 1895–1952* (Niwot: University Press of Colorado, 1993), 421; Lewis Wood, "High Court Blocks Bridges' Expulsion; Deportation Ruled Out by Supreme Court," *New York Times*, June 19, 1945, 9; "Trials of Harry Bridges," *New York Times*, Apr. 9, 1950.
32. "Sails with 249 Reds," *Washington Post*, Dec. 22, 1919, 1; Goldman, *Living My Life*, vol. 2, 717.
33. Carl W. Ackerman, "Emma Goldman Mentor of Czolgosz, McKinley's Slayer, Declare U.S. Investigators," *Washington Post*, Dec. 22, 1919, 1; Ann Hagedorn, *Savage Peace: Hope and Fear in America, 1919* (New York: Simon & Schuster, 2007), 413–14.
34. Goldman, *Living My Life*, vol. 1, 11; Alice Wexler, *Emma Goldman: An Intimate Life* (New York: Pantheon Books, 1984), 30–31; Weil, *The Sovereign Citizen*, 58–59. Goldman was born in Kovno, which was then a part of the Russian Empire but is now in Lithuania.
35. Wexler, *Emma Goldman*, 38.
36. Falk, *Emma Goldman*, vol. 2, *Making Speech Free, 1902–1909* (Berkeley: University of California Press, 2005), 309 (excerpts from Examination of Emma Goldman before Board of Special Inquiry, Apr. 6, 1908) [emphasis added].
37. Goldman, *Living My Life*, vol. 1, 13–18, 37, 185.
38. Falk, *Emma Goldman*, 432 (reprinting Charles Willis Thompson, "An Interview with Emma Goldman," *New York Times*, May 30, 1909).
39. Falk, *Emma Goldman*, 435–36 (reprinting Thompson, "An Interview with Emma Goldman"). However, Goldman had played a behind-the-scenes role in a failed assassination attempt on Henry Clay Frick, an American industrialist who ruthlessly opposed unions. Wexler, *Emma Goldman*, 67, 107–9.
40. Falk, *Emma Goldman*, 288–89 (reprinting letter from Oscar S. Straus to Edwin W. Sims, Washington, DC, Mar. 9, 1908).
41. Weil, *The Sovereign Citizen*, 15–29.
42. Weil, *The Sovereign Citizen*, 56, 136–42.
43. Weil, *The Sovereign Citizen*, 56.
44. "Woman Anarchist May Be Deported," *San Francisco Call*, Apr. 9, 1909; Weil, *The Sovereign Citizen*, 59 (quoting letter of John Gruenberg, immigrant inspector, Ellis Island, NY, to Sargent, May 27, 1908); Falk, *Emma Goldman*, 426 (reprinting letter from Assistant United States Attorney Chambers to Charles J. Bonaparte, Attorney General, Apr. 22, 1909).
45. Falk, *Emma Goldman*, 394 (reprinting letter from Emma Goldman to unknown recipient, Jan. 1909); Wexler, *Emma Goldman*, 231–36; Wexler, *Emma Goldman in Exile*, 9–18.
46. Goldman, *Living My Life*, vol. 2, 594; Wexler, *Emma Goldman*, 275 (quoting letter from Emma Goldman to Stella Ballantine, July 8, 1918).
47. Weil, *Sovereign Citizen*, 195 (quoting Emma Goldman, "A Woman Without a Country")
48. United States v. Stuppiello, 260 F. 483 (D.C.N.Y. 1919).
49. Weil, *Sovereign Citizen*, 1, 92–107.
50. Department of Justice Circular No. 3663, Mar. 25, 1942, from Attorney General Francis Biddle to all US Attorneys, quoted in Weil, *Sovereign Citizen*, 100; Weil, *Sovereign Citizen*, 136–37;

"U.S. House of Representatives. Committee on Un-American Activities. 1945–1969," https:// catalog.archives.gov/id/10462072.

51. Peter B. Flint, "Paul Novick Is Dead; Editor, 97, Helped Start Yiddish Daily," *New York Times*, Aug. 22, 1989, https://www.nytimes.com/1989/08/22/obituaries/paul-novick-is-dead-editor -97-helped-start-yiddish-daily.html.

52. "Faces Denaturalization," *New York Times*, Aug. 26, 1953, 52; Peter Kihss, "'Treason' Charge Made at Inquiry," *New York Times*, Mar. 16, 1957, 8; Alden Whitman, "James J. Matles, a Top Official of Electrical Workers, 66, Dies," *New York Times*, Sept. 17, 1975; Weil, *Sovereign Citizen*, 136–42.

53. Weil, *Sovereign Citizen*, 2.

54. "Sidney Roger: A Liberal Journalist on the Air and on the Waterfront: Labor and Political Issues, 1932–1990," vol. 1, oral history interview by Julie Shearer, 1989–90, Regents of the University of California (1990), at 333–34.

55. "Mr. Bridges Convicted," *New York Times*, Apr. 5, 1950.

56. "Verdict Revokes Bridges' Citizenship; Hallinan and MacInnis Face Jail," *San Francisco Examiner*, Apr. 5, 1950, 8; "Sidney Roger," at 334; "Harry Bridges Convicted of Lying about Red Ties," *Los Angeles Times*, Apr. 5, 1950, 1, 10; "A Kiss for Bridges," *Spokane Daily Chronicle*, Apr. 5, 1950.

57. "Speed Up Deportation Moves, Nixon Urges," *Los Angeles Times*, Apr. 5, 1950, 12; "Let Deportation Proceedings Stick," *La Crosse Tribune* (WI), Apr. 7, 1950, 4; "Good Riddance," *Star Press* (Muncie, IN), Apr. 5, 1950.

58. John F. Allen, "Judge Delays Decision on Bridges Citizenship," *San Francisco Examiner*, Apr. 12, 1950, 5.

59. "Bridges Hears Case Argued in High Court," *New York Times*, May 5, 1953, 16; Transcript of Oral Argument, Bridges v. United States, 346 U.S. 209 (1953).

60. Bridges v. United States, 346 U.S. 209 (1953).

61. Luther A. Huston, "Supreme Court Frees Bridges under Statute of Limitations," *New York Times*, June 16, 1953, 1; "Bridges Is Jubilant," *New York Times*, June 16, 1953, 21.

62. Kutler, *American Inquisition*, 149.

63. Michael T. Kaufman, "Noriko Flynn, 79, Advocate for Unions and Civil Rights," *New York Times*, Feb. 17, 2003, B7.

64. Linda Charlton, "Bridges, Once a 'Troublemaker,' Takes Place of Honor in Capital," *New York Times*, Jan. 18, 1978, A14; Mark Magnier, "Labor Leader Bridges Leaves Behind a Legacy," *Maritime News*, Apr. 2, 1990, https://www.joc.com/maritime-news/labor-leader-bridges-leaves -behind-legacy-founder-ilwu-dies-emphysema_19900402.html; Wolfgang Saxon, "Harry Bridges, Docks Leader, Dies at 88," *New York Times*, Mar. 31, 1990, 11; "Harry Bridges Day," SFGate, July 28, 2001, https://www.sfgate.com/opinion/editorials/article/Harry-Bridges-Day-2896069.php; "Let Harry Bridges Occupy His Plaza Eternally," *SFGate*, Nov. 5, 2011, https://www.sfgate.com/opinion /editorials/article/Let-Harry-Bridges-occupy-his-plaza-eternally-2324195.php.

65. Cherny, "Harry Bridges and the Communist Party," at 11.

66. Charlton, "Bridges, Once a 'Troublemaker,' Takes Place of Honor in Capital."

67. Cherny, "Harry Bridges and the Communist Party," 15–16.

68. Nelson, *Workers on the Waterfront*, 145; Cherny, "Harry Bridges and the Communist Party," 15.

69. The Communist Party archives also refute the testimony of some of the witnesses who claimed to have firsthand knowledge that Bridges was a member of the Communist Party. Cherny, "Harry Bridges and the Communist Party," 14.

70. Schrecker, *The Age of McCarthyism*, 5.

CHAPTER 8: EXPELLED CITIZEN

1. *A Forgotten Injustice / Una Injusticia Olvidada*.

2. "Over a Million Mexican-Americans Were Expelled in the 1930s. Now History Is Repeating Itself," *Sunday Edition*, CBC Radio, Mar. 23, 2018, https://www.cbc.ca/radio/thesundayedition /the-sunday-edition-march-25-2018-1.4589621/over-a-million-mexican-americans-were-expelled -in-the-1930s-now-history-is-repeating-itself-1.4589640; Wendy Koch, "U.S. Urged to Apologize for 1930s Deportations," *USA Today*, Apr. 5, 2006, https://usatoday30.usatoday.com/news/nation /2006-04-04-1930s-deportees-cover_x.htm.

3. Koch, "U.S. Urged to Apologize for 1930s Deportations"; *A Forgotten Injustice / Una Injusticia Olvidada*.

4. *A Forgotten Injustice / Una Injusticia Olvidada.*

5. Emilia Castañeda de Valenciana, interview by Christine Valenciana, Sept. 8, 1971, transcript, Lawrence de Graaf Center for Oral and Public History, California State University, Fullerton (hereinafter Emilia Castañeda Oral History); *Examination of Unconstitutional Deportation and Coerced Emigration of Legal Residents and U.S. Citizens of Mexican Descent During 1930s,* Testimony of Emilia Castañeda (hereafter 2003 California Senate Hearing).

6. Emilia Castañeda Oral History.

7. "Unemployment Statistics During the Great Depression," U-S-History.com, https://www.u-s-history.com/pages/h1528.html.

8. Emilia Castañeda Oral History.

9. Emilia Castañeda Oral History.

10. *Emilia Castañeda—American Citizen;* Testimony of Emilia Castañeda, 2003 California Senate Hearing.

11. Juan Ramon García, *Operation Wetback: The Mass Deportation of Mexican Undocumented Workers in 1954* (Westwood, CT: Greenwood Press, 1980), 14.

12. Hoffman, *Unwanted Mexican Americans in the Great Depression,* 9.

13. Fernando Saúl Alanís Enciso, *They Should Stay There: The Story of Mexican Migration and Repatriation During the Great Depression,* trans. Russ Davidson (Chapel Hill: University of North Carolina Press, 2017), 13.

14. Lawrence A. Cardoso, *Mexican Emigration to the United States, 1897–1931* (Tucson: University of Arizona Press, 1980), 35, 38, 91. Estimating the number of immigrants to the United States from Mexico during the first few decades of the twentieth century is difficult due to poor recordkeeping, and estimates differ. Another source states that the "total Mexican-origin or heritage population of the United States in 1930 was probably at least 1.5 million," of which approximately 639,000 were Mexican nationals, and the rest Mexican Americans who were descendants of the former citizens of Mexico living in the Southwest at the end of the Mexican-American war. Brian Gratton and Myron P. Gutmann, "Hispanics in the United States, 1850–1990: Estimates of Population Size and National Origin," *Historical Methods* 33, no. 3 (Summer 2000): 137–53.

15. Enciso, *They Should Stay There,* 13.

16. Testimony of Susan Dunbar, 2003 California Senate Hearing; Diane Bernard, "The Time a President Deported 1 Million Mexican Americans for Supposedly Stealing U.S. Jobs," *Washington Post,* Aug. 13, 2018, https://www.washingtonpost.com/news/retropolis/wp/2018/08/13/the-time-a-president-deported-1-million-mexican-americans-for-stealing-u-s-jobs/; Hoffman, *Unwanted Mexican Americans in the Great Depression,* at 18.

17. Arthur G. Arnoll, General Manager of the Los Angeles Chamber of Commerce, to Dr. George P. Clements, Manager of Los Angeles Chamber of Commerce's Agricultural Department, Feb. 25, 1931, quoted in Marla Andrea Ramìrez, "The Making of Mexican Illegality: Immigration Exclusions Based on Race, Class Status, and Gender," *New Political Science* 40, no. 2 (2018): 322; Testimony of Emilia Castañeda, 2003 California Senate Hearing; "35,000 Mexicans Leave California," *New York Times,* Apr. 12, 1931, 5.

18. Douglas Monroy, *Rebirth: Mexican Los Angeles from the Great Migration to the Great Depression* (Berkeley: University of California Press, 1999), 25.

19. Monroy, *Rebirth,* 25.

20. Antonio Olivo, "Ghosts of a 1931 Raid," *Los Angeles Times,* Feb. 25, 2001, https://www.latimes.com/archives/la-xpm-2001-feb-25-me-30223-story.html; Balderrama and Rodriguez, *Decade of Betrayal,* 73–74.

21. Balderrama and Rodriguez, *Decade of Betrayal,* 75.

22. In re Osterloh, 34 F.2d 223, 224 (S.D. Tex. 1929); National Commission on Law Observance and Enforcement, *Report on the Enforcement of the Deportation Laws of the United States* (Washington, DC: Government Printing Office, 1931), 133, 135, https://curiosity.lib.harvard.edu/immigration-to-the-united-states-1789-1930/catalog/39-990097354190203941.

23. *A Forgotten Injustice / Una Injusticia Olvidada* (quoting Western Union telegram from Charles P. Visel, director of the Los Angeles Citizens Committee on Coordination of Unemployment Relief, to Colonel Arthur M. Woods, US government coordinator, Unemployment Relief, Washington, DC, Jan. 6, 1931).

24. Camille Guerin-Gonzales, *Mexican Workers and American Dreams: Immigration, Repatriation, and California Farm Labor, 1900–1939* (New Brunswick, NJ: Rutgers University Press, 1996), 81; Testimony of Susan Dunbar, 2003 California Senate Hearing (quoting letter from C. P. Visel to Crime and Unemployment Committee, LA Chamber of Commerce).

25. *A Forgotten Injustice / Una Injusticia Olvidada.*

26. Testimony of Professor Kevin Johnson, 2003 California Senate Hearing; Kevin R. Johnson, "The Forgotten Repatriation of Persons of Mexican Ancestry and Lessons for the War on Terror," *Pace Law Review* 26, no. 1 (2005): 1–26.

27. Hoffman, *Unwanted Mexican Americans in the Great Depression,* 8–9; *A Forgotten Injustice / Una Injusticia Olvidada*; Testimony of Susan Dunbar, 2003 California Senate Hearing, quoting June 4, 1931, letter from member of LA Chamber of Commerce.

28. Testimony of Susan Dunbar, 2003 California Senate Hearing, quoting May 16, 1938, and Aug. 9, 1938, letters from the Superintendent of Charities to the Board of Supervisors, Los Angeles County.

29. Hoffman, *Unwanted Mexican Americans in the Great Depression,* 84; Alex Wagner, "America's Forgotten History of Illegal Deportations," *Atlantic,* Mar. 6, 2017, https://www.the atlantic.com/politics/archive/2017/03/americas-brutal-forgotten-history-of-illegal-deportations /517971/; Ed M. Koziarski, "Lost Citizens," *Chicago Reader,* Apr. 16, 2009, https://www.chicago reader.com/chicago/lost-citizens/Content?oid=1098523; Enciso, *They Should Stay There,* 6–7, 156.

30. Testimony of Susan Dunbar, 2003 California Senate Hearing (quoting June 8, 1931, letter from the Department of Charities to the Board of Supervisors, Los Angeles County); Testimony of Susan Dunbar, 2003 California Senate Hearing.

31. Brian Gratton and Emily Merchant, "Immigration, Repatriation, and Deportation: The Mexican-Origin Population in the United States, 1920–1950," *International Migration Review* 47, no. 4 (Winter 2013): 945, 950; Hoffman, *Unwanted Mexican Americans,* 126 (estimating more than 415,000 repatriated); US Commission on Civil Rights, *The Tarnished Golden Door: Civil Rights Issues in Immigration* (1980), 10, 44–45; "'Decade of Betrayal': How the U.S. Expelled Over a Half Million U.S. Citizens to Mexico in 1930s," *Democracy Now!,* Feb. 28, 2017, https://www.democracy now.org/2017/2/28/forgotten_history_in_1930s_us_deported.

32. *A Forgotten Injustice / Una Injusticia Olvidada.*

33. *A Forgotten Injustice / Una Injusticia Olvidada.*

34. Koch, "U.S. Urged to Apologize for 1930s Deportations."

35. Koch, "U.S. Urged to Apologize for 1930s Deportations"; Delia Fernández, "Mexican Repatriation, 1930–1935," in *50 Events That Shaped Latino History: An Encyclopedia of the American Mosaic,* vol. 1, Lilia Fernández, ed. (Santa Barbara, CA: Greenwood, 2018), 339.

36. Emilia Castañeda Oral History; Testimony of Emilia Castañeda, 2003 California Senate Hearing; Steve Boisson, "Immigrants: The Last Time America Sent Her Own Packing," https:// www.historynet.com/immigrants-the-last-time-america-sent-her-own-packing.htm.

37. Emilia Castañeda Oral History; Testimony of Emilia Castañeda, 2003 California Senate Testimony.

38. Testimony of Emilia Castañeda, 2003 California Senate Hearing; Emilia Castañeda Oral History.

39. Emilia Castañeda Oral History; Testimony of Emilia Castañeda, 2003 California Senate Hearing.

40. Balderrama and Rodriguez, *Decade of Betrayal,* 262; Testimony of Susan Dunbar, 2003 California Senate Hearing.

41. Balderrama and Rodriguez, *Decade of Betrayal,* 262; Testimony of Susan Dunbar, 2003 California Senate Hearing (quoting May 28, 1934, letter from Pablo Guerrero to LA County).

42. *A Forgotten Injustice / Una Injusticia Olvidada*; Koziarski, "Lost Citizens."

43. *A Forgotten Injustice / Una Injusticia Olvidada.*

44. Emilia Castañeda Oral History.

45. Emilia Castañeda Oral History; *A Forgotten Injustice / Una Injusticia Olvidada*; Rodriguez and Balderrama, *Decade of Betrayal,* 275; Testimony of Susan Dunbar, 2003 California Senate Hearing.

46. Testimony of Emilia Castañeda, 2003 California Senate Hearing.

47. S.B. 670, "Apology Act for the 1930s Mexican Repatriation Program," 2005, http://www .leginfo.ca.gov/pub/05-06/bill/sen/sb_0651-0700/sb_670_bill_20051007_chaptered.html; Leslie Hiatt, "How My 4th-Grade Class Passed a Law on Teaching Mexican 'Repatriation,'" *Rethinking Schools* 32, no. 4 (Summer 2018), https://www.rethinkingschools.org/articles/how-my-4th-grade -class-passed-a-law-on-teaching-mexican-repatriation; Lani Cupchoy, "The Fifth-Graders Who Put Mexican Repatriation Back Into History Books," *Yes! Magazine,* Aug. 4, 2016, https://www .yesmagazine.org/democracy/2016/08/04/the-fifth-graders-who-put-mexican-repatriation-back -into-history-books/.

48. "Over a Million Mexican-Americans Were Expelled in the 1930s. Now History Is Repeating Itself," *Sunday Edition*, CBC Radio, Mar. 23, 2018, https://www.cbc.ca/radio/thesundayedition /the-sunday-edition-march-25-2018-1.4589621/over-a-million-mexican-americans-were-expelled -in-the-1930s-now-history-is-repeating-itself-1.4589640.

49. "Over a Million Mexican-Americans Were Expelled."

50. "Over a Million Mexican-Americans Were Expelled"; Koch, "U.S. Urged to Apologize for 1930s Deportations."

51. David C. Gutiérrez, "A Historic Overview of Latino Immigration and the Demographic Transformation of the United States," in *The New Latino Studies Reader: A Twenty-First-Century Perspective*, ed. Ramón A. Gutiérrez and Tomás Almaguer (Oakland: University of California Press, 2016), 110; Elizabeth Blair, "In Confronting Poverty, 'Harvest of Shame' Reaped Praise and Criticism," *Weekend Edition Saturday*, National Public Radio, May 31, 2014, https://www.npr.org /2014/05/31/317364146/in-confronting-poverty-harvest-of-shame-reaped-praise-and-criticism.

52. Gutiérrez, "A Historic Overview of Latino Immigration," 110–11.

53. Stewart Hillhouse, "We Asked for Workers. We Got People Instead," *Medium*, May 28, 2018, https://medium.com/the-go-do-project/we-asked-for-workers-we-got-people-instead -8b040ed37238.

54. Natalia Molina, *How Race Is Made in America: Immigration, Citizenship, and the Historical Power of Racial Scripts* (Berkeley: University of California Press, 2014), 143.

55. "Wetbacks Nabbed, L.A.," *Los Angeles Times*, June 19, 1954, 7.

56. Kelly Lytle Hernández, *Migra! A History of the U.S. Border Patrol* (Berkeley: University of California Press, 2010), 187; "Wetbacks Nabbed," *Los Angeles Times*, June 19, 1954, 23; "Patrols Raid Wetback Haunts in Crackdown," *Pasadena Independent*, June 18, 1954, 39.

57. "Fast Moving Raiders Nab 500 in L.A. Wetback Roundup," *Los Angeles Times*, June 18, 1954, A1.

58. Louis Hyman and Natasha Iskander, "What the Mass Deportation of Immigrants Might Look Like," *Slate*, Nov. 16, 2016, https://slate.com/news-and-politics/2016/11/donald-trump-mass -deportation-and-the-tragic-history-of-operation-wetback.html.

59. Ngai, *Impossible Subjects*, 155.

60. García, *Operation Wetback*, 174–75; Hernández, *Migra!*, 184.

61. Ngai, *Impossible Subjects*, 155, 156; Yanan Wang, "Donald Trump's 'Humane' 1950s Model for Deportation, 'Operation Wetback,' Was Anything But," *Washington Post*, Nov. 11, 2015; Dara Lind, "Operation Wetback, the 1950s Immigration Policy Donald Trump Loves, Explained," *Vox*, Nov. 11, 2015; James McEnteer, *Deep in the Heart: The Texas Tendency in American Politics* (Westport, CT: Praeger, 2004), 78.

62. García, *Operation Wetback*, 194–95, 225.

63. Rodolfo Acuña, *Occupied America: A History of Chicanos*, 3rd ed. (New York: Harper & Row, 1988), 265; García, *Operation Wetback*, 201, 216.

64. Testimony of Emilia Castañeda, 2003 California State Senate Hearing.

CHAPTER 9: TWENTY-FIRST-CENTURY CITIZEN

1. Elisabeth Bumiller, "McCain Draws Line on Attacks as Crowds Cry 'Fight Back,'" *New York Times*, Oct. 10, 2008, A12.

2. Bumiller, "McCain Draws Line on Attacks as Crowds Cry 'Fight Back'"; "From 2008: McCain Corrects Woman Calling Obama an 'Arab,'" CNN, https://edition.cnn.com/videos/politics /2015/09/18/mccain-2008-presidential-campaign-audience-question-on-obama-as-arab.cnn.

3. "From 2008: McCain Corrects Woman Calling Obama an 'Arab,'" CNN, https://edition .cnn.com/videos/politics/2015/09/18/mccain-2008-presidential-campaign-audience-question-on -obama-as-arab.cnn; "McCain Volunteer Sends Out 'Obama Is an Arab' Letters," *Uptake*, Oct. 11, 2008, http://theuptake.org/2008/10/11/mccain-volunteer-sends-out-obama-is-an-arab-letters.

4. Greg Jaffe, "One Moment from McCain's 2008 Run Made Clear His Character and Foretold Trump's Rise," *Washington Post*, Aug. 26, 2018; Ben Smith and Byron Tau, "Birtherism: Where It All Began," *Politico*, Apr. 22, 2011, https://www.politico.com/story/2011/04/birtherism-where-it -all-began-053563.

5. Barack Hussein Obama II, Certificate of Live Birth, https://obamawhitehouse.archives.gov /sites/default/files/rss_viewer/birth-certificate-long-form.pdf; Corky Siemaszko, "Obama's High School Basketball Coaches, Teammates Remember 'Barry,'" NBC News, Jan. 13, 2017, https://www .nbcnews.com/storyline/president-obama-the-legacy/obama-s-high-school-basketball-coaches -teammates-remember-barry-n700986; "The Choice 2012, Kristen Caldwell Interview," *Frontline*,

June 27, 2012, https://www.pbs.org/wgbh/pages/frontline/government-elections-politics/choice
-2012/the-frontline-interview-kristen-caldwell/; Jess Henig, "It's Official: Obama 'Born in the
U.S.A.,'" FactCheck.org, Nov. 1, 2008, https://www.factcheck.org/issue/obamas-birth-certificate
/page/2.

6. The claim was first raised in a lawsuit brought by a supporter of Obama's main rival in the
Democratic primaries, Hilary Clinton, though Clinton never supported it. Ben Smith and Byron
Tau, "Birtherism: Where It All Began," *Politico*, Apr. 22, 2011, https://www.politico.com/story
/2011/04/birtherism-where-it-all-began-053563.

7. Ashley Parker and Steve Eder, "Inside the Six Weeks Donald Trump Was a Nonstop
'Birther,'" *New York Times*, July 3, 2016, A1; Amy Davidson Sorkin, "Trump Is Still Lying About
Birtherism," *New Yorker*, Sept. 20, 2016, https://www.newyorker.com/news/amy-davidson/trump
-is-still-lying-about-birtherism; Michael D. Shear, "With Document, Obama Seeks to End
'Birther' Issue," *New York Times*, Apr. 27, 2011, A1; Dan Pfeiffer, *Yes We (Still) Can: Politics in
the Age of Obama, Twitter, and Trump* (New York: Hachette, 2018), 119.

8. Sorkin, "Trump Is Still Lying About Birtherism"; Pfeiffer, *Yes We (Still) Can*, 121.

9. Shear, "With Document, Obama Seeks to End 'Birther' Issue"; C-Span, "Release of President Obama's Birth Certificate," https://www.c-span.org/video/?299220-1/release-president
-obamas-birth-certificate.

10. Kyle Dropp and Brendan Nyhan, "It Lives. Birtherism Is Diminished but Far from Dead,"
New York Times, Sept. 23, 2016, https://www.nytimes.com/2016/09/24/upshot/it-lives-birtherism
-is-diminished-but-far-from-dead.html. That same poll reported that the proportion of respondents who doubted Obama had been born in the United States dropped to 38 percent in September 2016.

11. Bob Bauer, "Michael Cohen Reminded Us Why Trump's Birtherism Matters," *Atlantic*,
Mar. 4, 2019.

12. Fourth Amended Class Action Complaint at 12–13, Castro v. Freeman, No. 1:09-cv-00208
(S.D. Tex. June 1, 2011); Jazmine Ulloa, "Born to Be Barred," *Texas Observer*, May 13, 2010, https://
www.texasobserver.org/born-to-be-barred.

13. "The Treaty of Guadalupe Hidalgo," National Archives, https://www.archives.gov/education
/lessons/guadalupe-hidalgo; Josue David Cisneros, *The Border Crossed Us: Rhetorics of Borders,
Citizenship, and Latina/o Identity* (Tuscaloosa: University of Alabama Press, 2014), ix; Omar S.
Valerio-Jiménez, *River of Hope: Forging Identity and Nation in the Rio Grande Borderlands* (Durham, NC: Duke University Press, 2013), 10.

14. In re Pagan, 22 I&N Dec. 547, 548 (BIA 1999); In re Matter of S.S. Florida, 3 I&N Dec. 111,
116 (BIA 1948); "Western Hemisphere Travel Initiative," US Customs and Border Protection, https://
www.cbp.gov/travel/us-citizens/western-hemisphere-travel-initiative. A state-issued enhanced driver's license comes with a radio frequency identification chip that contains biographic and biometric
data, as well as a machine-readable bar code. "Enhanced Drivers Licenses: What Are They?," https://
www.dhs.gov/enhanced-drivers-licenses-what-are-they?utm_source=google&utm_medium=google
&utm_term=(not%20provided)&utm_content=undefined&utm_campaign=(not%20set)&gclid
=undefined&dclid=undefined&GAID=1819430119.1574537127.

15. Fifth Amended Class Action Complaint at 11–13, Castro v. Freeman, No. 1:09-cv-00208
(S.D. Tex. June 1, 2011), https://www.clearinghouse.net/chDocs/public/IM-TX-0033-0007.pdf.

16. Rachel E. Rosenbloom, "From the Outside Looking In: U.S. Passports in the Borderlands," in *Citizenship in Question: Evidentiary Birthright and Statelessness*, ed. Benjamin N. Lawrance and Jacqueline Stevens (Durham, NC: Duke University Press, 2017), 135; Fourth Amended
Class Action Complaint at 12, Castro v. Freeman.

17. Fifth Amended Class Action Complaint at 11–12, Castro v. Freeman; Rosenbloom, "From
the Outside Looking In," 136; Bingham and Arnpriester, *Unmaking Americans*, 127; "Citizenship
for Midwives' Deliveries Questioned," *Houston Chronicle*, July 21, 2008.

18. Rosenbloom, "From the Outside Looking In," 133–34; Bingham and Arnpriester, *Unmaking Americans*, 127.

19. Fifth Amended Class Action Complaint at 11–13, Castro v. Freeman; Ulloa, "Born to Be
Barred."

20. 22 C.F.R. §§ 51.40, 51.42; 8 U.S.C. § 1503. Courts have divided on the question of whether
the government or the individual bears the burden of proof in some situations. Bingham and
Arnpriester, *Unmaking Americans*, 139–43; "Citizenship Evidence," US Department of State—Bureau
of Consular Affairs, https://travel.state.gov/content/travel/en/passports/how-apply/citizenship
-evidence.html, accessed Dec. 13, 2019; Saja Hindi, "Colorado Man Denied Passport Despite U.S.

Citizenship, ACLU Law Suit Alleges," *Denver Post*, Apr. 19, 2019, https://www.denverpost.com /2019/08/19/colorado-man-denied-american-passport-aclu-lawsuit.

21. Fifth Amended Class Action Complaint at 13–14, Castro v. Freeman.

22. Craig Robertson, *The Passport in America: The History of a Document* (Oxford, UK: Oxford University Press, 2010), 160–66.

23. John Torpey, *The Invention of the Passport: Surveillance, Citizenship and the State* (Cambridge, UK: Cambridge University Press, 2000), 97–101.

24. Meagan Flynn, "U.S. Citizen Freed After Nearly a Month in Immigration Custody, Family Says," *Washington Post*, July 24, 2019; "The Constitution in the 100-Mile Border Zone," ACLU, https://www.aclu.org/other/constitution-100-mile-border-zone, accessed August 24, 2020.

25. William Finnegan, "The Deportation Machine," *New Yorker*, Apr. 29, 2013.

26. Finnegan, "The Deportation Machine."

27. Stevens, "U.S. Government Unlawfully Detaining and Deporting U.S. Citizens as Aliens," 622, 624n58, 630; Testimony of Kara Hartzler, Attorney, Florence Immigrant and Refugee Rights Project, *Problems with ICE Interrogation, Detention, and Removal Procedures*, Hearing before the Subcommittee on Immigration, Citizenship, Refugees, Border Security, and International Law of the Committee on the Judiciary, House of Representatives, 110th Cong., 2nd Sess., Feb. 13, 2008; email from Kara Hartzler to author, August 12, 2020.

28. Today, noncitizens are prohibited from voting in most elections. During the colonial era, however, noncitizens were permitted to vote in a number of jurisdictions, and noncitizen voting continued in some states until the early twentieth century. Jamin B. Raskin, "Legal Aliens, Local Citizens: The Historical, Constitutional, and Theoretical Meanings of Alien Suffrage," *University of Pennsylvania Law Review* 141, no. 4 (Apr. 1993): 1397–417.

29. Fish v. Kobach, 309 F. Supp.3d 1048, 1067 (D. Kan. 2018).

30. Fish, 309 F.Supp.3d at 1075–79.

31. Christa Case Bryant, "In Kansas Voter ID Trial, a Clash of Two Visions for America," *Christian Science Monitor*, Mar. 20, 2018, https://www.csmonitor.com/USA/Justice/2018/0320 /In-Kansas-voter-ID-trial-a-clash-of-two-visions-for-America; Fish v. Kobach, 309 F. Supp.3d at 1081, 1102; Emily Bazelon, "A Crusader Against Voter Fraud Fails to Prove His Case," *New York Times*, June 19, 2018.

32. Stephen Koranda, "State Panel Says Kansas Woman Can Vote, Despite Lack of Citizenship Document," July 25, 2016, KMUW, https://www.kmuw.org/post/state-panel-says-kansas-woman-can-vote-despite-lack-citizenship-document; Bryant, "In Kansas Voter ID Trial, a Clash of Two Visions for America"; Fish v. Kobach, 309 F. Supp.3d 1048, 1078–79 (D. Kan. 2018).

33. Afroyim v. Rusk, 387 U.S. 253, 268 (1967); Weil, *The Sovereign Citizen*, 5.

34. Department of Homeland Security, Office of Inspector Gen., OIG-16-130, "Potentially Ineligible Individuals Have Been Granted U.S. Citizenship Because of Incomplete Fingerprint Records," Sept. 8, 2016, 7, https://www.oig.dhs.gov/assets/Mgmt/2016/OIG-16-130-Sep16.pdf; US Citizenship and Immigration Services, "USCIS Partners with Justice Department and Secures First Denaturalization as a Result of Operation Janus," press release, Jan. 10, 2018, https://www .uscis.gov/news/news-releases/uscis-partners-justice-department-and-secures-first-denaturalization -result-operation-janus; Department of Homeland Security, *US Immigration and Customs Enforcement Budget Overview, Fiscal Year 2019 Congressional Justification*, https://www.dhs.gov/sites /default/files/publications/U.S.%20Immigration%20and%20Customs%20Enforcement.pdf; "The Department of Justice Creates Section Dedicated to Denaturalization Cases," Department of Justice, Office of Public Affairs, Feb. 26, 2020, https://www.justice.gov/opa/pr/department-justice -creates-section-dedicated-denaturalization-cases.

35. Transcript of Oral Argument at 27–30, Maslenjak v. United States, 137 S. Ct. 1918 (2017) (No. 16-309).

36. "USCIS Partners with Justice Department and Secures First Denaturalization As a Result of Operation Janus."

37. Masha Gessen, "In America, Naturalized Citizens No Longer Have an Assumption of Permanence," *New Yorker*, June 18, 2018.

38. Trial Transcript at 293, United States v. Khan, No. 3:17-cv-965 (M.D. Fla., Apr. 2, 2019).

39. López, *White by Law*, 1.

40. "Trump Says He Is Seriously Looking at Ending Birthright Citizenship," Reuters, Aug. 21, 2019, https://www.reuters.com/article/us-usa-immigration-trump/trump-says-he-is-seriously -looking-at-ending-birthright-citizenship-idUSKCN1VB21B; Paul LeBlanc, "Trump Again Says He's Looking 'Seriously' at Birthright Citizenship Despite 14th Amendment," *CNN Politics*,

Aug. 22, 2019, https://edition.cnn.com/2019/08/21/politics/trump-birthright-citizenship-14th-amendment/index.html; Stephen Collinson, "Trump Slams 'Crazy, Lunatic' Constitutional Amendment in Midterm Endgame," *CNN Politics*, Nov. 2, 2018, https://edition.cnn.com/2018/11/02/politics/donald-trump-immigration-midterms-missouri/index.html; Esther Yu Hsi Lee, "How Many Candidates Have 'Taken Advantage' of Birthright Citizenship, but Oppose It?," *Think-Progress*, Aug. 19, 2015.

41. Rogers, "Trump Encourages Racist Conspiracy Theory About Kamala Harris."

42. Brief for the United States [Conrad] at 49–51, United States v. Wong Kim Ark, 169 U.S. 649 (1898).

43. Wong Kim Ark v. United States, 69 U.S. 649, 682, 693.

44. Michael Fix, "Repealing Birthright Citizenship: The Unintended Consequences," Migration Policy Institute, Aug. 2015, https://www.migrationpolicy.org/news/repealing-birthright-citizenship-unintended-consequences, accessed Dec. 12, 2019; Sen. Sumner, 40th Cong., 3rd Sess., *Congressional Globe* (Feb. 5, 1869), S 903; Galiski, *14: Dred Scott, Wong Kim Ark & Vanessa Lopez*.

SELECTED
BIBLIOGRAPHY

ACADEMIC JOURNALS

Berger, Bethany R. "Birthright Citizenship on Trial: *Elk v. Wilkins* and *United States v. Wong Kim Ark.*" *Cardozo Law Review* 37, no. 4 (2016): 1185–258.

Borome, Joseph H., ed. "The Autobiography of Hiram Rhoades Revels Together with Some Letters by and About Him." *Midwest Journal* 5 (Winter 1952–53): 79–92.

Calavita, Kitty. "The Paradoxes of Race, Class, Identity, and 'Passing': Enforcing the Chinese Exclusion Acts, 1882–1910." *Law & Social Inquiry* 25 (2000): 1–40.

Cherny, Robert W. "Constructing a Radical Identity: History, Memory, and the Seafaring Stories of Harry Bridges." *Pacific Historical Review* 70, no. 4 (November 2001): 571–99.

———. "Harry Bridges and the Communist Party: New Evidence, Old Questions; Old Evidence, New Questions." Unpublished paper prepared for the panel "Negotiating Boundaries: The Communist Party and the Public Arena." Annual meeting of the Organization of American Historians, April 4, 1998.

Christgau, John. "Collins Versus the World: The Fight to Restore Citizenship to Japanese American Renunciants of World War II." *Pacific Historical Review* 54, no. 1 (1985): 1–31.

Cott, Nancy F. "Marriage and Women's Citizenship in the United States, 1830–1934." *American Historical Review* 103, no. 5 (December 1998): 1440–74.

Epps, Garrett. "The Antebellum Political Background of the Fourteenth Amendment." *Law and Contemporary Problems* 67, no. 3 (2004): 175–211.

Kent, Andrew. "The Constitution and the Laws of War During the Civil War." *Notre Dame Law Review* 85 (2010): 1839–1930.

Kerber, Linda K. "The Meaning of Citizenship." *Journal of American History* 84, no. 3 (1997): 833–54.

Larrowe, C. P. "Did the Old Left Get Due Process—the Case of Harry Bridges." *California Law Review* 60, no. 1 (1972): 39–83.

Lewis, John, and Archie E. Allen. "Black Voter Registration Efforts in the South." *Notre Dame Law Review* 48, no. 1 (1972): 105–32.

Ngai, Mae M. "Legacies of Exclusion: Illegal Chinese Immigration During the Cold War Years." *Journal of American Ethnic History* 18, no. 1 (Fall 1998): 3–35.

Rawley, James A. "The General Amnesty Act of 1872: A Note." *Mississippi Valley Historical Review* 47, no. 3 (December 1960): 480–84.

Rice, Daniel B. "The Riddle of Ruth Bryan Owen." *Yale Journal of Law & the Humanities* 29, no. 1 (2017): 1–71.

Russ, William A., Jr. "The Negro and White Disfranchisement During Radical Reconstruction." *Journal of Negro History* 19, no. 2 (April 1934): 171–92.

Stevens, Jacqueline. "U.S. Government Unlawfully Detaining and Deporting U.S. Citizens as Aliens." *Virginia Journal of Social Policy & the Law* 18, no. 3 (2011): 606–720.

Thompson, Julius E. "Hiram Rhodes Revels, 1827–1901: A Reappraisal." *Journal of Negro History* 79, no. 3 (Summer 1994): 297–303.

Volpp, Leti. "Divesting Citizenship: On Asian American History and the Loss of Citizenship Through Marriage." *UCLA Law Review* 53, no. 2 (2005): 405–83.

ARCHIVAL MATERIALS AND MANUSCRIPTS

Bridges, Harry Renton File. Record Group 85, Records of Immigration and Naturalization Services, 1787–2004, Records Relating to Harry Bridges, 1920–1965, File Unit 12020/25037(1). National Archives and Records Administration at San Francisco–San Bruno, CA.

Carrie Dunlap Papers. University of Miami Archives & Special Collections, Otto G. Richter Library, Miami, FL.

Haw Moy File 1756. Record Group 276, US Court of Appeals for the Ninth Circuit, National Archives and Records Administration at San Francisco–San Bruno, CA.

Hiram Revels Collection. Schomburg Center for Research in Black Culture, New York Public Library, New York, NY.

Johnson, Andrew. "Proclamation 134—Granting Amnesty to Participants in the Rebellion, with Certain Exceptions." May 29, 1865. The American Presidency Project, UC Santa Barbara, https://www.presidency.ucsb.edu/documents/proclamation-134-granting-amnesty -participants-the-rebellion-with-certain-exceptions.

Kurihara, Joseph. "Murder in Camp Manzanar." Unpublished manuscript, April 1943. https://ddr .densho.org/media/ddr-densho-67/ddr-densho-67-18-mezzanine-7bf03dbfab.htm.

Minnie Moore Willson Papers. University of Miami Archives & Special Collections, Otto G. Richter Library, Miami, FL.

Revised Dred Scott Case Collection. Washington University in St. Louis, MO. http://digital.wustl .edu/dredscott.

United States v. Wong Kim Ark, El Paso Case 802(7), WTX097A1. Equity Case Files Relating to Deportation of Chinese 1892–1915, National Archives and Records Administration—El Paso, TX.

Wong Kim Ark Case File No. 11198. Admiralty Case Files, 1851–1966, United States District Courts, Northern District of California, San Francisco, Record Group 21, Archival Research Catalog (ARC) Identifier 296013, National Archives and Records Administration at San Francisco–San Bruno, CA.

Wong Kim Ark File 12017/42223. Immigration and Naturalization Service, Record Group 85, Archival Research Catalog Identifier 296477, National Archives and Records Administration at San Francisco–San Bruno, CA.

BOOKS

Balderrama, Francisco E., and Raymond Rodriguez. *Decade of Betrayal: Mexican Repatriation in the 1930s*. Rev. ed. Albuquerque: University of New Mexico Press, 2006.

Bernstein, Arnie. *Swastika Nation: Fritz Kuhn and the Rise and Fall of the German-American Bund*. New York: St. Martin's Press, 2013.

Blight, David W. *Race and Reunion: The Civil War in American Memory*. Cambridge, MA: Harvard University Press, 2001.

Bredbenner, Candice Lewis. *A Nationality of Her Own: Women, Marriage, and the Law of Citizenship*. Berkeley: University of California Press, 1998.

Brown, Rudd. *Ruth Bryan Owen: Congresswoman and Diplomat*. CreateSpace Independent Publishing Platform, 2014.

Collins, Donald E. *Native American Aliens: Disloyalty and the Renunciation of Citizenship by Japanese Americans During World War II*. Westport, CT: Greenwood Press, 1985.

Diamond, Sander A. *The Nazi Movement in the United States, 1924–1941*. Ithaca, NY: Cornell University Press, 2001.

Dorris, Jonathan Truman. *Pardon and Amnesty Under Lincoln and Johnson*. Chapel Hill: University of North Carolina Press, 1953.

Dray, Philip. *Capitol Men: The Epic Story of Reconstruction Through the Lives of the First Black Congressmen*. Boston: Houghton Mifflin, 2008.

Du Bois, W. E. B. *Black Reconstruction in America: Toward a History of the Part Which Black Folk Played in the Attempt to Reconstruct Democracy in America, 1860–1880*. Originally 1934. New Brunswick, NJ: Transaction Publishers, 2013.

Epps, Garrett. *Democracy Reborn: The Fourteenth Amendment and the Fight for Civil Rights in Post–Civil War America*. New York: Henry Holt, 2006.

Falk, Candace, ed. *Emma Goldman: A Documentary History of the American Years*, vol. 2, *Making Speech Free, 1902–1909*. Berkeley: University of California Press, 2005.

Fehrenbacher, Don E. *The Dred Scott Case: Its Significance in American Law and Politics*. New York: Oxford University Press, 1978.

Finkelman, Paul. *Dred Scott v. Sandford: A Brief History with Documents*. Boston: Bedford Books, 1997.

Foner, Eric. *Reconstruction: America's Unfinished Revolution, 1863–1877*. New York: HarperCollins, 1988.

———. *The Second Founding: How the Civil War and Reconstruction Remade the Constitution*. New York: W. W. Norton, 2019.

García, Juan Ramon. *Operation Wetback: The Mass Deportation of Mexican Undocumented Workers in 1954*. Westwood, CT: Greenwood Press, 1980.

Goldman, Emma. *Living My Life*, 2 vols. New York: Alfred A. Knopf, 1931.

Hager, Ruth Ann (Abels). *Dred & Harriet Scott: Their Family Story*. St. Louis: St. Louis County Library, 2010.

Hoffman, Abraham. *Unwanted Mexican Americans in the Great Depression: Repatriation Pressures, 1929–1939*. Tucson: University of Arizona Press, 1974.

Irons, Peter HH.H. *A People's History of the U.S. Supreme Court: The Men and Women Whose Cases and Decisions Have Shaped Our Constitution*. Rev. ed. New York: Penguin Books, 2006.

———. *Justice at War: The Story of the Japanese American Internment Cases*. Berkeley: University of California Press, 1983.

Ishida, Gladys. "The Japanese American Renunciants of Okayama Prefecture: Their Accommodation and Assimilation to Japanese Culture." PhD diss., University of Chicago, 1955.

Jones, Martha S. *Birthright Citizens: A History of Race and Rights in Antebellum America*. Cambridge, UK: Cambridge University Press, 2018.

Kettner, James H. *The Development of American Citizenship, 1608–1870*. Chapel Hill: University of North Carolina Press, 1978.

Kurihara, Joseph Yoshisuke. *Autobiography, Speeches, and Statements*. Berkeley: Bancroft Library, University of California, Berkeley, 1946.

Larrowe, Charles P. *Harry Bridges: The Rise and Fall of Radical Labor in the United States*. New York: Lawrence Hill, 1972.

Lee, Erika. *At America's Gates: Chinese Immigration During the Exclusion Era, 1882–1943*. Chapel Hill: University of North Carolina Press, 2003.

López, Ian Haney. *White By Law: The Legal Construction of Race*. New York: New York University Press, 2006.

Martin, David, and Peter Schuck, eds. *Immigration Stories*. New York: Foundation Press, 2005.

Murray, Robert K. *Red Scare: A Study in National Hysteria, 1919–1920*. New York: McGraw-Hill, 1955.

Ngai, Mae M. *Impossible Subjects: Illegal Aliens and the Making of Modern America*. Princeton, NJ: Princeton University Press, 2004.

Quin, Mike. *The Big Strike*. Olema, CA: Olema Publishing Company, 1949.

Reeves, John. *The Lost Indictment of Robert E. Lee*. Lanham, MD: Rowman & Littlefield, 2018.

Salyer, Lucy E. *Laws Harsh as Tigers: Chinese Immigrants and the Shaping of Modern Immigration Law*. Chapel Hill: University of North Carolina Press, 1995.

Smith, Rogers M. *Civic Ideals: Conflicting Visions of Citizenship in U.S. History*. New Haven, CT: Yale University Press, 1997.

Tamura, Eileen H. *In Defense of Justice: Joseph Kurihara and the Japanese American Struggle for Equality*. Urbana: University of Illinois Press, 2013.

Thomas, Dorothy Swaine, and Richard S. Nishimoto. *The Spoilage: Japanese-American Evacuation and Resettlement During World War II*. Berkeley: University of California Press, 1946.

Thompson, Julius Eric. *Hiram R. Revels, 1827–1901: A Biography*. New York: Arno Press, 1982.

VanderVelde, Lea. *Mrs. Dred Scott: A Life on Slavery's Frontier*. Oxford, UK: Oxford University Press, 2009.

Vickers, Sarah Pauline. *The Life of Ruth Bryan Owen: Florida's First Congresswoman and America's First Woman Diplomat*. Tallahassee: Sentry Press, 2009.

Weil, Patrick. *The Sovereign Citizen: Denaturalization and the Origins of the American Republic*. Philadelphia: University of Pennsylvania Press, 2012.

Wexler, Alice. *Emma Goldman: An Intimate Life*. New York: Pantheon Books, 1984.

Yung, Judy. *Unbound Feet: A Social History of Chinese Women in San Francisco*. Berkeley: University of California Press, 1995.

GOVERNMENT DOCUMENTS
Hearings, Debates, and Public Announcements
Amendment to the Women's Citizenship Act of 1922. Hearing Before the Committee on Immigration and Naturalization, House of Representatives, 71st Congress, 2nd Session, on H.R. 10208, March 6, 1930.
Arguments and Hearings Before Election Committee No. 1, House of Representatives: Contested Election Case of William C. Lawson v. Ruth Bryan Owen from the Fourth Congressional District of Florida, 71st Congress, 2nd Session, 1930.
Congressional Globe
Congressional Record
Examination of Unconstitutional Deportation and Coerced Emigration of Legal Residents and U.S. Citizens of Mexican Descent During 1930s. Hearing Before the California Senate Select Committee on Citizen Participation, July 15, 2003.
Hearings Before the President's Commission on Immigration and Naturalization, US Congress, House of Representatives, September 30, 1952.
Investigation of Un-American Propaganda Activities in the United States. Hearings Before a Special Committee on Un-American Activities, House of Representatives, 76th Congress, 1st Session, May–June 1939.
President Gerald R. Ford's Remarks Upon Signing a Bill Restoring Rights of Citizenship to General Robert E. Lee. S.J. Res. 23, 89 Stat. 380, August 5, 1975. https://www.fordlibrarymuseum.gov/library/speeches/750473.htm.
Problems with ICE Interrogation, Detention, and Removal Procedures. Hearing Before the Subcommittee on Immigration, Citizenship, Refugees, Border Security, and International Law of the Committee on the Judiciary, House of Representatives, 110th Congress, 2nd Session, February 13, 2008.
Relative to Citizenship of American Women Married to Foreigners. Hearings Before the Committee on Immigration and Naturalization, House of Representatives, 65th Congress, 2nd Session, December 13, 1917.
Statement of US Representative John L. Cable, "American Citizenship Rights of Women," in *Hearing before a Subcommittee of the Committee on Immigration, United States Senate, Seventy-Second Congress, Second Session, on S. 992, S. 2760, S3968, and S. 4169* (Washington, DC: US Government Printing Office, 1933). https://www.loc.gov/law/find/hearings/pdf/0014160126A.pdf.

Government Reports
Commission on Wartime Relocation and Internment of Civilians. *Personal Justice Denied.* Seattle: University of Washington Press, 1997.
National Commission on Law Observance and Enforcement. *Report on the Enforcement of the Deportation Laws of the United States.* Washington, DC: US Government Printing Office, 1931. https://iiif.lib.harvard.edu/manifests/view/drs:4673882$137i.
US Commission on Civil Rights. *The Tarnished Golden Door: Civil Rights Issues in Immigration,* 1980.
US Department of Commerce and Labor, Bureau of Immigration and Naturalization. *Report of the Commissioner-General of Immigration,* July 1, 1907.
US Department of Homeland Security, Office of Inspector Gen., OIG-16-130. *Potentially Ineligible Individuals Have Been Granted U.S. Citizenship Because of Incomplete Fingerprint Records,* September 8, 2016.
US Department of State, Bureau of Consular Affairs. *Citizenship Evidence.* https://travel.state.gov/content/travel/en/passports/how-apply/citizenship-evidence.html.
US Immigration Commission. *Abstracts of Reports of the Immigration Commission, with Conclusions and Recommendations and Views of the Minority.* Washington, DC: US Government Printing Office, 1910.
Western Defense Command and Fourth Army. *Final Report: Japanese Evacuation from the West Coast, 1942.* Washington, DC: US Government Printing Office, 1943.

LEGAL CASES
Abo v. Clark, 77 F. Supp. 806 (N.D. Cal. 1948).
Afroyim v. Rusk, 387 U.S. 253 (1967).
Ah How v. United States, 193 U.S. 65 (1904).
Baumgartner v. United States, 322 U.S. 665 (1944).

Bridges v. California, 314 U.S. 252 (1941).

Bridges v. United States, 346 U.S. 209 (1953).

Bridges v. Wixon, 326 U.S. 135 (1945).

Castro v. Freeman, No. 1:09-cv-00208 (S.D. Tex., June 1, 2011).

The Chinese Exclusion Case, 130 U.S. 581 (1889).

Commonwealth v. Bleischwitz, 14 Pa. D. & C. 170 (Court of Common Pleas of Pennsylvania, Montgomery County, 1930).

Dred Scott v. Sandford, 60 U.S. 393 (1857).

Ex parte (Ng) Fung Sing, 6 F.2d 670 (W.D. Wash. 1925).

Fish v. Kobach, 189 F.Supp.3d 1107 (D. Kan. 2016).

Fong Yue Ting v. United States, 149 U.S. 698 (1893).

Haw Moy v. North, 189 F. 89 (9th Cir. 1910).

In re Matter of S.S. Florida, 3 I&N Dec. 111 (BIA 1948).

In re Osterloh, 34 F.2d 223 (5th Cir. 1929).

In re Pagan, 22 I&N Dec. 547 (BIA 1999).

In the Matter of Harry R. Bridges: Findings and Conclusions of the Trial Examiner (1939).

Li Sing v. United States, 180 U.S. 486 (1901).

Mackenzie v. Hare, 239 U.S. 299 (1915).

Maslenjak v. United States, 137 S. Ct. 1918 (2017).

Minor v. Happersett, 88 U.S. 162 (1875).

Mitchell v. Wells, 37 Miss. 235 (1859).

Mrs. Alexander's Cotton, 69 U.S. 404 (1864).

Plessy v. Ferguson, 163 U.S. 537 (1896).

The Prize Cases, 67 U.S. 635 (1863).

Rogers v. Bellei, 401 U.S. 815 (1971).

United States v. Khan, No. 3:17-cv-965 (M.D. Fla., Apr. 2, 2019).

United States v. Kuhn, 49 F. Supp. 407 (S.D.N.Y. 1943).

United States v. Wong Kim Ark, 169 U.S. 649 (1898).

ORAL HISTORIES

Castañeda de Valenciana, Emilia. Interview by Christine Valenciana. September 8, 1971. Transcript, Lawrence de Graaf Center for Oral and Public History, Mexican American Project, Repatriation in the 1930s, California State University, Fullerton.

Mexican American Oral History Project: Repatriation in the 1930s. Center for Oral and Public History. California State University, Fullerton.

Roger, Sidney. "Sidney Roger: A Liberal Journalist on the Air and on the Waterfront: Labor and Political Issues 1932–1990 Volume I." Interview by Julie Shearer. 1989 and 1990. Oral History Center, Bancroft Library, University of California, Berkeley, 1998.

Schmidt, Henry. "Secondary Leadership in the ILWU, 1933–1966." Oral history conducted 1974–81 by Miriam F. Stein and Estolv Ethan Ward. Regional Oral History Office, Bancroft Library, University of California, Berkeley, 1983.

Schwartz, Harvey, ed. *Harry Bridges: A Centennial Retrospective: An Oral History of the Origins of the ILWU and the 1934 Strike.* 2001. Harry Bridges Institute, San Pedro, CA.

———. *Harry Bridges: An Oral History About Longshoring, the Origins of the ILWU and the 1934 Strike.* International Longshoreman and Warehouse Union Oral History Collection, Labor Archives and Research Center, San Francisco State University, San Francisco, CA.

Ueno, Harry Yoshio. Interviewed by Sue Kunitomi, Arthur A. Hansen, and Betty Kulberg Mitson for the Japanese American World War II Evacuation Oral History Project, Part IV: Resisters. October 30, 1976. Arthur A. Hansen, ed. Oral History Program, Japanese American Project. California State University, Fullerton.

PERIODICALS

"C.I.O. to Sea." *Time*, July 19, 1937.

Epps, Garrett. "The Citizenship Clause Means What It Says." *Atlantic*, October 30, 2018.

———. "The Struggle over the Meaning of the 14th Amendment Continues." *Atlantic*, July 10, 2018.

Finnegan, William. "The Deportation Machine." *New Yorker*, April 22, 2013.

"General Robert E. Lee's Parole and Citizenship." *Prologue Magazine* 37, no. 1 (2005).

Gessen, Masha. "In America, Naturalized Citizens No Longer Have an Assumption of Permanence." *New Yorker*, June 18, 2018.

Lind, Dara. "Operation Wetback, the 1950s Immigration Policy Donald Trump Loves, Explained." *Vox*, November 11, 2015.

Smith, Ben, and Byron Tau. "Birtherism: Where It All Began." *Politico*, April 22, 2011.

Swanberg, W. A. "The Spies Who Came in from the Sea." *American Heritage* 21, no. 3 (1970).

Ulloa, Jazmine. "Born to Be Barred." *Texas Observer*, May 13, 2010.

"Visit to Dred Scott." *Frank Leslie's Illustrated Newspaper*. June 27, 1857. https://cdn.loc.gov/service /pnp/ds/12400/12470v.jpg.

Wagner, Alex. "America's Forgotten History of Illegal Deportations." *Atlantic*, March 6, 2017.

Warren, Robert Penn. "Jefferson Davis Gets His Citizenship Back." *New Yorker*, February 25, 1980.

VIDEOS AND FILMS

Emilia Castañeda—American Citizen. Dir. Pedro Pablo Celedòn. Voces Vivas Project, Barefoot Productions, 2011. https://vimeo.com/25163159.

A Forgotten Injustice/Una Injusticia Olvidada. Dir. Vincente Serrano. MeChicano Films, 2009. https://www.youtube.com/watch?v=YQilGizg4BU.

14: Dred Scott, Wong Kim Ark & Vanessa Lopez. Dir. Anne Galiski. 2014. Graham Street Productions.

A Night at the Garden. Dir. Marshall Curry. Marshall Curry Productions, 2017. https://anightat thegarden.com.

"1934 Longshoremen's Strike." YouTube video, 1:04. September 19, 2007. https://youtu.be/aOAFEi1Yc9M.

"Release of President Obama's Birth Certificate." C-SPAN, April 27, 2011. https://www.c-span.org/video /?299220-1/release-president-obamas-birth-certificate.

IMAGE CREDITS

Chapter 1 p. 12: *Frank Leslie's Illustrated Newspaper*, June 27, 1857

Chapter 2 p. 30: Mathew B. Brady/Library of Congress (1870)

Chapter 2 p. 30: Mathew B. Brady/Library of Congress (1865)

Chapter 3 p. 50: National Archives and Records Administration

Chapter 4 p. 74: *Wisconsin State Journal*, Feb. 4, 1913

Chapter 5 p. 92: Library of Congress

Chapter 6 p. 112: Associated Press; Densho Encyclopedia/courtesy of Henry Fujita

Chapter 7 p. 136: AP Photo/Ernest K. Bennett; Library of Congress

Chapter 8 p. 158: AP Photo/Damian Dovarganes; LA Plaza de Cultura y Artes

Chapter 9 p. 174: US Senate, Office of Senator Kamala Harris

INDEX